*Believe*

# LEIGH-ANNE PINNOCK

WITH NATALIE MORRIS

# Believe

HEADLINE

First published in 2023 by
HEADLINE PUBLISHING GROUP

1

Cataloguing in Publication Data is available from the British Library

Hardback ISBN 978 1 0354 0349 3
Trade paperback ISBN 978 1 0354 0350 9

Designed and typeset by EM&EN
Printed and bound in Great Britain by Clays Ltd, Elcograf S.p.A.

Headline's policy is to use papers that are natural, renewable and recyclable
products and made from wood grown in well-managed forests and other
controlled sources. The logging and manufacturing processes are expected
to conform to the environmental regulations of the country of origin.

HEADLINE PUBLISHING GROUP
An Hachette UK Company
Carmelite House
50 Victoria Embankment
London EC4Y 0DZ

www.headline.co.uk
www.hachette.co.uk

*To my Grandma Norma and Nanny Doreen,*

*I hope I have made you both proud.*

# Contents

# CHAPTER ONE

# Awakening

'You are a queen.
You are fierce.
You are powerful.'

'Eight years we have waited for this moment!' I yelled into the microphone and the crowd roared back at me. I could feel tears stinging hot at the corners of my eyes. I blinked hard to hold them back.

'Eight years!' I yelled again. The crowd screamed, thousands of voices swelling up into the night air. The most beautiful noise. I'm used to hearing big crowds. It is always an amazing feeling. But this was something else. This was next level. The sound worked its way into my chest and my heart banged against my ribs. Adrenaline fizzed through my veins. Next to me, my bandmates wrapped their arms around my shoulders and for a moment, we clung together in the middle of the stage, our blue-and-orange PVC costumes sticking to each other's skin. The night was warm, and the air was clear. Above us, a black sky glowed white and orange in the light radiating from the stage.

The crowd was in a frenzy. They were desperate to see us. Even from backstage, we'd heard them screaming and chanting from the moment we'd arrived. I couldn't wait to get out there. This is why we do what we do – to perform in front of our fans, to hear them singing our lyrics back to us, to see their joy radiating all around us – there is no feeling like it. As we got into our positions for our big entrance, I closed my eyes and let the adrenaline crash over me in waves. Silently, I repeated my mantras to myself – the words I always say before a performance – positive affirmations that help me unlock my other persona. Beyoncé has Sasha

Fierce. I don't have a name for mine, but she comes out the moment I step on stage.

*You are a queen. You are fierce. You are powerful. You are a queen. You are fierce. You are powerful.* I think these words over and over until they are all I can hear in my head. Then it's time to go on stage. A kind of stillness comes over me in the seconds before I see the audience. The calm before the storm. I hear the music start up and my heart skips a beat.

It was the perfect time of year to visit Brazil. March 2020, just before the pandemic hit and the world shut down, we were blissfully ignorant of the chaos that was to come in the following weeks. It still felt like winter in the UK, but we stepped off the plane in São Paulo to balmy heat, blue skies, and nights that were warm enough to party on the beach. But we weren't there for the weather, or for the parties. We were there for our fans. For years, our South American followers had been begging us to come to Brazil, and for one reason or another, it just had never happened. We knew our followers in that part of the world are passionate; we had received so many messages from them over the years – they were desperate for us to come. So when we got the invitation, I knew we had to make it happen, no matter what. Performing in Brazil was something that meant a lot to me. As soon as we started the rehearsal process, I began to feel excited. We knew this was going to be a special performance. And it didn't disappoint.

From the moment we stepped out onto that stage and the lights hit us, it felt like fireworks were going off all around us. It was an explosion of noise, colour and pure joy. None of us could contain it. We could feel the love pulsing out towards us from the crowd as they sang our songs word for word, screamed non-stop, and danced like they were at a rave. The vibes were infectious, and it made us raise our game. We were hitting our routines with even more energy; we went for the high notes that sometimes scared us; our harmonies seemed to sound even smoother. That performance encapsulated everything we are about, who we are as a band, why we do what we do. It was the best performance we had ever done – we all knew it. I felt the emotion rise in me like a bubble in my chest, and it threatened to pop.

You might be wondering where these intense feelings were coming from. Surely I was used to this? I had been part of the band for years at this point. We had already sold millions of records, released multiple albums, toured all over the world, performed on the biggest stages and at the most astounding venues. We had fans who followed our every move, who dedicated so much time to us, who stood outside in the freezing cold for hours just to catch a glimpse of our faces. As a member of one of the biggest girl bands in the world, why was this performance hitting me in this way? Why was I on the brink of tears, suddenly overwhelmed? What was it about this trip that felt so different?

As soon as we touched down in Brazil, we felt like megastars. It was completely unreal. The only other time we had ever felt like that was when we visited Japan. Our fans had found out where we were staying and they'd crowded around outside the hotel, waiting for us. The noise was deafening when we arrived, and every time I looked out of the window I could see them there, hundreds of them, waving banners up towards us, screaming every time they saw a curtain twitch. It was wild. These fans were something special, and they made us feel amazing. It was like we had been catapulted into a different level of fame. But it wasn't just this that was making me feel so tearful. It was something deeper.

'I told myself I wasn't going to cry!' I yelled into the microphone. The girls clung to my arms, and we took a second to simply be in the moment, to appreciate it fully.

That's when the crowd started to chant:

'Leigh-Anne! Leigh-Anne! Leigh-Anne!'

My name. They were chanting *my* name.

I let the tears come. Finally. They fell from me in waves of relief. I couldn't hold them back. I closed my eyes and let them roll down my cheeks. I knew I was ruining my stage makeup, but I didn't care. They were happy tears, but they were also tears that had been building for an impossibly long time. Tears of recognition, of shared experience, of solidarity. The crowd got even louder. Their voices wrapped around me, and I felt held by them. I felt seen. For maybe the first time since joining the band, I felt loved. *Really* loved. It's hard to admit that I hadn't felt this level of love until that point. I didn't want to believe it. But it was true. In that moment, though, hearing my name chanted in unison by thousands of fans, I knew I belonged on that stage. For the first time, I felt I had as much right to be there as the other girls. I had waited eight years for that feeling. Eight long years of feeling less-than, of feeling invisible, of questioning my worth and my purpose. And now here, at last, this incredible crowd was telling me that they saw me, that they appreciated me, that I was worthy of that stage, worthy of the spotlight. I felt euphoric. It was a feeling of pure happiness, but also some-thing else, something like vindication. I finally realised that the disconnect I had been feeling over the last eight years was not all in my head. I hadn't been making it up, and I wasn't mad. This appreciation, this love that I was feeling on stage, this was what had been missing all along. Why had I never felt this before? Why was it such a shock to hear our fans chant my name? These were questions I would slowly answer over the following months and years, but this was the start of something new – a new phase in my career, and bigger than that – it was the beginning of a new stage in my life.

Earlier that day, before the stage and the lights and the crowds, we had gone down to see the fans who were camped outside our hotel. There was one interaction that will stay with me forever. As I moved down the line of fans, one guy caught my attention, and we started talking. He was Black.

'You are an inspiration to so many Black Mixers,' he said, referring to the Little Mix fandom.

That was it. I was gone. I started crying immediately. In the UK, and in most places we visited and performed across Europe, the majority of our audiences are white. I didn't get to meet many Black fans, so to hear someone – a Black fan – call me an inspiration, to hear how much love they have for me . . . I was unprepared for it. Nobody had ever said this to me before.

His words felt like a turning point. Like a pinprick of light in the corner of my mind, helping me to finally see something that had always been there. At this time, I hadn't yet spoken publicly about race. I hadn't even come to terms with these issues in my own mind. I still had so much pent-up emotion, frustration and sadness that was all wrapped up in my experiences of race that I hadn't even begun to unpick. Something had been building and building within me, without me even knowing exactly what it was, and this conversation released a pressure valve. Yes, I was crying because I felt loved and because every fan in Brazil made me feel incredibly special, but more than that, I was crying because this fan *saw me*; he saw my struggle. He took the time to make sure I knew I was valued. I can't tell you how much I needed to hear that.

After the show we went out for drinks to celebrate, and I confided what I was feeling with Jade and two of the dancers I was close to – King and Claude. I tried to tell them what the show had meant to me, but I was in my feelings, and I kept being overwhelmed by all these emotions. I couldn't stop crying, and I didn't understand why. I couldn't figure out why I had never felt like this before. After all the shows, all the tours, all the hundreds of performances I had done over the years, why had I never felt that level of love? Why had I never felt like the crowd had truly *seen* me in this way before? King and Claude immediately understood what I was talking about. They got it. They helped me talk it through and to figure out where this emotion was coming from. They told me this was just the start for me, that I would have my time, that I would figure out how to thrive. It was such a beautiful moment of reflection, and looking back, I know everything they said to me was right.

This trip to Brazil *would* be the beginning of something new. An awakening. From this moment, I began my journey towards figuring out where I fit, and how to turn that into something powerful. A weight had been pressing on my chest ever since they called out Little Mix as the winners of *The X Factor* back in 2011 – potentially even before that. I had to figure out why. Why was I regularly coming off stage and bursting into tears? Why did I feel like I had to dim my light and make myself smaller? Why was there always this disconnect, this sense of uncertainty that I couldn't figure out?

It still makes me sad that it took so long to get to this point. But everybody has to start somewhere. To understand how I got to this moment, I have to look backwards. Back to the start. The journey I am on now began with a little girl. I think about her often – her dimples and frizzy hair, her painful shyness, and her quiet determination. I hold her dreams close to my heart, the dreams that I pushed so hard to achieve for her. Have I done enough? Have I done that little girl proud? Everything I do, every boundary I break, every conversation I start, I do it for her – the little girl who lives inside me – and all the little girls who watch me on stage, all the Mixers who have ever wondered where they belong. This is for all of you.

# CHAPTER TWO

# Family

# 'Don't mess with a Pinnock!'

My family is a tough bunch. That's how we have been raised. Our parents taught us to stand up for ourselves, to be strong and resilient, to go after what we want no matter what anyone says. Mum – Deborah – worked relentlessly to build her career as a teacher, and to provide us with a good life. Dad – John – worked just as hard establishing his own business. He was also a fighter. Literally. He was a champion boxer for a large part of my childhood. I took so many of my values and my work ethic from watching Mum and Dad when I was a child – they inform everything about my character. But we'll get back to my parents. To really learn anything about me, we have to go back a bit further – back to my grandparents. I'll start with Nanny Doreen. My angel. The woman who showed me what kindness was, who showed me that love was a limitless thing.

Losing Nanny Doreen was my first loss, my first experience of death and grief. At seven years old, I'm not sure exactly what I understood about what had happened, but I knew it was unbearably sad; I knew I would never see my beloved Nanny again. It makes me cry now whenever I think about losing her. Hearing my mum wail into the phone when she got the news, watching Dad's heart shatter in front of my eyes at her funeral. She was only in my life for such a short amount of time, but she made the biggest impact on me and on everyone she met. She was a true angel. The kindest, most loving person I have ever known, and I am still heartbroken that I didn't get more time with her. Whenever

13

# BELIEVE

I meet people who are my age or older who still have their grandparents, I want to grab them by the shoulders and say to them: 'Please cherish your grandparents! Go and see them – make the effort!' I would give anything to still have my Nanny here with me today.

Nanny Doreen was Dad's mum. She adored him. She was obsessed with him. They were closer than close. Nanny Doreen was truly a supermum. She had six children, and our dad was her youngest. Somehow, she still had enough love left in her for my sisters and me – she doted on us. I'd sing for Nanny too. She was always excited to hear me, and she would encourage me so much. My sisters and I would put on a talent show for her in her living room, and I sang 'Viva Forever' by the Spice Girls. Whenever I hear that song, I think of her. I like to think that I'm like her. At least, I hope I am. I hope I have taken on even a fraction of her kind nature, her gentleness, her ability to love so openly and so boundlessly. I try to emulate her as much as I can. I show it in my love of animals, in the love I feel for my parents, my sisters and their children, and now with my own babies. It's my small way of keeping her with us and making sure the legacy she built with this family is passed on through the generations.

I think about Nanny's bravery a lot. She was a white woman who married a Jamaican man in the 1960s and then had five mixed-race children. When they were all out together, people used to stare at them and would cross over and walk on the other side of the street. I can't imagine what that must have felt like. Nanny's husband, my Grandad Steve, came over to the UK as part of the Windrush generation, and when their relationship ended, he moved back home to Jamaica. He has never spoken about the hostility and racism he faced while he was in England. I imagine the memories are painful. I can understand that – the feeling of burying that kind of pain, not being able to find the words to properly explain it. Grandad Steve is my last remaining grandparent. We spent a lot of time with him growing up because we visited him in Jamaica every year, without fail. That bond is special. He not only ties me to my dad and to my family's history, but he is also a crucial link to my Jamaican heritage. I cherish him for so many reasons.

On the other side of the family, my mum's dad was from Barbados, which makes me part Bajan. We didn't spend as much time with my Grandma Norma and Grandad Luther. Grandad Luther wasn't pleasant to Grandma Norma, and everybody knew it. Obviously, Mum didn't like that and as a result, we never really got on with him. When he passed away, we all started spending a lot more time with Grandma Norma. It was a bitter-sweet reality, and sad that it took something like that to enable us to be closer with her. But with Grandad Luther gone, I must admit that things were easier. We built a beautiful, meaningful relationship with Grandma Norma before she died.

One afternoon, Grandma Norma came round to our house because we were celebrating somebody's birthday. I came into the kitchen to find her dancing, twirling around the room, her arms above her head, with the widest smile. She looked so happy. She passed away shortly after that day. I wish we had got closer to her sooner. I wish we'd had more special times like that together.

One thing I will say about Grandad Luther is that the man could cook. He made the most delicious coleslaw I have ever eaten in my life. It was *serious*. I have never had coleslaw that tasted as good as his. He made us all these traditional Bajan dishes that we loved. One of my favourites was his gungo pea stew served with rice. We did have fun at their house, too. We would go round on Boxing Day and fill our bellies with Grandad's food. There would be music and singing, always singing.

☆

My mum worked in Tesco as a cashier when I was little. She grafted hard and got promoted to manager, which was a really big deal. She was such a driven person, and as soon as my sisters and I got a bit older, she knew she hoped to do more with her career. When I was at primary school, Mum decided to become a teacher, so she went to night school and got her qualifications. Obviously, I didn't appreciate it at the time, but I can't even comprehend how hard she must have been working to support her family, look after her three girls and study every evening. It's exhausting thinking about it. She was incredibly dedicated, and I knew she would stop at nothing to make her dreams come true. After she qualified, she got a job at a local school and her new teacher's salary meant we could move to a bigger house. That work ethic and exceptional drive to get what she desired stuck with me. I absorbed that tenaciousness, that determination. Mum passed all of those qualities down to her daughters and led by example. But I also struggled with how work took so much of her time. I missed her.

I was always jealous of the kids who had parents who were around to pick them up from school and drop them off in the morning. I used to get so upset that I didn't have that – I craved that wave and that cuddle at the school gates more than anything. But my parents were constantly working, so I was always with a childminder. That only intensified when Mum started studying to become a teacher. She was always in a suit. That's my image of her from those days, on her way out the door, or getting home, but always dressed for work.

My mum is the kind of woman who believes in tough love. She isn't particularly soft as a person; she isn't the type to fuss over you or spoil you. She can be emotional, she'll cry at movies, and she's passionate about the things she cares about, but you do have to work for her affection. She doesn't dish it out for free. She's tough, just like my sisters. She takes on other people's burdens, shoulders whatever stresses she is going through in life and faces them head-on. No nonsense. If I come to her with a problem, her response will likely be: 'Come on, Leigh-Anne, chin up. You can handle this.' Sometimes, when something is rough and I genuinely do need that support from her, I will have to sit her down and say to her, 'No, Mum. This really is too much.' Her go-to reaction is that there is nothing we can't handle. That's just what she's like. Mum didn't have an easy life. She had my oldest sister, Sian, when she was young, so then her entire focus became about building a life for herself and her daughters that was better than what came before. She is out here breaking generational patterns, creating something safe and lasting for her babies. You need to be tough and single-minded to make that happen. She always puts us first. Her girls. She is utterly selfless and she would do anything for us. That has always been true for as long as I can remember.

Mum's strength is genuinely awe-inspiring to me. Although I try to be like her, to take on some of these tough qualities, I'm softer than she is. I'm more emotional – I cry at everything; I show my affection enthusiastically and frequently. I'm more like my dad in that way. He's soft, like me.

Sometimes Dad would be around to take me to school – but I didn't love that either. He had this little red van for work, and I was mortified that he was dropping me off in a van. It was one of those inexplicable embarrassments you have as a kid. I couldn't even begin to explain it now, but at the time there was nothing more shameful to me than climbing out of that red van at the school gates. I used to ask Dad to drive a bit further on, to park around the corner, so no one would see me. How bloody ungrateful of me. Kids can be so thoughtless. My dad had worked since he was sixteen; he's had his own business for my entire life – and yet I thought his van wasn't good enough.

I was always a daddy's girl when I was little. I guess I still am now. Dad was a whirlwind of fun when we were growing up. Every weekend, every school holiday, he had some activity planned for my sisters and me. We loved being outside and my clearest memories with my dad are running around in the park, or at the beach. On special occasions, he would splash out and take us to funfairs, or to the zoo, but most of the time it was the simple things that kept us occupied. One of our dad's favourite things to do was to take us out on our bikes to The Dales, this wide expanse of soft green hills that seemed to go on forever. I felt such freedom as we flew over each rise, my heart jumping to my throat for a second as we whizzed down the other side, kicking my legs and letting the pedals spin out. We would get home, breathless and muddy, and collapse together in a pile on the sofa. Dad genuinely loved spending time with us and making our lives as fun as possible. He also believed in us, no matter what we wanted to do. Whether it was music lessons, acting classes, singing, dancing – he encouraged us to follow whatever passion had captured our attention that month. He wanted us to live like he did – he always did what made him happy.

As a boxer, Dad was always training. I vividly remember him shadow-boxing all the time. Constantly punching the air and dancing around on the balls of his feet, his fists high, protecting his face, before jabbing out in front at a blistering pace. He had four professional fights – which he won – before he retired. Undefeated! Then he discovered acting. He loved being on stage, and he was good at it. He played Othello in a number of local productions. We would sit in the audience, marvelling at his ability to morph into a different person. I remember the intense pride I felt when the audience applauded, and Dad stepped forward to take a bow. At the same time, he was running his business – fixing car axels. As the business grew, Dad had less and less time for his acting, but I know he still loves it. I'm sure he will go back to it one day.

I'm so proud of my parents, and what they did for us as a family. They are the ones who made us feel safe, who showed us what was possible if we set our minds to it. My mum's strength, determination and resilience, my dad's creativity, passion and insistence on finding the fun in everything he does – I think I embody these elements of them. They are painted on my face, in my eyes and lips and skin tone, the features that blend the two of them into one. But they are also woven into my character, my mind, my soul. I owe so much of who I am today to their individual journeys, and what they achieved together.

☆

My parents broke up for the first time when I was young, but I know I was old enough to understand what was going on because I wrote a letter to Santa begging him to make them get back together. I found the letter a couple of years ago. It read:

'Dear Santa. For Christmas I would really love my parents to get back together, please. P.S. and a Bop It Extreme.'

It's funny because I didn't really remember how I felt at the time they broke up, but that letter told me everything. I needed things to go back to how they were before. To have everyone under the same roof again. Mum and I moved out of the family home when she and Dad broke up. We didn't go far. We moved to a flat in the same area, a short distance away. My sisters stayed with my dad. Sairah and I weren't getting along at the time, so I didn't mind not living with her, but I know I missed living with my dad. Kids are malleable though; we can get used to anything. And that became my new reality for a while.

Then when Grandma Norma, Mum's mum, died, they got back together. Mum was broken after losing her mum, and Dad showed up for her. He was there for her in a way that she needed. I think that after losing his own mum – Nanny Doreen – years earlier, he knew the depth of that pain. He knew that she would need him. So they rekindled their flame. Mum and I moved back into our old home and we became a family again – all under the same roof. It felt like a miracle to me.

# FAMILY

I rarely saw my parents be affectionate with each other. They argued a lot. But they had their moments. One year, my sister held a party at our house on New Year's Eve. This was during the period Mum and Dad were back together, they had gone out somewhere and we were left to our own devices. Inevitably, the party got a bit out of hand. There were loads of kids in the house, loads of teenage boys, the music was too loud, people were drinking. Everything you imagine a group of teenagers would get up to in a parent-less house. At some point – it must have been a little while after midnight – Mum and Dad came home. I feel like the normal reaction in this situation for most parents would be to kick off, right? There would be shouting, the music would be cut off, all the kids would be kicked out. But not my parents. Instead, they started waltzing to the music, right there in the middle of the living room, in front of all of Sairah's friends. Full-on ballroom dancing to the noughties' hip-hop and R&B playlist we were blasting from one of our iPods.

At the time, we were mortified. Can you think of anything more embarrassing for a teenager than your parents acting all loved-up in front of your friends? But now, I look back at that moment with pride. It's nice to remember that they were happy, that they had real affection for each other.

It didn't last. A little while later – maybe a year or two – they ended their relationship again. They weren't meant to be together like that. They didn't work as a married couple. This time, no one moved out. They split up, but they stayed in the same house. I learned later that there were some financial issues keeping us all under the same roof – my mum wanted to sell and my dad didn't. But as with so many family issues, I was shielded from what was really going on.

That's what happens when you're the baby of the family. But despite all of this, the ups and downs, the moments of tension and uncertainty, we have always been and will always be a family unit. My parents didn't work out romantically, but they were still a partnership, and there was still love and mutual respect there. Above all, they had their love for their girls and their love for this family. People would always ask them how they did it. How we all still managed to go on holiday together and spend Christmas Day together as a family – even though my dad has a new partner now. But the answer is simple – we're always going to be Pinnocks.

Everyone in my family has a huge amount of pride around our name. We have this intense kind of patriotism for our tribe. Our Grandad Steve would say to us: 'You're a Pinnock. You're a Pinnock! Don't you forget that.'

My aunties and uncles always said it as well. It became this kind of mantra that we could all repeat to ourselves, and to each other, whenever we needed reminding of our inner strength. We Pinnocks are strong. We are resilient. We stick together. That's how it's always going to be. That resilience has carried me through some tough times. It's helped me hold my head up in moments that should have crushed me. I don't think I would have made it through the last few years if I hadn't had a strong sense of who I am and where I come from. No matter what's going on in my life, that knowledge will always ground me.

☆

My big sisters are my rocks. They always have been, and they always will be. Sian is my eldest sister. Technically, she's my half-sister. We have the same mum and different dads, but she's been in my life since I was a baby, so I see her as my whole sister – no need for any fractions. We have never even spoken about any kind of different label for our relationship – it wasn't necessary. My dad brought Sian up as his own. Sian still sees her biological dad, but she calls our dad 'Dad', too.

The age gap between us – eight years – felt wide when I was little. Growing up, she was closer to Sairah than she was to me, simply because they were closer in age. But I used to look up to Sian so much. She looks just like our mum. She always seemed so grown-up and glamorous. She had amazing clothes and designer shoes. She moved down to London and was living with our grandma while I was still young. She has never been afraid to strike out on her own and do her own thing. She is a free spirit, and I have always admired that energy within her.

Sairah is the middle child, my second big sister. There's only two years between us, which means we did almost everything together during our childhood. All my memories are infused with her presence. Everyone always says we look alike, and we were forever being asked if we were twins. We don't really see it. We had a closeness that is hard to even describe. We played together all the time, and I looked up to that girl like you wouldn't believe. I wanted to be her. At primary school, she and her friends dressed up as the Spice Girls for a 'Stars In Their Eyes' competition, Sairah was Mel B and she looked *so good*. The whole group looked spot-on. It felt like they *were* the Spice Girls. I watched Sairah in total awe. I looked at her up on that stage, in that leopard-print outfit, dancing around with her curls all wild, and thought, 'Oh my gosh, you are such a *queen.'* Obviously, they won the competition. I was bursting with pride.

But being that close in age meant we also clashed. A lot. We would fight like cat and dog. It got even worse as we got a bit older. I would take her ID so I could go clubbing when I was only around fifteen, and she would find out and be so livid that I had taken her passport. I stole her shoes and her clothes and wore them without telling her, or I would take ages to return them – classic little-sister behaviour. I was a nightmare. Sairah hated it, and she would be so horrible to me in return. She would call me 'ugly' all the time. She would say I was gross, or that she didn't want to hang out with me. She could be mean to me when she wanted to be. Sian would stick up for me in those times. She was my ally against Sairah's outbursts. There were definitely times when Sairah and I have had a love–hate relationship.

When I was in Year 8, I asked Sairah if I could borrow a coat. She was in her bedroom with her boyfriend at the time, and I banged on her locked door to ask. She shouted at me to go away. She said she was sleeping and that I should use one of the coats downstairs instead, but for some reason I was adamant I had to have the coat that was in her room. The door to Sairah's room was a bit broken. One part of the frame was loose – a piece of the wood would sometimes come out and we would have to pop it back in. I can't believe I thought this was a good idea, but I punched that loose piece of wood clean through, leaned through the gap, opened the door, strolled into Sairah's room, and took the coat. Sairah was so angry that she picked up the piece of wood from the door frame and smacked me over the head with it. I think I tried to fight back for a moment but ended up running away. I was probably concussed! This was the kind of madness we used to do to each other when our parents weren't around.

It's funny how things change over time and, in many ways, our roles as sisters have reversed as we have got older, but back then I think these flashes of anger and hostility came from the feeling that I was living under her shadow. Sairah was so confident and knew how to fill a space. Unlike me, she didn't shrink away from the spotlight – she chased it. She had a self-assurance that I could only dream of. She was just *giving it* all the time. So confident, so much swag. She was fiery as hell. And I was basically the complete opposite.

When I would sing for my family, Sairah would be my back-up dancer, but she would take the limelight with all these amazing moves while I was mumbling into the microphone, singing as quietly as I could. Sairah didn't get shy or nervous. She didn't seem to feel any of the fear that made me shrink whenever I was around too many people. I think part of me envied her for that. I felt as though I could never live up to her sparky personality. She was unafraid to take up space, to be loud, to be noticed. I wanted to be like her – but I didn't know how.

As much as we fought, I knew she always had my back. She was so protective of me. Fiercely protective. If I ever got into any trouble with anyone, with other kids at school, or people in our area, it didn't matter. Sairah would be there, backing me, always. One Christmas Eve I was out in a club with my friends. We were having fun. I was sticking up for one of my friends who was having an issue with another girl, but then the girl turned on me. She cornered me in the toilets of this club and started on me. She punched me, right in the face, so hard that I staggered backwards into one of the cubicles. But she wasn't done. She came at me again. Now, I am not a fighter, but this girl was coming for me – hard – and I had to protect myself. Instinct kicked in, and I started to fight back. It was chaos. At one point, I had her in a headlock. We were flailing our arms at each other, landing punches, kicks, scratches, crashing around this bathroom, bashing into the sinks, bouncing off the cubicle doors. I have no idea how long this fight went on for. It felt like forever, but at some point, I got away – I'm pretty sure she came out of the scrap worse than I did – and as soon as I was outside, I called Sian first, and then told Sairah. I was shaking and my voice was trembling as I explained to Sairah what had happened. I'd barely got to the end of the sentence before she was putting her shoes on. Sian drove the two of them and Sairah's boyfriend at the time down to this club. It didn't matter that it was Christmas Eve – there was nothing that was going to stop them from coming to help me. I came outside as they arrived, and Sairah had stormed ahead of the others, practically running towards me. She was livid.

'Who was it?!' she yelled at me. I looked around and spotted the girl who had punched me. I pointed towards her.

'It was her,' I said quietly. I felt scared about what was about to happen, but at the same time, powerful now that my sisters were there. They made me feel invincible, untouchable. Sairah spun round and locked eyes on this girl with a laser-focus. She didn't hesitate and walked straight

26

over to her. She is always so fearless. She pushed the girl hard and shouted, 'Don't fucking mess with my sister!' Then there's me, practically hiding behind her. I found my voice and piped up with, 'That's what you get when you mess with the Pinnocks!'

Honestly, it was like we had descended into an episode of *EastEnders*. It was so ridiculous. But that girl never bothered me again, and what I remember most from that festive night out is the speed with which my sisters were at my side. No matter what silly, dangerous, or downright stupid situation I might have got myself into, I knew I could always count on them. And as soon as they were with me, no one could touch me. I still feel that way about them now.

Sairah is the one who looks after this family. She holds everything together. She is that person, the glue, and always has been. Everyone goes to her for everything. Even our eldest sister goes to her. We all depend on her. I truly don't know how she manages it. She's the middle child, and it must be a lot for her. I feel bad for her when I see how much she does for all of us. We take a lot from her, and I watch as her feelings and her needs get pushed to the side. She has this persona of always being so strong – as though she has to be everyone's warrior – but then she forgets about her own feelings. She forgets that she needs things too. Sometimes I want her to think more about herself, to put herself first. But that's not who she is.

These days, my sisters are the most brilliant, brave, inspirational mothers to their children. Sian has three beautiful kids that we adore, and Sairah has two little boys. Sian's children and Sairah's eldest are pretty close in age and seeing them grow together has been so special. Sairah's second little boy was born three days after my babies, so it warms my heart to think that they will always have each other. They will grow up together. The next generation of Pinnocks. And I know we are going to raise them to be just as tough as we are.

# CHAPTER THREE

Early
Childhood

'Home is a
beautiful chaos.'

A home is so much more than bricks and mortar. That goes without saying, right? It isn't about how many bedrooms you have, or the size of your garden, the amount of square footage, or the proximity of your neighbours. Whether you're in a castle or a high-rise flat, the essence of a home is what happens within those walls, and how that space makes you feel. Home is a feeling, a warmth that spreads across your skin like a blanket, a light on in the kitchen and the smell of something delicious on the stove at the end of a long day. Home is comfort and familiarity, the knowledge that you will always be welcome, you will always belong.

I often have to grasp that feeling tightly in my hands and take it with me. Travelling the world for long stretches at a time isn't always easy, but thankfully I have realised that 'home' is not a singular place. For me, home is knowing I have someone to always call, it is a sense of safety, knowing that I have somewhere to return to, people who will show up for me and champion me no matter what. That feeling, that certainty, comes with me – wherever I go. And no matter how much I love touring, meeting new fans and working and performing in the furthest corners of the globe, there will always be a part of me that longs for home, that's counting down the days until I get to walk through that front door.

I'm a homebody at heart. My family's little rituals and traditions are the glue that holds me together. Our Sundays are sacred. Even though my mum and dad aren't together anymore, Sunday is such an important day in our family – for all of us. It is a day where we like to be under the same roof whenever it's possible. We eat, we laugh, we bicker and debate, we play music, we argue. There's always yelling, dogs barking, babies crying, kids screaming. My sister Sairah will be ranting about something, as usual. I'll probably disagree with my dad about something. It's a madhouse. On Sundays, our home is chaos. A beautiful chaos. But what matters is that we are all there.

My mum is at the heart of our home. A constant, reassuring presence. Dad is the sensitive one, the one who is quick to talk about his feelings or dish out hugs. Mum is more reserved. She holds back that outward affection. You have to work a bit harder for it. But that makes it even more special when you do see her softer side. A hug from your mum is different, isn't it? Whenever I've been away for a long time and I come home, I head straight to her, wrap my arms around her, and I feel instantly supported, like she has taken some of the weight off my shoulders. A mummy hug is different to a friend hug, or even a boyfriend hug. A mummy hug has a way of righting everything that's wrong with the world, even for just a moment. It's like everything slows down, or stops, and you feel safe.

Home is a place where I get to watch my family grow and evolve. We have a big family. Even back in the day, before my sisters and I started having kids, there were cousins everywhere, aunties and uncles. Endless Pinnocks. My dad has three brothers, one of whom has passed away, but also two sisters, so you can imagine the noise when we all got together under one roof. My mum has two siblings, but I didn't really know a lot of my extended Bajan family because we only went to Barbados a handful of times growing up – we weren't as close to them. But on the Jamaican side of the family, we were tight. The house would be full of laughter, always so busy. There was nothing calm about it. The walls hummed with our energy, with our noisy ways of loving each other.

The first home you live in will always occupy a special place in your heart. It is the place where you made your formative memories, where you had all your 'firsts', where you learned about what family means to you, the place you hopefully felt the safest. My first home was where I could learn to be myself. It was the place where I took my tentative first steps towards becoming the woman I am today. It was a safe space for me to experiment, to be silly, to be loud, to perform. And this meant the world to me because, for the first decade of my life, I found so much of the outside world overwhelming and scary. But our home was my haven.

What do I see when I try to picture the first house I lived in? It's funny how there are certain moments that I remember so vividly – the colours, the smells, a song that we used to play all the time, the feel of the carpet between my bare toes – and yet the wider picture, the house itself, is fuzzy and blurred by time. That first house in High Wycombe, the first place I ever lived. What do I remember about it? I know it wasn't big. I shared a room with Sairah; we had bunk beds. Our eldest sister, Sian, had her own room with a Tupac poster on the wall. The house was a terrace with neighbours connected on each side. There was a green out the front where all the kids in the neighbourhood would play together after school – we were always knocking for each other. Everyone knew everyone. Families would meet up in certain pubs; it was a small community in that sense. We had a garden out the back, but it was paved – there was no grass. Sairah once fell off the fence and cut her head open on the concrete. Our dog, Khalifa, was protective. He would stand at the fence for hours and bark at anyone who came past. If anyone put their hands through, he would go for them. I can remember the layout of the house, but the specifics are harder. I think there were dark-brown sofas in the living room. My overwhelming sense was that the decor was moody, in that way that homes in the nineties always seemed to be – dulled and a bit dark, like a sepia photo.

Our second house, I can recall more clearly. It was bigger. It had four bedrooms. This was the house we were able to move to after my mum got her new teacher's salary. My sisters and I couldn't believe it. All of a sudden, we had this massive garden, and all this space. It wasn't a mansion or anything, and it wasn't particularly fancy – but to us, it felt like we had stepped into a different world. My parents had worked so, *so* hard to be able to buy that house. It was a huge achievement for them. And the icing on the cake was that I had my own bedroom.

It was a tiny box room, and it didn't even have a door – it only had one of those beaded curtains hanging in the frame – but it was pure heaven. I had my own space for the first time, and I loved it. I asked for it to be painted green and yellow (I have always been in love with green, it is my life colour – my engagement ring, my car, my nails, all green). My little bed was covered in stuffed toys. I had monkeys everywhere, I had an obsession and fascination with them. I knew all these strange facts – did you know lemurs can hypnotise other monkeys? My ultimate dream was to go to Borneo to visit the orangutans.

My tiny bedroom was my sanctuary. I would hole up in there for hours. I loved reading and my shelves were brimming with Jacqueline Wilson books. *Lola Rose, Secrets, Tracy Beaker* – all the classics. I felt incredibly grateful to have a space that was all my own, a space for me to grow and figure out who I was, what I wanted to be. I look back on my time in that house and it feels almost sacred. The words that come to my mind are 'warmth', 'safety', 'support'. I felt so nurtured. Whatever I dreamed of doing, whatever I wanted to achieve, I was always given the space and the encouragement to go after it. I realise that not everyone has that, and it makes me feel so lucky for the home that we had. Looking back, I am so proud of what my parents achieved to get us into that space, to build that sense of safety for all of us.

My childhood homes were loud, busy, chaotic. We came together, all of us – grandparents, aunties and uncles, nieces and nephews – all the time, for parties, Christmases, birthdays, random Sunday afternoons. There was always music, laughter, bickering, constant chatter. There were babies and pets, the TV would be on, or the speakers would be blasting. We are not a quiet bunch. Where did I fit among all this beautiful chaos? Where was my place amid all that noise, the shouted conversations, and the big personalities? I can see her now. Timid as anything, easily scared. Always the baby of the family. My older sisters protected me, and I let myself be wrapped in cotton wool, coddled safely in the warm bubble of our home. I'm definitely still the baby. I don't think that ever changes – even now that I'm a grown woman with babies of my own.

I didn't mind being babied. It suited me. I was excruciatingly shy. Yes, the same person who now gets on stage and performs to millions would shrink herself to nothing every time she was in a room full of people. One of my earliest memories is of hiding behind my dad's legs, pressing my face into the denim of his jeans, whispering to myself over and over 'I hate peoples'. And I did. I hated crowds, I hated meeting new people or having to say hello to strangers, I hated anyone looking at me. I longed to blend into the background, not be seen, become invisible. It felt safer. But, despite this longing to be invisible, I also had a drive to perform. It's a contradiction, I know – it doesn't make sense, but it's just how I was. Painfully shy, yet desperate to sing. Somehow, both things were true. Being heard petrified me, but there was also a spark deep inside me that was desperate to be on stage – it often felt like these two sides of me were battling it out. My home environment let me explore this side of myself in a way that didn't paralyse me with fear.

You could see it whenever I jumped on the karaoke machine in our living room – which was a lot. Any kind of family day would usually feature singing. Boxing Day is the occasion that always stands out the most for me. Those memories are so clear. I can almost smell the Bajan and Jamaican cooking smells wafting from the kitchen, the sweet, spicy aroma of allspice and scotch bonnet chillies, brown stew chicken, curry goat and rice and peas. Of course, there were toys and piles of colourful wrapping paper, twinkling lights and tinsel draped over every surface, but it was the singing I always looked forward to the most at that time of year.

We had an old karaoke machine that would always be wheeled out and hooked up to the TV, one of those ones with the big white lyrics scrolling across a blue screen. I remember Auntie Marlene murdering 'Dancing Queen' one year, and both my grandmas were obsessed with ABBA. I would take centre stage (i.e. the middle of the living room), swaying slightly as the backing track started up, gripping the microphone tightly in both hands. It was my first taste of performance. That spark inside me leapt up into my chest as the music swelled and I raised the microphone to my lips to sing the first note. But the shyness bubbled up too. I would sing with my eyes cast down at the carpet, my feet planted on the floor, my body moving just the tiniest bit. I always made sure that the music was loud enough to practically drown me out. My family would tell me to sing louder, to turn the music down, but I couldn't do it.

We have a home video of one of these moments. It's grainy and looks intensely nineties. I'm singing in the living room, and the music from the karaoke machine is drowning me out. You can hear my mum, off-camera, telling me to turn the music down so they can hear me. I get stroppy, stomp my foot and yell 'no!' I couldn't have had a safer, more supportive or encouraging environment, but even with all of that, I wasn't able to let myself shine. The singing, though, I loved everything about it. The powerful ease with which I knew I could hit the notes, the feeling of controlling my voice like an instrument, hitting a high note or a harmony so that it made my skin tingle. I loved to sing, but fear made my voice small. It turned my volume down and kept me at little more than a whisper – but the spark never went out. In fact, it only got brighter. But it would take me a while to find the confidence to fan that flame.

I still find it hard to pinpoint what caused me to shrink like this, or where that fear and shyness came from. I was always told, in no uncertain terms, that I could do whatever I wanted, become whoever I wanted to be. We were all told this, both my sisters and I. I believed it, even then. But I was scared. I still get scared now. It's not that the fear or the shyness left me completely, it's more that I learned how to do the things I loved *despite* those things. They still live inside me now; that little girl who hates 'peoples' is still in there, but the fire is brighter now. It pushes me to chase my dreams, no matter how big or scary they might be.

For years, the idea of 'home' was something I had to carry with me. I had to create it for myself wherever I was. From when I moved into the *X Factor* contestants' house as a teenager, or when I rented my first apartment in London after joining the group, or when we toured around the world for months at a time – it meant my home was always somewhere new, a different hotel room every night, a tour bus, or an airport departure lounge. My family was Jade, Jesy and Perrie, our dancers, our management, our vocal coaches and makeup artists who travelled with us. We created a sense of home for ourselves, one that kept moving and changing, but still gave us that sense of comfort, the reassurance that we belonged together. I threw myself into it. The excitement of everything that was happening to us carried me along and helped me bury any homesickness, but it wasn't always easy, and as I've got older and started my own family, I've found myself longing for permanence and stability – for a home that is constant and still and steady.

I finally created that for myself when we bought our forever home in a quiet, green suburb outside of London – not too far from where I grew up in High Wycombe. My husband Andre and I wanted a permanent home for our family, to raise our children and grow older together. And there was something that drew me away from the city. I'd ideally be close enough to go into the capital for work, but it felt important to be able to leave, to have our family life away from the frantic pace of the city. I needed us to have space to breathe, to be close to the countryside, within walking distance of fields and woods and cows. That's what I grew up with, and I wanted my children to have the same. When they're bigger, I picture us spending our weekends going out for walks, getting muddy, traipsing through fields and trails and exploring the countryside. I think it's so important for them to have that link with nature, like my sisters and I had when we were little.

In many ways, I want to recreate the home I had as a child. That means it is a space where I can be the truest version of myself, where I don't have to hold back any part of who I am. Home is a sense of comfort, both in your surroundings and in your own skin. It's a feeling of being accepted for who you are, no matter what. I want that for myself, for my husband, and for our babies. I want them to feel like they can always be themselves, and that our home is a safe space for them to figure out who they are and who they want to be. I think about the green bedroom I had as a little girl, with the beads instead of a door, the shelves full of books and my bed full of monkey toys. I remember how it felt like my sanctuary, how proud I was of that little space, how I would lie on my bed and dream of my future, make detailed plans for the life I wanted to have. I want my little ones to have the space to dream big like I did, to dream even bigger.

In keeping with the traditions of my childhood, the home I have created for myself and my family has a touch of chaotic energy to it. It wouldn't be a home without it. And we are still working on the stability. At the time of writing this, Andre is playing football in Greece, so the babies and I split our time between Greece and the UK, and then I have my work to factor in, too. It's a balancing act, one that we are still working hard to figure out. It's tough not being together all the time, but it also means we appreciate each other so much more, and we make time to do as much as we can as a family, and spend real, quality time together as often as possible.

But no matter where we are, our priority is to create a home that feels like safety, security and, above all, an abundance of love. I wanted to fill my home with it. Every space where we exist as a family, the bedrooms, the kitchen, the living rooms, the rooms where we eat and sleep and work and play, these rooms are full with love. I want my children to know where they belong, and that isn't only here in the UK. Like me, they also have Caribbean heritage – from both my side of the family, and their dad's. I was lucky to have spent all that time in Jamaica while I was growing up. I feel the Jamaican sunshine in my bones, in my blood. It's an integral part of who I am, who I've been and who I want to become. What an amazing thing to feel like you have two homes, two places where you belong. My heritage lives within me, within my children, and will always make us proud.

# CHAPTER FOUR

*Heritage*

'Jamaica has half of my heart.'

I'll never forget the day Jamaica's football team qualified for the World Cup. It was 1997, and I was six years old. The qualifying game was a huge deal in my house. Everyone took it seriously. Very seriously. Jamaica had never made it to the World Cup before, and now only ninety minutes of football stood in their way. It was an historic moment, particularly for my Jamaican family. By kick-off, the nerves were bubbling, and we all crowded around the TV to watch. My sisters and I sat cross-legged on the carpet, packed tightly between the knees and feet of the adults. I felt myself leaning forward, inching closer to the screen every time Jamaica had the ball. I willed them to win so badly. Every time one of their players got the ball, I urged them on in my mind. Run faster, run faster, shoot, *shoot!*

I got my wish, and a Jamaican player slotted the ball into the back of the opposing net. Our little living room erupted like we were in the stadium. Everyone jumped to their feet, fists smashed into the air, guttural roars filled the room. It scared the shit out of me. I had never witnessed my family produce such an enormous noise before. I scrambled to my feet and ran behind the sofa, pressing the palms of my hands against my ears and squeezing my eyes shut. The sudden explosion of screaming and yelling was overwhelming – but so was the pride. Being Jamaican has always meant a lot to us, and this was a moment worth celebrating, worth pissing off the neighbours with our deafening cheers. I pulled myself up and peeped over the back of the sofa cushions to see my family still clinging to each other, beaming with joy. I stared hard at the little Jamaican flag in the corner of the TV screen: black, gold and green.

Half of my heart is in Jamaica. We even spent Christmas there once, and we stayed with Grandad. His name is Byron, but he goes by his middle name, so we call him Grandad Steve. My sister Sairah and I loved spending time with Grandad Steve when we were small. I couldn't always understand him, though. His accent was thick and lyrical, and he often slid into patois mid-sentence. It sounded so beautiful, but I always had to ask him to speak a bit slower for me. That Christmas, I must have been about eight. Grandad Steve had decorated his home with multicoloured paper streamers, shiny tinsel and plasticky ornaments dotted on every surface – I'm sure it would be considered tacky as hell now, but we were delighted. Sairah and I had one present each – we both got a doll – and it was one of the best Christmases of my life. We couldn't get over it being hot at Christmas. It felt like the whole world had turned upside down. Everything was unfamiliar. All of our normal seasonal routines were up in the air. It made us giddy.

We could barely contain our excitement when we went to the beach – *at Christmas!* The beach was about an hour's drive from my Grandad's, he didn't have a pool or anything, so every time we came to visit, we would throw our stuff in the car and head down to the ocean whenever we could to escape the tropical heat. We loved being near water. On the drive to the beach, Sairah and I would sit in the boot of the car – there was enough space for us to sit up and look out the back window. I forget why we did this. It might have been because there wasn't enough space, but maybe we just liked it. When we got to the beach, they would open the boot and we would run towards the water like excitable puppies. After we tired ourselves out building sandcastles and splashing at the edge of the ocean, we sat down for a Christmas lunch of fresh fish, lobster and festival – a sweet, fried dumpling that goes perfectly with spicy Jamaican food.

In the mornings, we would eat green banana or ackee and saltfish, followed by fresh fruit and hard dough bread for breakfast. Brown stew and jerk chicken, curry goat, rice and peas. That was what we would dream about for weeks after we came home – the food. Grandad Steve didn't cook, but he always had someone there who would make food for all of us, sometimes a housekeeper, sometimes a girlfriend. For years, there would be a different young woman staying with Grandad every time we went to visit. But then he met Annette. They got married when I was fourteen and we have called her 'Grandma' ever since. She looks after him, and that's what we care about the most. That, and her cooking. Grandma Annette makes the most mouth-watering bread-fruit salad, full of vegetables, green beans, peppers and sweetcorn, mixed together with mayonnaise. I honestly don't know how she gets it to taste so good.

The entire ritual of going to Jamaica has always filled me with joy. I love every single moment of it. From packing a bag full of beach clothes, to the excitement at the airport, to stepping off the plane and breathing in a lungful of warm air. It's the smell of it. So familiar, and instantly comforting. It always feels like home from the moment my foot hits the earth. And the heat of it. Wow, I loved that. Never needing a jacket. Warmth sinking into my bones, my skin darkening into a golden, syrupy glow. Nothing but bright,

bright sunshine from morning to night. There's a part of me that was supposed to exist in a warm climate. I feel like I'm solar-powered, and the Jamaican sun supercharges my spirit.

As a child, I never thought of these trips in terms of connecting with my heritage. I didn't attribute much significance to it than visiting Grandad Steve. It was just what we did. But looking back, I know that part of my love for Jamaica was to do with the sense of belonging. I never felt out of place. I never had to question whether I was meant to be there. I didn't have the words to articulate this feeling back then, but I can see it now.

It's a forty-minute drive from the airport to Grandad Steve's, and we would stick our heads out the window all the way and wave at the people selling food at the stalls on the side of the road. The sweetest, fat oranges – that are green, not orange – and fleshy coconuts filled with syrupy water. In the evenings, we would sit on the veranda and play Ludo with Grandad for hours, or crowd around him while he sat in his chair and watched Westerns. In the mornings, we woke up to the sound of birdsong and the breeze rushing through the palm leaves. Grandad had goats, we were obsessed with them and we loved to feed them. At some point, one of our cousins would visit and braid our hair. I loved turning up to school with all these silky braids cascading down my back. My friends would go wild for them.

In Jamaica, my sister and I felt freer than we ever did at home. We had cold showers and got eaten alive by hungry mosquitos; we ran barefoot through the rural terrain for hours without anyone telling us to behave or to come home. The air felt cleaner and fresher; there was endless space to play and explore. There were fewer rules, fewer conventions designed to keep children quiet and contained. It was so far removed from our suburban existence in High Wycombe. It was intoxicating and glorious. Being there was so good for us. It was good for our dad, too.

Dad is so close to Grandad Steve. They are the ultimate bros. I love seeing them together, watching how they interact with each other. There is so much love, respect and real friendship between them. I feel so lucky – for my dad and for us – that he has this relationship. Not all of Dad's siblings were close to Nanny and Grandad Steve like he has always been. I'm grateful that my sister and I got to have them play such prominent roles in our lives, and that we got to visit literal paradise so often. How many people can say that?

We didn't have everything we wished for when we were little; we weren't well-off, and some of the kids at school would brag about getting new clothes, or the latest trainers, as kids do. But we never felt any jealousy or resentment about not having the newest games or the coolest clothes, because we knew our parents were scrimping and saving all year to take us back to Jamaica. I would choose those memories over box-fresh Nikes or the latest PlayStation any day of the week.

My connection with Barbados is less defined than with Jamaica because we didn't spend nearly as much time with Grandad Luther. Grandad Luther also lived in the UK all the time we knew him, so we didn't have the same kind of need to go and visit his birth country when we were little. Barbados is as much a part of my heritage as Jamaica is, but I don't feel that inherent connection in the same way.

There's no deeper reason to this than the fact that I'm less familiar with the country.

Don't get me wrong, I love Barbados. It's a stunningly beautiful place with extraordinary landscapes, people, food, music and culture. Every time I go there, I discover something new to love about it. Around a decade ago, I visited family while I was out there, and it was such a special trip. Just like in Jamaica, inhaling that warm Caribbean air and feeling the sunshine hot against my skin, helping me breathe easier. But I don't have the same memories attached to Barbados. I don't have that feeling of recognition and familiarity. The last time I was there it felt amazing to connect with family – but I know I can go deeper. I want to truly feel that sense of belonging like I do when I'm in Jamaica. Because I'm Bajan as well – this is who I am, and I don't want to deny or ignore that part of myself. It hasn't been a conscious decision. It's almost inevitable that I don't have the same special bond as I have with Jamaica. But I hope to deepen my bond with Barbados in the future, to find those roots for myself, build my own links and forge a stronger relationship with that side of my heritage. There's no time limit on connecting with your history, with your roots. I know I will get there in my own way when it feels right.

My Caribbean heritage is incredibly important to me. It's something that flows through me and influences so much about who I am. From the food I make, to the books I read, to the lessons I know I will teach my children when they are old enough. My heritage influences the music I listen to and the music I want to create. There is an island rhythm in me that I know has been passed down to me from both of my grandads. I want to honour the gift of their lineage, make sure it is a loud and proud part of my identity, my work, my family. Going to visit is as natural and as vital to me as breathing. It has to happen on a regular basis. No matter what is going on with my career or the wider landscape of my life, I always have to make time to go back. I don't feel complete without it.

There are, of course, challenging things about feeling as though you exist between two worlds. There are times when I am searching for that sense of belonging, when I feel like something is missing, or that I've been stretched too thin, as though I am sometimes trying to exist with my feet straddled across two worlds, always missing something or someone. But it's the other side of this reality that I think about the most – the unique joy of having two worlds to call your own. The ability to blend seamlessly across cultures, to infuse British traditions with Caribbean spice, the abundance of love pouring out from different corners of the globe. I am incredibly grateful to have access to so much love. It feels infinite. And I'm grateful that my heritage has given me gifts of acceptance, tolerance and understanding. It's a special thing to exist in two spaces at once, to have two homes, to find belonging in multiple places. I will never take that fact for granted.

My heritage is my pride, my power, and has shaped me into the determined fighter I am today. Everything my parents and their parents endured – from migration to the UK, the hostility they faced here, the racism, the systemic disadvantages, the judgement because of their interracial families – all that hardship made them strong, spirited, hard-working. They passed these characteristics down to me. I have experienced my own struggles, but I know it doesn't even scratch the surface of what my elders and my ancestors would have faced over previous generations. I take so much strength in knowing that I am forged from them, that their resilience is now my resilience, that they are looking down at me, willing me to succeed. I know I am a product of their sacrifice, and that thought keeps me going.

My children will know their heritage. I've taken them to Jamaica now that they're old enough, and will continue to do so as they grow up. They will know the white sands and crystal-clear blue oceans like I do, they will know the lush mountains, they will run in long grass chasing rain-bow-coloured butterflies and tiny green lizards. I want them to feel the warm breath of the Caribbean breeze against their cheeks. I will make sure our culture and our heritage seep into the fabric of our lives and are an integral part of who we are and what we do as a family. My girls have Black dolls to play with; we watch TV shows with Black charac-ters and read stories about Black and mixed-race families. I want them to see themselves represented, feel proud of who they are, and to know they can achieve anything they want to achieve. I also want them to know how hard they will have to work for it. Like my parents, and their parents before them, I have grafted for everything in my life. I would never expect anything to be handed to me on a plate. I want to make sure my children have the same mentality. Although they will have more available to them than I had in my childhood, I will do whatever I can to make sure my babies know the value of working hard. I'm trying to lead by example.

# HERITAGE

The importance of my heritage has inspired me recently: I'm learning to cook. My mum is a seasoned cook and on Sundays, she makes amazing Caribbean meals for all of us, but I learned how to make traditional Jamaican food from my sister. Sairah sends me recipes and then walks me through the steps, teaching me how to do it. It has taken practice, and when Andre and I do it at home, it isn't always successful – it has been hit and miss in the past – but I'm determined to stick with it. It's a case of trial and error. Many errors. But these days, I have pretty much got a Jamaican Sunday roast nailed. The shopping and all the prep is so long, it takes basically all day. The rice and peas, the curry goat, the coleslaw, the salad, the plantain – I do it all. It is so worth it. When we finally sit down together, as a family, to this incredible feast with so many different elements and dishes, it is a beautiful thing, and it tastes like home.

# CHAPTER FIVE

*School*

'Formative years'

My primary school was relatively small and located on the outskirts of High Wycombe. Both my sisters went to the same school, but I don't have many memories of us all being there at the same time. Sian had practically gone to big school by the time I started, and Sairah was two years above – and even that feels like a huge gap when you're six.

Just like at home, I was painfully shy and mostly quiet at primary school. I never got into any trouble, but I never really let myself shine, either. I hated maths – the numbers didn't make sense to me. I loved English and reading, anything to do with books. And, of course, music – unsurprisingly, that was always my favourite subject. I think I was clever. I always did well in my work and felt confident with my homework and group projects, but I never let myself really embrace any of my wins because I hated the spotlight being on me. I would never volunteer for anything or put my hand up to answer questions.

I had one teacher, Mrs Francis, who I adored. She was always encouraging, pushing me in this gentle way to come out of my shell and to make my voice heard. I'm sure she could see something in me, that I had potential in there lurking behind this wall of shyness I had built up around me. In my school report, Mrs Francis described me as 'a worrier'. She would always say to me: 'Leigh-Anne, stop worrying! You worry too much.'

What I had to worry about at age six, I can't imagine. It makes me sad to think about that anxious little girl, riddled with fears and concerns, when all I should have been thinking about was learning and playing and having fun. I honestly can't say why my mind was wired like that when I was little. But there was something holding me back, preventing me from letting my full self shine through. Part of it might have been to do with the stark lack of diversity at my school.

I was one of four Black girls in the whole school, and only one of those girls had dark skin. We all gravitated towards each other instantly – I think even at that age, we sensed that we needed to stick together. Shanice, the dark-skinned girl, and I became pretty much obsessed with each other. We were joined at the hip. BFFs. We sat together in every class we could and after school we would go to each other's houses for dinner or for sleepovers. At weekends we had play dates together – at the park, or the cinema. But our favourite thing was to play silly games together. It didn't matter where we were or what we were doing. We could always entertain ourselves. When I was with Shanice, all that shyness dissipated, and I became the real Leigh-Anne. Goofy, silly, loud, confident.

As we grew up, we shared books, trading our favourite Jacqueline Wilsons back and forth, and discussing every detail of each plot at length. We spent hours and hours playing *The Sims* on our desktop computers at home. This was back when we had to dial up to connect to the internet and the computer sounded like it was about to take flight every time we loaded a new upgrade of the game. We were obsessed. Shanice would make these awesome houses and mansions from scratch – with multiple layers, roof gardens, swimming pools and balconies with hot tubs. She was a pro. I was more interested in love stories. I would create families and couples, and there would always be boyfriends and affairs – lots of drama.

When we weren't on the computer, we were making up our own games. We used to pretend we had our own TV show which we called 'Sugar Fantasy'. It was like *SMTV Live*, or *CD:UK* – one of those Saturday morning shows that had pop stars performing songs and interviews with celebrities and silly game show segments. On our show, we had a song that we would always sing at the beginning, then we would welcome everyone and host 'interviews' about our favourite celebrities in front of a pretend audience. We filmed ourselves creating made-up soap operas, acting out scenes and improvising. All we ever did was laugh. That's what I remember most vividly about those times. The kind of deep laughter that makes your belly hurt and your face ache.

Shanice was so creative; she came up with the most immersive games that became our whole world. I always admired her for the ridiculous, absurd things she was able to think up. Like me, Shanice was always shy and quiet at school, but we came alive when we were together. We created a safe space for us both to unleash our creativity. We gave each other confidence. We even performed together. The 'Stars In Their Eyes' competition was a big deal at our school – I had watched Sairah win as one fifth of the Spice Girls a few years earlier – so we decided to have a go. We performed the 3LW song 'No More', which we were obsessed with at the time. I never would have been able to get on that stage if Shanice wasn't by my side. She was my other half.

Shanice and I bonded over culture, too. Her family was from St Vincent and there were lots of traditions and rules in her family home that I recognised and could relate to as a fellow Caribbean. Her mum was always cooking, and I loved her food. I would often be invited to family parties with tons of relatives, which almost felt like being in Jamaica and visiting my Grandad Steve. It was a huge reason we were drawn to each other, I'm sure of it. I was friends with lots of white girls at school too, but Shanice and I had this common bond, this implicit understanding of each other's lives. It was easier, comfortable, safe. I never had to explain anything to her. Not about the food I ate at home, or the music we listened to, or about how my skin would tan so quickly in the sun, or my different hairstyles. She just got it. In a way that my white friends would never have been able to.

The overwhelming whiteness of my primary school created other problems for me, too. My hair was a constant source of stress. My curls are Afro-textured, my hair gets dry easily and has a lot of volume, but the coils are softer and looser than my sister Sairah's, for example, and it also has more of a fineness to it because of my white European heritage. Back then, in the late nineties and early noughties, we didn't have many resources to help us care for our hair. As a result, I don't have the best memories about it.

It seems wild that something that seems so frivolous and superficial can have such a big impact on your day-to-day life, but Black hair is always political. It is never just about a certain style or texture; it is about how you are perceived because of how you wear your hair. It's about beauty standards that told us – relentlessly – that Black hair isn't beautiful. It's about the judgement you receive if your hair looks 'messy', 'wild' or 'unprofessional', and it's also about the shame you feel if you're unable to look after your hair in the best way.

I felt this sense of shame regularly. My mum tried her best, bless her. She really did, but she just didn't know what to do with it. This was before there were tutorials on Instagram and YouTube explaining how to protect and style Afro and mixed-race hair, and in the shops we would be lucky to find one product that we could actually use. Mum relied on Pink Oil Moisturiser; that was all we had. It came in this lurid pink bottle, and it didn't smell particularly enticing. The moisturiser was too heavy for my hair and made it greasy and lank. Mousse didn't work either – it made my curls crispy and strangely rigid. I needed something in between, something to moisturise and to give definition and hold to my curls, but nothing too thick. That product didn't exist, or if it did, we had no way of accessing it. So, the struggle continued.

Mum would blow-dry my hair every week on a Sunday so she could send us to school with it straight. I don't blame her at all for doing this, she was a busy working mum with three kids to look after and blowing our hair straight was the easiest thing, but it's such a shame that we did that to our beautiful curls for so many years. I developed an intense complex about my hair being frizzy or messy and was obsessed with making sure it was sleek and straight, or that the curls were perfectly smooth – which, obviously, was an entirely unreasonable expectation. I was constantly pressing my palms against my scalp, flattening out my hair, trying to force it smooth, sleek and straight. I needed it to be as flat as possible.

# BELIEVE

In our later years at primary school, we had weekly swimming lessons. During each lesson, I would make sure to dunk my head so my curls would smooth out in the water and hang perfectly against my back. I loved how my hair looked when it was wet. I prayed it would stay like that all day. But then, inevitably, it would dry, and to my dismay, the frizz would return. It always returned. That was just the natural formation of my hair, and I had absorbed the message that it was not OK, that I had to fundamentally change it in order to be acceptable, in order to be beautiful.

I was self-conscious and embarrassed about my hair, plus my experiences at school didn't help. I would look at my white friends and long for their silky locks that swished over their shoulders. Why couldn't I look like everyone else? Their hair was beautiful, I thought mine was not. I wasn't actively teased or bullied about my hair, but there were a few instances of unkindness that reaffirmed this message in my mind. Sometimes in secondary school, the kids sitting behind me in class would throw scrunched-up pieces of paper at my hair. I wouldn't feel it or notice, but the tiny balls of paper would stick in my curls, and it could take me hours to realise they were there. A little white speck would fall at my feet, or I would spot people pointing when they thought I wasn't looking, or hiding their faces and trying not to laugh. I would shake my hair and pull madly at the paper, trying to get every scrap out as quickly as I could. It was mortifying.

Shanice always had her hair in beautiful, intricate braids. I wonder if she ever struggled with her hair like I did. I'm not sure we ever spoke about it. We were too young to fully understand or vocalise the impact of this kind of pressure. Shanice and I drifted in secondary school. We were put into different classes and made our own circles of friends. It was sad that we didn't stay close as we got older, but that's just what happens. I will always have those memories with her, and I will always be grateful for the ways she encouraged me to express my creativity from such a young age – I owe her a lot for that – and for giving me such a fun and hilarious time in my life. We reconnected recently, and I have her number now. It's nice to know that she is still there, that there is the possibility of us growing closer again now we are adults.

At primary school, I started entering talent competitions. All of them. They would take place during assemblies, or after school, and I would carefully choose the song I wanted to sing and practise in my bedroom for hours to get it perfect. But when it came to the actual performance, something didn't connect. It was like there was a battle going on inside me. The part of me who fought to perform, who loved nothing more than singing and dancing on stage, went up against the part of me who was still deeply terrified by crowds, who still hated being heard and longed to melt into the shadows. It meant my performances were pretty terrible. Not because I couldn't sing – I knew that I could – but because fear was holding me back.

The time I sang Whitney Houston's 'I Wanna Dance With Somebody', I hit every note perfectly. But it didn't matter, because I made sure the backing track was so loud that the audience could barely hear me. Another girl in my year sang an Avril Lavigne song – she even dressed like her. She had the stripy tie, the chains on her cargo pants, even the mesh sleeves – she must have raided Tammy Girl. She shouted her way through the song. It was terrible. But she won. I was so upset. I couldn't understand why no one was seeing my talent – even though it was clearly because I wasn't *letting* anyone see it. Another time I sang my heart out on the stage. My eyes were closed, and I felt like my voice was strong and clear, but when I opened my eyes, I realised everyone in the crowd was talking. No one was listening to me. It was so tragic. But it was my own fault. I wasn't singing loudly enough; the music was too loud; I wasn't selling it. As much as I wanted it – to be on that stage, to perform, to show people what I could do – I wasn't yet ready to truly believe in my talents. And if I didn't believe in it, how could I expect anyone else to?

When I went to secondary school, I felt my confidence start to build – very slowly – and a big part of that was because of who I had around me. The school itself was in the centre of town. It was your average comprehensive secondary school, not posh, but not particularly rough either. We wore navy-blue blazers, grey trousers, and a tie striped with light blue and navy. There was a real mix of kids there, of all different academic abilities, from different families, with different backgrounds. Moving to big school is always a wrench. You go from being the biggest fish in a small pond to being a tiny tadpole in the ocean. At least that's how it felt in Year 7. But the most notable thing for me was the significant increase in diversity. I had gone from being one of four Black people in the whole school to suddenly being surrounded by kids of all different ethnicities. I was no longer in the tiniest minority. I felt more able to be myself, my complete self. It felt good.

I built a solid group of friends around me quickly when I started secondary school. I was the kind of girl who was friends with everybody. I had lots of different circles, but then I had my core group as well. The first friend I made was a girl called Tannisha. She was the strongest person I had ever met. She was so fierce. I admired her because she didn't take any shit from anyone, ever. She had my back from day one – and still does, to this day. The way that girl would protect me, I have never had a friend stand up for me in such a selfless way like that. If I was ever in any trouble, or got into any arguments, she would be there, no questions asked, ready to fight for me.

Like Shanice, Tannisha's family was also from St Vincent. I loved going round to her house because her mum would cook up the most amazing food. Her fry-ups at the weekends were out of this world. I was always round there for gatherings and family events. I even went to some christenings. In our first year of school, Tannisha and I bonded over a project we had to work on. We had to build a castle. It was a competition, so we spent the entire weekend working on it. At the time, we were obsessed with Daniel Bedingfield's album, specifically the song 'He Don't Love You Like I Love You'. We would play this song over and over again, and belt it out as loud as we could. We won the castle competition, and we were ecstatic because we had worked ridiculously hard on it.

I then started to become friendly with a girl called Hannah. She was already in a friend group with two other girls, Astrid and Leah, so I ended up joining their group, and Hannah and I got closer and closer. Tannisha and I drifted at this point; she found a new group. We were still friends, but never as close as during those first couple of months at school. My friendship with Hannah, though, that one was enduring. She is still my best friend today.

Hannah knew nothing about R&B music, and I made it my mission to educate her. I made her mixtape CDs that I burned on my desktop computer at home, with all my favourites on there. Joe, Jagged Edge, 3LW, Usher. I made it clear to Hannah that she had to know this music. I encouraged her to love it as much as I did. As a duo, we were so silly. Hannah never took anything seriously, and we just spent all our time laughing hysterically. It reminded me of my friendship with Shanice in that way. I had a webcam on my computer at home and we spent an enormous amount of time doing photoshoots in front of it, pulling the silliest faces and busting up laughing until we could barely breathe. She was my right arm. We were never without each other – at school, at the weekends, all the time. If I was ever on my own in the corridors, people would ask me where Hannah was, why we weren't together. Everyone was so used to seeing us as a pair.

My girlfriends were my world at school. I looked forward to going in every morning because I knew I got to hang out with them for eight hours and that made me so excited. Even though we were such a big group of friends, there was rarely any drama. There was no bitchiness or nastiness, no one was ever left out or excluded. We didn't talk behind each other's backs or argue every other day. Now, people ask me how I have managed to keep such a solid group of friends. I think the only explanation is that I have been incredibly lucky. My favourite group chat on WhatsApp is a huge group with all the girls from school. To still have that connection, more than twenty years after we first met each other – that is special. I'm so grateful I met them. They keep me grounded. They remind me where I come from; they remind me that I am loved and supported. I can't tell you how many times I have needed them over the last decade. My female friendships are deeply, vitally important to me.

I knew what we had was special, even back then. I think that's why I was always so quick to defend them. They were the only times I ever remember getting into any real trouble at school – when I was standing up for my friends. I was willing to lay everything on the line for them. And often, I wouldn't think about the consequences.

When I was around fifteen, Rosie – one of the girls in our group of friends – was being picked on by some other girls. I was with her when I noticed it happening once, and I confronted the bullies. One of the girls who was being mean stepped up to me and got in my face. It escalated, and all of a sudden, she had her hand gripped in my hair, so I reached up and grabbed her hair, too. Then we were scuffling; some blows were thrown. She ended up with a mark on her face. The teachers found out about it. But it was the other girl who ended up getting suspended, not me. The head teacher pulled me into her office to talk about it, though. I was sitting opposite her, separated by this big oak table between us. I looked at my lap and fidgeted nervously with the edges of my blazer. I hated getting in trouble. The head teacher told me I was only still in school because I was a first-time offender, and that the behaviour was 'out of character' in her opinion. She told me that if this had happened in the real world, I would be the one going to prison because I was unscathed and the other girl was the one with the mark.

'You have to understand what the consequences would be in the real world, Leigh-Anne,' she said to me. 'People won't give you a pass.' I hung my head and nodded towards my shoes. I promised her it would never happen again. What she told me stuck with me for many years after that incident.

Despite the occasional spot of trouble, the teachers loved me. Generally, I was a peacemaker. I had this ability to nip arguments in the bud and calm people down, and I think the teachers saw that skill in me. Overall, I was sensible. I was reliable and worked relatively hard. I wasn't one of the super-popular girls – the girls who were beautiful and always had makeup and the best clothes – and I wasn't one of the rebels either – the ones who were cool because they didn't try hard with schoolwork. But I was friends with everyone. I think that was why I was made a prefect, and then a senior prefect, and ultimately, Head Girl. I had a way of shifting effortlessly between different social circles, keeping on the right side of practically everyone. It meant that, although I wasn't the smartest girl in the school, having that position of authority made sense for me.

I felt honoured to be appointed Head Girl. Seeing that my teachers had so much faith in me helped my confidence to bloom. I could feel myself coming further out of my shell with every year that passed. I was blossoming. Becoming the person I was supposed to be. With the teachers on my side and a fiercely supportive group of friends surrounding me in everything I did, I began to feel more powerful. I started speaking up more and becoming more assertive in my opinions.

In English, it must have been a GCSE class because we were reading *Lord of the Flies*, our white teacher was reading a passage out loud, and she said the N-word. I was stunned. Hearing the word in that context caused a visceral reaction in my body, like a shiver of disgust and anger.

I put my hand up, and said, 'Miss, you can't say that word.'

'Well, that is the word that's in the book. And this is the language they would have used at the time,' she said. Her voice sounded so stern. But I didn't back down.

'But you can't say that word – it's racist,' I said. My voice was clear.

No one else said anything. All the other students were silent. Eventually, the teacher dismissed my concerns, brushing them off like I had said something silly, and then got on with the class. I'm sure she probably said the word again. And she never apologised or anything. I don't think she thought she had done anything wrong. But I was proud of myself for speaking up. I could feel my confidence growing. This wasn't the same girl who hid behind her dad's legs when there were too many people in the room. This wasn't the same girl who sang as quietly as possible with the backing track pushed up to full volume.

Secondary school felt like the beginning of me. The person I knew I could be, and the person I was to become. I began to step into a different version of myself. A version that was stronger, bolder, more resilient. It felt like an unlocking of my potential. And this was just the beginning.

# BELIEVE

Head Girl was chosen by the teachers. I had to go through an interview process and I worked hard preparing my answers for the questions. I really wanted to get this title. It felt like I had something to prove. I needed to solidify this new, confident version of myself. So I worked hard to get it. In the interview, I said my aim was to hold more talent competitions, and encourage students to explore their creativity – everything from music to performance and theatre. When I became Head Girl, I wasn't the best at it. The Head Boy, who was strong academically, did so much, and I barely did anything. But I stuck to my promise about creating talent shows. And, of course, I entered one of the shows myself.

This time I was ready for it. In a way, I had been preparing for this moment for years, for the entire time I was at school. Our school talent shows were a big deal, and each time I entered one, I felt myself blossom a little further into the person I knew I could become. I thought back to my first year of secondary school. Eleven-year-old Leigh-Anne didn't even make it through the audition stages. My friend and I wanted to perform together, but they didn't put us through. I felt crushed by that, I knew they made the wrong decision, but also, looking back – I wasn't ready.

Then, two years later, something had shifted. I decided to sing Sisqo's 'Incomplete' for that year's show. It was such a beautiful song, and I knew I could do it justice. I practised for days, hours after school, before school, at the weekends. I wanted it to be perfect. The nerves were still there, and right before I went on stage, my teacher pulled me aside and we did a breathing exercise. She showed me how to pull the air into my lungs and then let it out slowly, over and over, until the fear turned into something more purposeful, something I could harness for my performance. It helped massively. I stepped onto that stage and started to sing. My voice was much louder than the backing track, clear, strong, and hitting every note just like I practised. The crowd was stunned. Their eyes were all fixed on me. They were listening, really listening. They cheered loudly when I finished singing and I won the competition. It is still one of the proudest moments of my life.

In Year 11, as Head Girl, competing in a talent show I had organised myself felt like the culmination of everything I had worked for up until that point. The shy little girl was finally fading into the background, and I could feel the power that came with finally believing in my abilities. Instead of competing on my own like in previous shows, I performed with a group of my closest friends. We opened with the classic 'Ain't No Sunshine', followed by a rap verse from one guy and beatboxing from another, and then I went into an original song I had written myself whilst a couple of my girlfriends were dancing. It was a mash-up with so many different elements, and I felt immense pride during the performance as the crowd went wild. This time I didn't even need the backing track, I got up on that stage and sang in front of the entire school acapella.

My confidence had reached a new level, and that was in large part down to my friends who encouraged me, backed me up and smashed it on that stage right next to me. We won the talent show, and I just remember thinking – *yes, this is what I am meant to do*. The end of secondary school was looming on the horizon, and I was starting to piece together what I wanted to do with the rest of my life. I knew

I needed to feel that high again, the buzz of performing on stage.

This was the start of something special. It was time to go after the thing I desired more than anything in the world. I finally felt ready for it. But of course, I was also a teen-ager, and that meant there were passions other than singing beginning to enter my life.

# CHAPTER SIX

## Young Love

'When I fall
... I fall hard.'

My A Levels were derailed because I fell in love. I didn't do as well as I knew I could have because I simply stopped caring about school or exams or getting into university. I stopped caring about anything other than him. He became my entire world, and the rest of it just sort of melted away at the edges. He was all I could see. He was all I wanted.

I am a hopeless romantic. I always have been. I fall in love easily and I fall hard. I give my all to someone and I expect the same back. I don't do love half-heartedly; I don't play it cool or pretend I'm not bothered. And when I was a teenager, I was even more intense about it all. My first love crashed into my life like a wrecking ball, and it left me spinning, gasping for air. I understand when someone calls a relationship a 'whirlwind'. That is how I felt: swept up in something beyond my control, half drowned in it, spun off my feet.

I was around sixteen when I met him. I'm going to call him Nathan, but that's not his real name. I can only tell this story from my perspective. I'm sure he has his own version of events, too. In true noughties'-teenager style, we met on MSN Messenger. He was a friend of a friend, and we just started talking one evening after school on the chat site. He was a little less than two years older than me, and he was trouble. Everyone in the area seemed to know his name. He always seemed to have a bit of money, and I never got a straight answer about how he earned it. But I didn't care about any of that. If anything, his 'bad boy' reputation only made him more interesting.

# BELIEVE

On our first date, we went to the cinema. I developed intense feelings for him quickly, and I think he did for me as well. Then my sister found out who I was dating, and she kicked off. Sairah knew about Nathan's reputation and she did not want me going out with him. She told Mum and Dad, and from that moment they all decided he was bad news. They never gave him a chance. Nobody did. But they knew how much I loved him. I was obsessed with this boy. They wouldn't have been able to keep us apart even if they had tried.

It started so well. He told me everything I wanted to hear and made me feel so loved. For me, everything was about him. My life began to orbit around him and what he wanted. I saw him all the time, after school, every weekend. I couldn't get enough. I would have been with him every second if I could have. Very quickly, it started to become toxic. Nathan could feel my dependence on him. He knew he had me wrapped around his finger because I loved him with such intensity, and he started to exploit that.

He stopped making an effort. He was always cancelling plans with me at the last minute, forgetting to call me back, ignoring my texts. He started to treat me like an afterthought, when for me, he was always at the forefront of my mind. I began to realise that I was planning everything. We only ever did romantic things if I was the one to make the effort to organise it and persuade him to go. One Valentine's Day, I planned a romantic night away for the two of us. I spent the whole day in London getting everything I needed. I bought new underwear, rose petals, champagne – the works. I wanted to get to the hotel early to set the room up with candles and flowers – the kind of thing I had seen in the romcoms I watched religiously with my friends at sleepovers. That was the kind of romance I dreamed of – big, obvious, undeniable. I was so excited and had been planning the whole evening, meticulously, for weeks. All Nathan had to do was book the hotel room. Just that one job. I had given him all the details he needed; he simply had to book it.

I was at Hannah's house getting ready and feeling excited about the night ahead, and it got to about an hour before we were supposed to be at the hotel, and I asked Nathan if he was picking me up. He kept stalling and stalling until, eventually, he admitted it.

'I didn't get the room. I couldn't book it in the end.'

I just stared at the message on my phone. Wow. I was crushed. He knew how much effort I had put into this night, how much it meant to me, and how excited I was. And now none of it was happening. My girlfriends were meeting up that night, so instead I went with Hannah to a girls' night at one of our other friend's houses. I was so angry; I took the rose petals I had bought and threw them out the window. Dramatic, I know. But this was just the norm for us. Nathan brought so much drama into my life. All the time. If this sounds like an insignificant incident, the context is that these little let-downs and disappointments happened on a regular basis. Constantly. I have so many memories of sitting on Hannah's bed and getting a text from Nathan that would make me cry or rage. The accumulation of so many moments like this, when I loved this boy so hard, was almost unbearable. But I took it, I took all of it, because I couldn't imagine my life without him in it.

This went on for a long time. We would break up and get back together, have screaming rows before a passionate reconciliation. I continued to love him with every molecule in my body, even when he treated me like shit. I couldn't help it. I couldn't extricate myself from his hold over me, from the love I felt for him. He kept me in that space, he kept me coming back to him, over and over. In my eyes, he could do no wrong.

The relationship became increasingly toxic. He was frequently horrible to me; he never made me feel good. I think by this point I was only in love with the idea of him. A made-up version of Nathan I had in my head, who was nothing like the real thing. Looking back, I realise that this was inevitable. How could we possibly build anything that looked like a future together when our history was so full of drama? But I was still a teenager, and I thought the strength of my love for him was enough. I thought that was all that mattered. But eventually, we started to crumble.

I cheated on him. It's the only time I have ever cheated on anyone in my life. And it didn't make sense, because how could I do that to someone I loved so completely, so overwhelmingly? But that was the reason why. I was pouring so much love into him, and getting so little in return that it was starting to drive me mad. I was craving love, touch, passion. I longed to feel desired, needed, protected – and Nathan did not make me feel any of those things. He had made me feel so shit for so long, but instead of getting myself out of that situation, I went looking for what I needed from someone else. I think part of me wanted to hurt him, too. Maybe I was looking for a reaction. Looking for him to show me, finally, that he did love me as much as I loved him.

It wasn't just a one-time thing with this other guy. We entered into a kind-of affair. We kept hooking up in secret. He made me feel loved, and I know part of me enjoyed the thrill of it, the risk and the fact that we knew we were doing something wrong. The affair went on for months . . . or maybe it was only weeks. When you're a teenager, everything feels so significant, so important. It felt like I was holding this secret knowledge for such a long time. People found out about us, and a friend of a friend told her boyfriend, and word eventually got back to Nathan.

He lost his temper with me. He was so angry. He was screaming and yelling and slamming things. I was horrified, and again returned to this central fact that was always at the forefront of my mind in those years – *I can't lose him.* I didn't want him to leave me. I was terrified of him ending it. So I denied and denied and denied. *It isn't true, it's all lies; that isn't what happened.* I stuck to it. Defending and reiterating my lies, over and over, until somehow, I managed to convince him. He calmed down and we survived it. I stopped seeing the other guy, and everything just blew over. We carried on, just like before, with the arguments, the disappointments, and this desperate need to try to get him to love me in the way I wanted to be loved.

The rumours about me lingered, though. I suddenly felt like everyone in Wycombe was against me. Nathan was well known in certain circles, and now everyone thought I was this villain who had broken his heart. People seemed to love to stir things up about me. Some girls – who I think wanted Nathan to be single – seemed to take a lot of joy in trying to tear me down and painting me as an awful person. At the time, I was getting more into music, writing and recording songs, meeting people in the industry. One guy, someone I knew had stirred things up in the past between Nathan and me, asked if I would feature on his rap song. I said no. Why would I want to record a song with someone who had spoken about me behind my back? So he wrote a song about me, calling me a 'slag', saying I would never succeed, slating me in every way possible. He put the song on YouTube and it felt like every person in my area watched it. He didn't stop there. He kept making these hate songs – always about me. He made four of them in total. It was a nightmare. It felt like everyone in town was talking about me. I even retaliated and made a song about him, which is the most embarrassing thing I have ever done. I should have just ignored them, but I felt trapped. It was as though I was being attacked from every angle. In that moment, I thought the best thing to do would be to stand up for myself.

It didn't help, and the cycle of rumours and hate continued. The whole town was against me. At least, that was how it felt. I stopped going into High Wycombe town centre on my own. I began to realise that I couldn't stay in this place forever. I knew I would have to have a fresh start somewhere new. And all of this started because I got mixed up with the wrong boy. If I hadn't met Nathan, none of this would have happened. I wouldn't have felt like an outcast in my own home town. I hated him for that.

I have regrets from this time in my life. I was young and dumb and making some terrible decisions. But the experience taught me a lot of valuable lessons, too. I learned to have more respect for myself; I learned to trust my instincts. I learned that it's important to put my needs above what is expected of me, or any childish notions of what romance is supposed to look like. Sometimes, love isn't enough. Particularly when you're not being treated with respect or kindness. Someone telling you that they love you isn't enough if they aren't showing it in how they interact with you every day.

I also learned that real love requires friendship. Nathan was never my friend. He didn't even act like he particularly liked me as a person. I learned that kind of treatment isn't good enough. In relationships, I want a lover, yes, but I also need a friend. I need someone who I can talk to about everything. Someone I can trust with my deepest, darkest secrets, someone who I feel safe to be my true self around. I need someone I can laugh with. I want to laugh every day. I want to laugh until my stomach hurts and my face muscles cramp up. That's friendship, and that's love.

With Nathan, everything was pure drama. Stress after stress, scandal after scandal. And after a while, you begin to believe that is normal. That's what love is, and that is what a relationship has to look like. But that's not who I am. I'm a silly, lighthearted person. I always have been. I think about what I'm like with my friends, the ridiculous jokes I have with Hannah, the way we laugh together over the most foolish things. That's what I need in a partner. I never want to be with anyone who makes me feel like I can't be silly, or real, or that I can't laugh at the stupid things I find funny. I want someone who lets me be myself. And, above all, I don't want any drama. I think I've had enough relationship drama to last me a lifetime.

I want someone who is family. Someone who feels like a comforting presence in my life. A safety blanket who makes me feel warm, secure. Who makes me feel loved. That is all I have ever wanted. Nathan was the opposite of a champion. I don't think he ever really hoped for me to do well. I almost threw away my future because of him. It feels almost unbelievable to think I gave him five years of my life. I was still with him throughout my early *X Factor* journey. He was the one I called the moment after we won. But our visions weren't aligned. I knew I had to set myself free to fulfil my potential. Ultimately, my dreams were what released me from the hold he had over me. I was reaching for it all: the moon, the stars and the sky. I wasn't going to allow him to keep me tethered to the earth.

# CHAPTER SEVEN

## Auditions

'Finding my voice'

It is such a cliché to say that everything happens for a reason. But here I am, saying exactly that. There is a reason clichés become clichés – it's because often there is truth in them. That is certainly what I have found. Maybe the stars aligned for me, or I manifested my dreams by wishing for them so hard, or maybe the gods of fate decided my path for me long ago. I don't know what it was, but I know something bigger was at play, mapping out my destiny, nudging me in the right direction. I believe that so completely, and honestly, I don't know how else to explain the series of events that led me to *The X Factor*.

It started with Nathan, and the years I lost to that toxic love affair. Rather than studying for my A Levels, I was wrapped up in this messy romance. My love for him was the only thing that mattered to me. It certainly mattered a lot more than my English coursework or my psychology revision. I lost focus entirely. My attendance was poor. I wasn't able to get to school on time, I was busy getting ready, faffing, talking to Nathan on the phone. Anything other than getting to school. And my grades suffered. I stopped caring. So, it wasn't too much of a surprise that when it came to results day, I didn't have what I needed to get into my first-choice university.

I was disappointed – mostly in myself – but I wasn't devastated. I think I knew in the back of my mind that I wasn't meant to go to university. Part of me suspected there was a different path I was meant to be following. I didn't know which path yet, but I knew the destination. I had a clear picture in my mind. I was going to be a star. I knew it. I *knew* it in my heart. I look back over old Facebook statuses, back from 2009 when your status used to be in third person, and they all said things like: 'Leigh-Anne will soon hit Madison Square Garden'; or: 'Leigh-Anne is going to have a smash-hit number-one record.' I was convinced. I thought all I needed to do was believe. I genuinely believed I could will it into reality. But I also knew I would have to work. Hard.

The first time I tried to get a tattoo, I was sixteen. I took my sister's ID to the tattoo parlour and showed the guy what I wanted. I can't even remember what it was. He was all ready to ink me up, but then I saw the needle and got immediately lightheaded. The room swam in front of my eyes and I lurched off the little bed with the plastic cover and ran to the bathroom. I threw up everywhere. When I emerged, wobbly on my feet, face tinged with green, he took one look at me and shook his head firmly.

'You're not getting a tattoo today, sweetheart.'

The second time I was more prepared. I was eighteen, legally of age now, and I braced myself when the needle came out. I managed to keep it together. No passing out. No vomit. I chose the word 'Believe', spelled out in black cursive, with the letters curling delicately into each other. It's printed on the back of my neck. From that moment, it has always been my mantra in life. I knew that if I could believe in myself, there would be no limit to what I could achieve. I know it sounds a bit corny, but it's a life philosophy that has genuinely never let me down. And I needed buckets of belief in that year after my failed A Levels.

# AUDITIONS

A lot of my friends disappeared off to university, and I was stuck in Wycombe. A town where I felt increasingly unwelcome, tainted by my relationship with Nathan and the rumours and drama that swirled around us. I felt lost for a while. I got a job at Pizza Hut. I thought about re-applying for university. I was toying with the idea of studying social work because I wanted to help people, but it never came to anything. My love for music was still the overwhelming desire in my life. I still daydreamed of sell-out tours and accepting BRIT Awards whenever I had a spare minute between serving pizzas and fizzy drinks. I knew I had to follow my dream. It was like a calling.

After work and at the weekends, I spent all my free time writing songs and singing. I saved every penny from my waitressing shifts and used the money to go to London to meet people in the industry, songwriters, producers, people who had access to recording studios. I posted my music on MySpace and Facebook and started interacting with industry people online, sending them links to my work, trying to connect with useful contacts who could help me sign to a label or get representation. I started linking up with people in my local area who were involved in the business. There was this one guy, Fox, who was an eccentric character, but he believed in my talent. Another guy, called Bubble, was a big help. I wrote and recorded with him whenever I could. One time, my dad drove me to London after I saw an advert for a music business manager. I auditioned, but the whole experience was strange. Nothing came of it. The entire industry felt impenetrable. I just didn't know how to crack it. I couldn't get myself noticed. I didn't seem to be able to put myself in front of the right people or make myself stand out. I was doing everything in my power, working so hard, and it just wasn't happening. It was incredibly frustrating. And for every person who believed in me, there was someone who didn't. The negative energy continued to flow from certain people in Wycombe, people who were intent on watching me fail, who told me I would never amount to anything. People who did everything they could to keep me in a box.

There were months of this. Every time I doubted myself, I touched the tattoo on the back of my neck and told myself to be strong, that it would all fall into place. But it was getting harder to keep the faith. One day, I was sitting on my sofa at my mum's house, contemplating life, when I saw the audition form for *The X Factor*. I had sent off for the form online and almost forgotten about it, but there it was, on the table. What the hell. What did I have to lose? Absolutely nothing. I didn't put too much thought into it; I just filled it out and sent it off. Easy as that. This huge, life-altering step began with this tiny, quiet moment on my mum's sofa. Nothing dramatic, no huge revelations, no lightning bolts. It was all quite random. But if it wasn't for everything I had been through the year before, if I hadn't messed up my A Levels and I had gone to university like I planned, none of this would have happened. I wouldn't have been sitting on my mum's sofa, contemplating life. My dreams of Madison Square Garden would have evaporated in a world of halls and freshers' week, exams and meetings with lecturers who would have encouraged me to get a 'real job'. Everything that led to me sending off that application form – it all happened for a reason.

I was still so young at this point. Still a *teenager*. And yet, I felt like *The X Factor* was my last chance. It's ridiculous when I think about it now. Of course, I had so much time ahead of me, and I know now that I would have done whatever it took to make my dreams a reality. But at that time, I felt like this was it. This was my one shot. This was my chance to get out of Wycombe, to prove everyone who had doubted me wrong. I had to make it count.

There were three auditions you had to make it through before you got in front of the actual judges. For each one, I had to travel to London, prepare songs, get all dressed up and ready to perform. There was so much that went into each stage, and that's before you even get anywhere near a TV camera. For these early auditions, you're only in front of producers and researchers. For one of them, I sang 'Only Girl (In the World)' by Rihanna. We were all in these little individual booths with a couple of producers watching and listening to you, but the rest of the room could hear you, too. Something shifted during that audition – people were stopping to listen; I could feel eyes around the room turning to look at me. Someone said, 'Oh wow,' as I was singing. I kept going. When I finished, I could tell by their faces I had impressed them. That's when I started to get excited. If I could impress at this stage, who knows how far I could take this? My hand fluttered to the back of my neck, my fingers tracing the outline of my tattoo.

I got through. I was there with my parents and a friend of mine who had also auditioned. She didn't get through and she was, understandably, pretty upset about it. So I had to keep my happiness contained. I couldn't act too giddy while she was grappling with the rejection. But inside, my heart was doing somersaults. The next stage was a phone interview. I didn't have to sing; they just wanted to chat. I think the producers were ensuring I was confident or 'sparky' enough to feature on the TV auditions stage, in front of the judges. They wanted to make sure I had something about me.

My phone rang while I was in a music studio in London, recording with one of the contacts I had made through my MySpace page.

'Oh my god. It's them. It's them!' I was expecting the call, and I recognised the number. I knew it had to be the producers. I ran out of the recording booth and answered the phone. The conversation is a blur. They wanted to know more about me, who I was, my background, the kind of music I wanted to make. I was garbling, high on adrenaline. I must have been speaking at 100 miles per hour. But when I hung up, I had a feeling that it had gone well. I could tell they liked what I was saying, that they liked me. There was a buzzy, confident feeling in my chest, but I didn't want to acknowledge it, just in case I had read it wrong.

A few days later, I received another call. This time telling me what I had been longing to hear. I was through to audition in front of the judges. Relief flooded through my body like warm sunshine. I held the phone away from my ear for a second and just stared at it, letting the words properly sink in. They told me the date and time I had to be in London, and what I needed to prepare for the audition. When you watch *The X Factor*, you have no idea how much goes into the process before you see people walk on stage in front of the judges. I had no clue. The clever editing and smoke and mirrors make it seem as though you simply turn up on an audition day, queue for hours and then eventually come face-to-face with Simon Cowell. But that isn't how it works at all. The program creators don't just let anyone rock up and sing. The people you get to see have already been through weeks of auditions and whittling down to those who are the most talented, or – let's be honest – those who are the best entertainment value for TV.

In the time between getting that phone call and singing in front of the judges, I went on a girls' holiday to Ibiza. I was so excited about the audition, I was telling everyone I met about it. I remember being on a boat party, whizzing across the Mediterranean Sea with the hot sun against my back and a cold cocktail in my hand, telling everyone who would listen that I was going to be on *The X Factor*, to watch out for me on TV. I was so hyped, and so confident. I was certain it was all going to work out, that this was my moment. I had belief coursing through my veins. It all felt within my grasp.

I partied hard in Ibiza. Too hard. By the time I got home, I was run down, sick, and my voice was a mess. The judges' audition was the following day, and my throat was dry and scratchy. I didn't know how I was going to be able to hit the notes. I was downing so much water and overdosing on throat sweets, but nothing was helping. Before I knew it, I was stepping into the room to face the judges and the TV cameras and the audience sitting at home, judging me. I had been nervous at the earlier auditions, but this was a different level. The pressure of the moment felt like a physical weight pressing down on my skull, constricting my lungs. This was the first moment where it felt real. I had no choice but to give it everything I had. I swallowed hard as I brought the microphone up close to my mouth, ignoring the scratching pain in the back of my throat.

# BELIEVE

The room was big and echoey, with high ceilings. In the middle was the stage area with hot, blinding lights pointing towards it from every angle and a brightly coloured back-drop. Cameras pointed from at least three positions in front of me, and two behind me. In the shadows at the edges of the room, there were producers, directors, lighting engineers and sound engineers, dressed in black and clutching clip-boards, talking quickly into little walkie-talkies or holding a finger to their ear to listen to instructions coming through a headset. I was told to walk to the centre of the room and face the judges. In front of me there was a long table. You know the one. You've seen the setup. The four judges sat in a line. On the table in front of them were bits of paper with information about me, but they weren't looking at the paper, they were looking at me. Their eyes followed me as I walked to the central point in front of the main camera. I met their gaze and couldn't believe who I was about to sing for. Tulisa, Gary Barlow, Louis Walsh, Kelly Rowland. Superstars. It was the first time I had ever seen famous people up close. It felt like I was watching TV. The most successful musicians and music professionals I had ever been in the presence of, and they were about to listen to me sing.

I was scared. Of course I was. Walking to the centre of the room, I could barely feel my legs. My limbs felt like they were filled with jelly. But I wasn't going to let that stop me. I let the fear drain out of my body and replaced it with something solid, something that felt like determination. And joy. I loved performing. I loved to sing. I had a hunger to be heard, to be noticed. And now it was happening. My face cracked open into the biggest smile. I told them my name

90

and what I was going to sing. I had been preparing for this moment – in one way or another – for my whole life.

I knew my voice wasn't where I needed it to be. I had to rely on something else. I was singing 'Only Girl (In the World)' again, and I decided to give them a show. As soon as the music started, an indescribable energy pulsed through me and I started bouncing around all over the stage. I was dancing, jumping up and down, lifting my arms towards the judges, running from one side of the stage to the other. I was performing with everything I had. I tried to show off my personality, to bring a bit of spice and attitude. It was the first time I had ever moved on stage. I had never danced while I was singing before. I had never thought about the performance element, or anything beyond my singing. It felt good. The judges were responding well to it, too. I could feel them vibing with me. I finished, breathing hard. I knew it had gone well.

They asked me to sing another song. They wanted to hear that I could control my voice, too. So I sang Louis Armstrong and Ella Fitzgerald's 'Summertime' acapella. Even with my sore throat, I managed to pull off a strong performance. My vocals held out. The adrenaline pulled me over the line, and my desire to succeed kept me going. Bowing out at this stage simply wasn't an option. I had to get through. I had to make this work.

I got four yeses. All four of the judges agreed to see me again. Gary Barlow said I was a 'little star'. *Gary Barlow* thought I was a star! Tulisa said she loved my energy. So all of that bouncing around the stage had most definitely paid off – they liked it. They liked me. They could see something in me. I felt vindicated, like I could scream from the roof-tops, to shout as loud as I could until the people in my home town heard them, until the people who told me I would never be anything had to eat their words. But they were a small element in my mind. I wasn't doing this for anyone else's approval. The only person I needed to impress was myself. I was the only person I had to prove myself to. The little girl with the quiet voice, hiding behind the backing track, cling-ing to her dad's legs. I wanted to take that little girl's hand and show her what she was going to become, that everything was ahead of her.

Kelly Rowland mentioned that she could see me working well in a group. She was the first person to suggest that. It wasn't something I had even thought about before. My dream had always been to be a solo artist. I aspired to stand in the centre of the stage and belt out my songs in front of an adoring crowd. But I had never considered being in a group. It had simply never crossed my mind. When Kelly said this, I thought, *fine!* I was cool with the idea. They were the experts; they knew what would work best for me. And the thing I cared about most was making it through the audition, becoming a success, getting to sing for a living – in front of a crowd. I didn't care how that dream became a reality, whether it was me on my own, or me sharing a stage with other people. I wanted it, no matter what.

After the audition, I was on top of the world. Cloud nine. My head was spinning with it. It was the happiest I had ever felt. I went out to celebrate with my parents, and I called the rest of my family to tell them I had got through. There was so much screaming down the phone. Nobody could even get their words out. They were all so happy for me. I felt blessed to be surrounded by so much love, so much positive energy. I told them that I knew this was it. I knew this was going to be the start of something. Something huge. This kind of thing doesn't happen to people from High Wycombe. I had lived such a small-town life up until this point. It felt like I had stepped into a tornado and was about to be picked up and transported to a different, more magical life. Everything was about to change. I was ready for it.

# CHAPTER EIGHT

## Bootcamp

'Becoming Little Mix'

The word 'bootcamp' has gruelling connotations. It makes you think of military operations, or a horribly intense kind of fitness class with a personal trainer yelling in your face, screaming at you to work harder. It made perfect sense to call this stage of the audition process 'Bootcamp'. It *was* gruelling. Not in the physical, army-crawling-across-the-floor sense, but mentally – it was a truly exhausting experience, one that demanded so much of me from the moment I arrived.

Despite the military name, Bootcamp doesn't take place on an army base. Instead, they put us all up in the same hotel. Hundreds of hungry musicians and singers, all in competition for the chance of a lifetime, all under the same roof – for a week. It was intense. There were some seriously big personalities in that space, and at times it felt like the walls of the hotel wouldn't hold them all. The energy was loud, showy, competitive, and it threatened to spill over. It felt like we had been pushed in at the deep end, fully immersed in the madness of the competition. All I could do was cling on and hope to ride it out for as long as physically possible.

I felt instantly intimidated. Walking through the corridors, I would see people huddled in little groups, riffing, harmonising, flexing their vocal talents as though they were already on stage. At one point, a guy jumped on the piano that was located in one of the communal spaces and started playing. Immediately, people gathered around and began singing, spontaneously breaking into different melodies, everybody desperate to hit those high notes, to show their range, show what they were capable of. It all felt incredibly stage-school. To be honest, I found it a bit cringe. This wasn't me. At all. As much as I love performing, I'm not the kind of person to just stand up and start singing in front of a group of friends (not unless I'm really drunk!). It's not my style, and it feels like showing off. But it was incredibly daunting because everyone was *so* good. It felt like every single person there was amazing. Suddenly, I was surrounded by people who ached for this dream as much as I did, people who had trained in singing and dancing, people who had been exposed to more opportunities than I ever had. As much as I believed in myself, I couldn't help but feel a little out of my depth. I had never been around so much talent before. This wasn't High Wycombe anymore, and I wasn't just going to sail through these auditions. I knew the competition was going to be intense. Underneath that surface fear, though, I still had my belief, running through my heart like a central thread. I knew I had a right to be there, too. I felt capable and ready for the challenge. I never questioned my talent.

On the night we arrived, the producers threw a party for everyone. The Bootcamp performances and rehearsals took place in a huge mansion near the hotel. It had endless rooms and was surrounded by so much greenery. It was one of the fanciest houses I had ever seen. The perfect setting for a party. But I made a point of not going. I heard later that there was lots of alcohol and a hot tub, everyone was drinking. It sounded like a recipe for disaster. I wanted to chill and rest my voice. I didn't fancy being hung-over, or giving myself a sore throat from doing too many tequila shots and having screamed conversations with people I had only just met. Weirdly, it almost felt like it was a bit of a test, like the producers were trying to whip up some drama between the contestants. It's a good tactic – get everyone drunk and remove all our inhibitions. But I wasn't up for it. I'm glad I didn't go in the end.

The whole thing was such an intense experience. Every day we had rehearsals and performances. We were up at the crack of dawn and working relentlessly until bedtime. You had to be 'on' all the time. Every moment was a performance, not just when you were on stage. Every interaction with the other contestants, even just talking to the crew and producers – it felt like you were under this laser-focused scrutiny all the time. It was a lot. Every night I collapsed into bed; the tiredness was deep in my bones like a constant ache. I was running off excitement and adrenaline and little else.

That year – the 2011 competition – was the most brutal Bootcamp ever, or so the headlines said at the time. There were 186 acts due to take the stage in front of the judges, the first time we would sing in front of them again since our initial auditions, but before we even got to perform, the judges (or rather, the producers) decided to send forty acts home. Great TV, but less great for the people who were putting their hopes and dreams on the line. Producers, directors and audiences live for the drama – I understand that. But that was forty people – or more than that, as some of those acts were groups – who would have their hearts broken in the name of entertainment. It was impossible to be unaffected by the tension. We all dreaded going home. I wanted to stay more than I had ever wanted anything in my life. It was this clawing need that filled my whole body. Every minute I was by myself, every night before I fell asleep, I would visualise it. Visualise myself progressing. I had to see that it was possible. I had to believe.

I made it through the first round, but the relief was short-lived. We were straight into competition mode. I was put into a big group, and we were told we were to do a performance together. Everyone in the group was *sick*. The talent from everyone was unreal. I felt so inspired by everyone I was working with. One guy in my group, Ashford – he and I just clicked. We understood each other instantly and gravitated towards each other. I loved rehearsing with him, and I admired so much about the way he approached each song. His mentality was a real calming force in an overwhelming, high-octane environment. Ashford and I are still close friends even now. My connection with him helped me feel confident about our performance, but I also knew our song was polished, our harmonies were on point, our choreography was tight. I knew we were in with a great shot of going through.

We walked onto the stage, and the music started. We threw ourselves into the performance, giving it everything. Our vocals sounded amazing. I was so happy with what I was doing; I felt in my element. I loved being on stage; I loved being watched by the judges. I was confident and bold. There was no hesitation, no second-guessing. But then something shifted. Around halfway through the song, one of the girls in our group did something we hadn't rehearsed. Mid-way through the performance, she was going to do a rap. But to everyone's shock, she abandoned the choreography we had decided on. I watched her as she peeled away from the group and stalked to the front of the stage, skipping down the steps towards the judges.

*What the hell is she doing?!* I thought. We were all staring at her, trying to keep performing, worrying she was going to mess it up for all of us. We hadn't discussed this – she had gone off-script. It felt like she had thrown us under the bus. She didn't stop at the bottom of the steps. She strutted in front of the judges' table, belting out her parts with everything she had. She got right in front of each judge, performing directly into their faces. She was giving the performance of her life, and we had become nothing more than her backing singers. I couldn't believe what I was seeing. But, as they say, the show must go on. I focused on what I was doing, what the group was meant to be doing. I stuck to the plan.

She did what she had to do. There's a part of me that understands why she did that. I know what it feels like to want something so badly that you will do anything to achieve it, to find a new level that you didn't even know you had inside yourself. I had done a similar thing at the initial auditions in London, when I had thrown myself around the stage, dancing to Rihanna in a way I had never done before.

That girl was the only person to make it through to the next stage. That was it. It was done. I was crushed. I couldn't believe it was over. Tears brimmed over my eyes and I cried until I felt empty and hollow, like everything had been scooped out of me. I called my mum and cried again. I told her I was sure it was over, that I hadn't made it. I would have to go home. I tried to picture it. Back to High Wycombe, back to grafting on social media, travelling in and out of London, desperately trying to be noticed again. It was unthinkable. It couldn't be over.

They led a group of us into a room, all the people who hadn't made it through to the next stage. I thought they were going to talk to us about going home, to confirm that the dream was dead in the water. I braced myself. But the bad news never came. Instead, they told us they were trialing us in groups. I remembered what Kelly had said at my first audition – that she could see me in a group. It felt like a lifeline. A group could work. As long as I was on stage, as long as I was singing – that was what I needed. It didn't matter how I got there.

I'd been officially moved into the 'groups' category, but I didn't have my own group yet. They tested lots of different combinations out, different voices, music styles and looks. They were looking for the perfect blend, people who just fit together naturally like jigsaw pieces. They hadn't found that thing yet, that magic spark. I don't know what it is that makes a group work. I don't think there's a perfect formula, or special equation. One blonde, plus two brunettes, a good handful of dancing ability, three cups of vocal talent, a dash of spicy personality, a pinch of humour. It doesn't work like that. I believe that for a group to work, there has to be a *real* connection. The personalities have to gel as much as the voices. It's a different kind of harmony, but just as important. And, *vitally*, we have to actually like each other.

I met Jesy first after we were put in a room together at the hotel, so we became pretty close in those first few days. Jesy was already good friends with Jade after she had got talking to her on the bus to and from Bootcamp, and so the three of us became a little squad. We loved each other's vibes from the minute we got together. I was quickly drawn to Jade. She was quiet and unassuming, which was refreshing in an environment with so many enormous personalities. She seemed super humble, super normal. We sensed we were similar to each other. I think we both knew we would be able to help keep each other sane, even when everything around us felt overwhelming.

We thought we should be a band. The three of us. It was perfect. We liked each other; we looked great together; we sounded amazing. So, when it came to them splitting people up into groups, we made sure we stood together as a tight little trio. But it didn't happen like that. They split us up. Jesy was put in a group with Perrie and two other girls. They were called Faux Pas. Jade and I were put into another group of three with another girl. We were called Orion. It wasn't what we had hoped for – we were sad that we were now competing against each other after becoming friends – but I was determined to make it work, regardless. The other girl in our group was lovely, and we had meshed well together, and I quickly enjoyed the dynamics of being in a group. I love collaborative work and it generated a real sense of fulfilment from practising together, arranging our voices to fit the songs, figuring out who was going to sing and when, and where we would all be on the stage. It felt like we could build something special together. Rather than diluting my voice, it felt as though it was being enhanced by the other girls' voices. I loved how it sounded.

The next stage of the competition was going to be the judges' houses, which was familiar to me from watching the show as a kid. The acts are flown off to a glamorous location. There are higher stakes, lots of tears. It felt like that was the point when shit started to get real. It was a huge leap forward. The stage before the live rounds, in front of a studio audience. Not only would we be mentored by one of the best in the business, but it would mean we were closer than ever to winning, to gaining more exposure than we could have ever dreamed of. Making it to the judges' houses felt impossibly huge. But so much of it was still entirely out of our control at that point. We were at the whims of the judges and the producers as they shunted us around into different groups, different combinations, trying out new things. It felt like I had whiplash. Things were changing so fast, I could barely keep up.

They decided they weren't going to let Orion or Faux Pas through to the next round. Another blow. But just as I was about to call my mum crying yet again, there was yet another twist in the tale. Jade and I were to be combined with Jesy and Perrie to make a new group. We knew the producers wanted a girl band for this year's competition, and they liked for each member to have a different appeal and a different look. I think the original plan was for the band to just be Jade, Jesy and myself. Perrie wasn't even in the equation until one of the producers heard her singing on her own backstage. That girl has a *voice*. He knew that she needed to be part of the group.

The whole process had been such a rollercoaster up until this point – so many ups and downs, so much uncertainty, so many moments I had been convinced I was going home – it was hard to feel settled, but eventually it sank in. This was the group. We were going through to judges' houses. They believed in us, and the moment I heard our voices come together for the first time, I believed in us, too. I often think about what it was that pulled the four of us together in the final version of the band. Why not another four? Why not a different combination? There was so much talent in those early auditions, so many people deserving to be on stage, deserving to have their talent heard. Why us?

Eleven years, five albums and over sixty million record sales later, I think I finally have the answer. We had that *thing*. That intangible thing that just pulsed around us, like an energy. There was magic in the air, and all of us could feel it from the first time they threw us in a room together. You might call it the 'X factor'. It just felt *right*. When we connect with each other, sparks fly – sparks of creativity, but also sparks of love and happiness. We spark joy in each other and do our best to spark joy in those around us. From the beginning, our values were aligned. We knew what we wanted, we knew the feeling we hoped to create. It wasn't about money or fame, that was never our priority. More than anything, we wanted to have fun, to love what we did, to spread that love to our fans. To do that, we had to love each other. And we did. Fiercely.

This was the moment Little Mix was born. Only, not quite. That wasn't our name originally. We sat down to brainstorm, and the first name we came up with was Infinite Bass. Truly terrible. The name we loved was Rhythmix. We were happy with that name, but there was already a charity that had the exact same name, so we had to change it – we were gutted. We knew we wanted the name to incorporate the word 'mix', but we were struggling to think of anything that felt right. It was Tulisa who finally named us.

# BELIEVE

'How about Little Mix?' she said. It was met with deathly silence. We hated it, I thought it made us sound like little kids. There was nothing 'little' about us. Not our voices, not our personalities. But it was too late. The wheels were in motion. All the judges and producers liked the name, so it just kind of stuck. We were Little Mix. Thankfully, over time, the name started to grow on us. We just got used to it, like you get used to anything. And then, by the time we had heard the name a million times, it became so normal we couldn't imagine being called anything else. It's funny to think that we hated it at first, when now that name is such an intrinsic part of our identity and our history.

In that moment, there wasn't much time to think about our new name. We were going to the judges' houses. Our biggest opportunity so far. But groups never win *The X Factor*. It had never been done in the history of the show, and we had only just met each other. How could we possibly compete with these polished solo acts, the girls who could stun a crowd into silence with their power ballads, the boy bands who always drew in thousands of teenage fans? We were the underdogs. We barely expected to last the week.

# CHAPTER NINE

## Judges' Houses

'Are you ready?'

Within days, or even hours, it felt like I had known the girls for a lifetime. You know those people who you just have an instant connection with? You're straight in, no need for the small talk or the polite 'getting-to-know-you' questions. Those people are special. You don't get many immediate bonds like that in your lifetime. But that's how it was with the others. It felt like we were able to skip all of that and plunge straight into the good part, the part where we were closer than close, best friends who talk to each other like sisters. They became my family overnight. We clung to each other as our lives became unrecognisable around us.

With everything that was going on, the strange and wonderful circumstances that had thrown us together, it was inevitable that our friendship was going to be intense. Teenage friendships so often are, but for us, everything was accelerated. We went from being strangers to working together, living together, spending every single second in each other's company, within a matter of days. We were united in this desperate longing to make our dreams come true, surrounded by the chaos of TV cameras, press attention, live performances. We had been thrust into a new, unfamiliar world, and we needed each other in order to survive. It didn't take long for us to know each other inside out, the kind of mutual knowledge and understanding that would ordinarily take years to develop.

We had a little time off before we had to go to judges' houses for the next stage of the competition. Boy, did we need it. Bootcamp had been a wild ride, and we were craving some time to decompress. We were still processing everything that had happened. I had to keep reminding myself that it was real, that I didn't dream it. We had made it to judges' houses. Out of thousands and *thousands* who auditioned, we were still in the running; we still had a shot. I said it to myself, over and over, but it still felt unreal. The other girls felt the same. We kept bursting into random fits of excitement – losing our minds, jumping around and screaming – out of nowhere. It was so hard to properly comprehend what was happening. I'm so glad we had each other during that strange time in limbo. We helped to keep each other grounded. We were still teenage girls, kids really, and despite the madness of the competition, we never lost our sense of fun.

On our break, we all went to stay at Perrie's mum's pub up north so we could have a week of spending time together, getting to know each other even more, making plans for the next stage of the competition. It was one enormous sleepover. We were in each other's pockets, doing everything together, going for walks, watching silly movies, staying up into the early hours talking, talking, talking. We got to know everything about each other, what we loved, what we hated, what was important to us, what made us tick. The more we discovered, the closer we became. It was like we were threading ourselves together, pulling the stitches tighter and tighter each day. There was so much laughter. The face-aching laughter that comes from somewhere deep and real.

But the main thing we did was work. We were always working. Every day, late at night, first thing in the morning. We were young, hungry and brimming with enthusiasm.

In our minds, there weren't enough hours in the day. We would have worked non-stop if it wasn't for annoying inconveniences like eating and sleeping. We were so hard-working because we all had the same vision. We yearned to be superstars. We knew we had all the elements; we had all the ingredients, and now it was up to us to make sure we lived up to our own expectations. We would huddle at every chance we got, singing, harmonising, writing, planning world domination. So many plans were made in that little pub in South Shields. We felt safe and cocooned in our self-belief, a little bubble of hope and happiness. Everything was ahead of us.

There is something sacred about beginnings. The start of something. There was a special quality about that early period in our journey, something pure and untainted. All we had was hope. That was it. We weren't famous. We weren't rich. We weren't anybody yet. We were just four girls who loved to sing and perform and were desperate to share that with the world. My memories of those days, of discovering who we were without any of the madness that would come later, are incredibly precious to me. Part of me thinks that this was the best bit of our entire journey. We had all the space to simply enjoy each other, and enjoy the delicious anticipation of the unknown. I would like to freeze those moments, bottle them up, so I could experience that simple happiness whenever I wanted. But we couldn't stay there. Time crashed into our little haven and pushed us forward, pushed us back to London, back into the chaos. It was time to go to the judges' houses.

BELIEVE

We flew out to Mykonos to stay with Tulisa and the other groups in this adorable villa. Perfect blue skies, blinding sunshine bouncing off a glittering sea, immaculate white buildings dotted along the winding hills. It was paradise. If we could forget for a moment why we were really there, it almost felt like the ultimate girls' holiday. The four of us were joined at the hip, sitting together on the plane, sharing rooms in our villa, soaking up the warm weather. We were still getting to know each other, swept along by our intense excitement.

But it most definitely *wasn't* a holiday. We were there to work, and we took it incredibly seriously. While the other groups were drinking or sunbathing or reading by the pool, we were rehearsing. Every single second, we were working. We wanted our performances to be the best they could be, to show off what we could do, all that we were capable of. We had this bubbling sense that the sky was the limit – that we could reach new heights – that's what kept us going, propelled us forward, pushed us to work harder and harder. That is honestly one of the things I loved the most about the group. We were so focused and all had our sights set on the same thing. The work ethic we had between us was off the charts.

We were so nervous, too. Only a handful of acts make it through this stage – maybe three or four groups would get to perform at the live shows, which would be the next stage of the competition. The cutting process was brutal, and we knew we could go at any moment. We had to stay ready. We knew from Bootcamp that the producers could decide to eliminate as many people as they cared to, at any point. Nothing was guaranteed. And as a result, it was impossible to ever feel settled or relaxed. But the adrenaline was a good thing. It coursed through our veins, giving us this boundless energy, a fierce exuberance that shone through our performances. We wanted it, and you could tell.

We had two songs to sing in front of Tulisa. The first one was 'Cry Me A River' by Justin Timberlake. We nailed it. Our arrangements, our harmonies, everything was so on point . . . and they didn't show it on the programme. We were so annoyed. They showed it on *The Xtra Factor*, the behind-the-scenes show on ITV2, but not the main show, the one everyone would see. The second song was 'Big Girls Don't Cry' by Fergie. In rehearsals, we sang that song flawlessly. We were buzzing with ourselves. It was perfect. But when we watched it back, it didn't sound perfect. One of the harmonies sounded much louder than the main melody, which threw everything off and made the whole thing sound not as good as we rehearsed. I am not the kind of person to blame the tools when a job goes wrong, but in this instance, I do wonder if there was something off with the levels or our microphones. I also wonder if things had been manipulated, if there was a decision to change the levels, or edit the song afterwards to make us sound off. I'm not sure. But all I know is the performance that went out to the millions of people watching at home was not the performance we knew we were capable of. Suddenly, everything felt precarious. We went from feeling hyped and confident to being seriously afraid that we were going to be sent home. That was one of the scariest moments. I almost wouldn't have minded being sent home if we had shown them exactly what we could do and we just weren't good enough, but I couldn't handle being eliminated if we hadn't lived up to our true potential yet.

Later, we found out that they *were* planning on sending us home. The rumour was that they didn't want us to make it to the live shows because girl bands never do well. They thought it would be a waste to put us through, only to see us get sent home in the first week of the live shows. Tulisa had to fight for us. She believed in us. She could see our talent, our drive, our hunger. She had our backs from the beginning and continued to fight for us throughout the entire competition. I will always be incredibly grateful to her for that. She really saw us.

Getting through that stage was the most euphoric feeling. When we got that 'yes', I couldn't believe what I was hearing.

'Girls, you've got something different about you,' Tulisa said. The four of us were lined up in front of the pool, gripping each other's hands tightly.

'Here's my issue though – you're all *so* young.' I felt my throat constrict. This was it. She was going to tell us no.

'Are you ready? I'm just not sure.' I wanted to scream at her that we were ready, that we had been ready for years. I had felt ready for this moment for as long as I could remember. I had dreamed it, wished it, willed it, and now it was within arm's-reach. But I didn't scream. None of us did. Instead, we edged closer to each other, turning inwards until we became a little semicircle, our arms pressed together, our breathing rapid. I could practically feel everyone's heartbeats fluttering in their chests. I dropped my chin to my chest and tried to control my breathing. I had never known nerves like it.

'I'm really sorry . . .' Tulisa said, 'but you're gonna have to do this all over again.' I didn't even hear the end of her sentence. It was drowned out by our screams. The joy and relief were overwhelming. We burst into life, tears dripping down our faces, jumping on the spot. Jade threw her arms out and pulled us into a vice-like hug. We pressed our foreheads together and I could feel hot breath and cool tears on my cheeks, all our emotions melting into one big ball. Tulisa came up behind us and wedged her way into the circle. We couldn't squeeze her hard enough.

Immediately afterwards, we huddled around Perrie's phone while she called her mum on speaker phone. We pressed our hands to our mouths so we couldn't give it away early.

'Mam?' she said, a slight tremor in her voice. 'Hi . . . um . . .'

'Oh, come on, Perrie, just tell us – I can't take the stress!' said Perrie's mum as we all tried not to laugh. Perrie nodded at us and held the phone in the centre of all of us.

'We're through!' we screamed in unison. What a moment.

This time in our journey was so precious. The start of everything. Only hope and opportunity ahead of us. Tulisa was right, we *were* so young – although we didn't feel it. And we were naive. How could we not be? We were teenagers. Were we ready for what was ahead? We never could have known what to expect. The scale of it, the speed of it all. It was so much to navigate, and so much to learn all at once. We were about to wade into a different world: of fame, fans and fortune – and those young women holding hands at the edge of the pool had no idea what they were in for.

Once you get on that machine, it's hard to hit the brakes. The wheels were in motion and we were gathering speed.

# BELIEVE

All of a sudden, it felt like life became a blur and we were hurtling into a new reality, one we had only dreamed about in our bedrooms. But that was all to come. Right then, in that moment, we were on cloud nine. I said I wish I could bottle this feeling, draw on it whenever I feel low. This is because it's so important for me to remember what it felt like at the start, the optimism, the happiness, because the years that followed would be so much harder. There were times when I felt like the girl who was jumping for joy in Mykonos, the girl who believed in herself, believed in her talent, had disappeared forever. There were times when I worried I would never feel that way again. I lost her for a long time. That's why I return to the beginning. To force myself to remember where I started, who I used to be, the confidence and strength I used to have – before I had it pummelled out of me.

We flew home from Mykonos in a daze of joy. It was slightly awkward because we were on the same flight as the acts who hadn't made it through, and they were obviously gutted, but nothing could stop our high. It felt like it was our positive energy keeping the plane in the air. We couldn't wait to land, we couldn't wait to push on to the next stage, to the live shows. We were always thinking about the future; we were impatient, running ahead of ourselves. What's next – what's next – what's next? I wish I could go back and pause it there. Pause myself in that moment, force myself to appreciate every second of that feeling, because it wasn't to last. Little Mix were at the beginning of everything, but for me, this was also the beginning of everything changing.

# CHAPTER TEN

# Defying the Odds

'We were going to show them all.'

As soon as we landed back in the UK, we started getting ready for the next stage of the competition. It felt like we had barely touched the ground before we were whisked off to something new. There wasn't a second to catch our breath or look back at everything that had just happened to us. We were being propelled forwards at top speed. The adrenaline of it all was addictive. We were itching to get started. But first, we had to move into the *X Factor* contestants' house.

Living in that house was genuinely one of the best experiences of my life. Maybe the most fun I have ever had. Ever. In a way, it felt like this was my university experience. I was still a teenager, living in a big house with a load of other young people I had only just met. We were all trying to figure out how to live on our own, how to look after ourselves, how to be adults, dreaming of the futures we were trying to build for ourselves. I imagined this would be what university halls would have been like. Just maybe with less sporadic singing and impromptu performances after dinner. There was a huge kitchen where we all made meals together, and a dining room where we would eat and chill out. There was a jukebox in the basement, and pool tables, so we would blast music as loud as we wanted and have these wild dance parties all night. There was a sense of freedom I had never felt before. I was out in the world, living the life I was meant to be living. Edging closer to my dream. It was all happening.

All the acts who were going to be performing in the live shows were living under this one roof. That meant it could also get intense at times, and there was drama. There were arguments, tensions between different groups, people would get with each other and try to keep it secret, but rumours would circulate. I had a couple of run-ins with fellow contestant Frankie Cocozza. This guy just *did not* like me. I don't know why, but we did not get on at all. One time, Frankie ate Jade's lasagna and then brazenly left the remains in the sink. He didn't even clean up after himself. Jade was upset because it was a disrespectful thing to do, but also because our meals were genuinely precious – we were so busy with rehearsals and preparing for the show that we didn't always have time to cook and eat properly, so having one of your meals vanish was a big deal. We found out Frankie was the culprit and called him out on it, but he barely reacted. He wasn't bothered that we were upset. Another time, he told one of the other girls that he didn't like me. Actually, he said it in much stronger terms than that. He said I was an 'ugly c-word'. I couldn't believe it when the girls told me what he had said. I was fuming. I confronted him and we ended up having a screaming match in the middle of the kitchen. I guess this is what happens when too many teenagers and young adults are left to their own devices.

These little negative moments didn't ruin my experience, though. My overwhelming memories from this time are of the fun we had. Jade, Perrie, Jesy and I became closer and closer. Our friendship cemented into an even more solid form. We spent our evenings curled up on each other's beds, huddled on sofas, planning, plotting, practising. We began to move as a unit. We were practically thinking as one.

I'm so grateful I got to experience that house. A coming-of-age accelerated and intensified, but with all the hallmarks

The journey I am on now began with a little girl. I think about her often – her dimples and frizzy hair, her painful shyness, and her quiet determination. I hold her dreams close to my heart, the dreams that I pushed so hard to achieve for her.

Have I done enough? Have I made that little girl proud? Everything I do, every boundary I break, every conversation I start, I do it for her – the little girl who lives inside me – and all the little girls who watch me on stage, all the Mixers who have ever wondered where they belong.

(*above, left*) Grandad Steve and Nanny Doreen.

(*above, right and below*) Grandma Norma and Grandad Luther.

Home is a beautiful chaos. Home is a place where I get to watch my family grow and evolve.

The house would be full of laughter, always so busy. There was nothing calm about it. The walls hummed with our energy, with our noisy ways of loving each other.

The moment that my life changed forever. Little Mix winning *The X Factor* in 2011, and being the first group to do so. This was real. We had done it.

(*above, left*) Promoting our very first album, *DNA*. You can tell this is over a decade old because it was at HMV, before streaming became dominant!

(*above, right*) One thing I loved about touring was how close we became with the dancers. They were a constant support in a high-stress environment.

(*right*) Glitz and glam in one of my favourite tour outfits.

(*left*) My sister, Grandad Steve, my dad and me.

(*below*) Jamaica will always be my second home. I will forever cherish the memories I hold and continue to make here.

Some snaps with all the amazing people who have supported me throughout my journey. I will always keep my family close. Plus, there's no party like a Pinnock party!

Climbing Mount Kilimanjaro for Sport Relief with a great group of people. The scenery was stunning, and I loved being so immersed in nature.

I had a lot of meaningful conversations and realisations on this trip and it spurred me into action. A rainbow appearing reminded me that something beautiful can come out of a storm.

There are so many special women in my life, true friends who are with you through the ups and downs and share all the milestones with you. Pregnancy included!

of growing up and experiencing a parent-free existence for the first time – just like I would have had if I had gone to university and become a student. But I'm also grateful that this stage was only the beginning of my journey. I often think about all the people who lived in that house with us, all the other acts who, like us, thought they were standing on the precipice of their dreams, who thought everything was about to happen for them. But for most of them, it didn't. They got to move into that house, do some of the live shows, get a tantalising taste of the excitement and joy of performing, of fame . . . only for it to come to nothing. I'm not sure how you're supposed to move forward after that. How you come to terms with a disappointment on that level. The threat of losing this opportunity hanging over me was enough to keep me pushing forward. I had never craved anything so badly.

But we were *not* the favourites. In fact, we were quite the opposite. Nobody on that first live show believed in us. Girl bands didn't do well. We knew that, we knew the history. Everyone expected Little Mix to be heading home in the first couple of weeks. There was one producer who had been instrumental in forming the Spice Girls. So when it came to girl bands, he knew his shit. He was working with us backstage, helping us to develop our performances, and he saw something in us. He knew what we could do, and he told people that they needed to keep an eye on us, that we were great. But still, no one took us seriously. We could feel it – the lack of belief, the dismissive attitude people had towards us – but we didn't let it get to us. Although we saw ourselves as the dark horses of the competition, in a way, it was reassuring to be in a position where the expectations were so low. It meant there was less pressure on us; no one was scrutinising us, or even thinking of us as a threat. We settled quietly into this role. We didn't need to be the biggest personalities in the room or be at the centre of any dramas. We preferred to keep our heads down, to work on our craft like we always had, and to let our performances do the talking. If they didn't believe in us now, that was fine. We were going to show them all.

As soon as the live shows started, we threw ourselves into rehearsals. We were at it constantly. In the house, there was a big gym that had a row of floor-to-ceiling mirrors all along one wall, and lots of floor space in front of the mirrors. That's where we rehearsed. Every day. For hours. Practising the songs over and over, drilling the steps endlessly – we would keep going until we genuinely couldn't put a foot wrong, until the moves felt fluid and natural and we hit the beats with an ingrained muscle memory. We weren't used to learning routines. None of us had done this before – singing and dancing in a full performance – not on this scale, and the pressure was intense. It only got harder as we progressed through the competition too, because each week there were more songs to learn, more dance routines, more vocal arrangements. Our heads were swimming with it.

The live shows were incredibly intense. You'll remember the structure. Every Saturday night, all the remaining acts take to the stage and perform a cover of their choice before facing the judges. Then there's a public vote where people at home phone in to save their favourites, and the two acts that come last in the vote have to perform for the judges. The judges then choose who to send home. Before each performance, there would be a succinct little montage of the rehearsal process, any dramas or issues that had happened that week. It was designed to show off a bit of our person- alities so viewers could get to know us, and to build some tension. Maybe there was a harmony we were struggling to hit. Maybe someone had been feeling homesick that week and struggled with their emotions. That's what the people at home got to see. But what they didn't see was all the rest of the work that went into getting those performances ready week in, week out. Because it was a lot. It was the hardest I had ever worked up to that point.

Every morning, we'd be up at the crack of dawn. The early starts were no joke. We had to go to bed before 10 p.m. because by the end of each day, we would be drained. We would fall into bed with that heavy, body-exhaustion that sucks you into the deepest sleep. The days were packed with perfecting our routines. At the start of each week we would decide which song we were going to perform, with some guidance from Tulisa and the producers, then as soon as that was decided, we would start planning our vocal arrangement of the song, then straight into rehearsals – choreography, dance rehearsals, vocal rehearsals, meetings with producers. All day, every day there were meetings and things to work on. It was relentless. Tulisa was such a huge support during this whole process. We saw her a couple of times per week, but she was always just at the other end of the phone if we needed to talk to her about anything. Once, she had us over to her place for dinner and made us curry goat – it was wicked. She was rooting for us so sincerely; she motivated us to succeed. Having people in your corner is so important in times like those.

That first live show was a whirlwind. There are a lot of performances from early in our journey that I struggle to watch because we were still learning, but whenever I watch this first live show, I feel so proud. For our first live performance, I genuinely think we killed it. I think I'm wearing one of the worst outfits I have ever seen – white denim shorts with sleeveless denim shirt, red socks and white trainers. We all had luminous eyeshadow, chunky jewellery. It was peak 2010s fashion, but we pulled it out of the bag. We sang a version of Nicki Minaj's 'Super Bass', and we opened the song with a rap. It was a high-energy, full-of-life performance, and we looked like we were enjoying every second. I'm so proud of us for nailing it because my god we were nervous, but it paid off.

'It's week one, and you are already the best girl band we have ever had on *The X Factor!*' Gary Barlow's comment during our judges' feedback had our jaws on the floor. We couldn't believe what we were hearing. The judges loved it. They showered us with praise. They loved our chemistry, our energy, our creativity. Kelly Rowland said we had tons of raw potential. We felt it too. It felt like we were off to a flying start. Of course, we were petrified getting on that stage for the first time, but we had gone into that week knowing what we wanted. We planned out our own arrangement, I wrote my own rap; we were the ones leading our own identity as a group – even from that first week. The judges and producers were really impressed that we had taken control. And that was how every week went from there. That fiery work ethic never faltered, and we were willing to put in the hours to get our performances to the standard we knew we could reach. We may have been young girls, but we were not about to be pushed around or told what to do. I have always loved that about us. It was also super important for us to stay focused on the work itself – because it would have been so easy to get caught up in all the other stuff that came with being on *The X Factor*.

Now that we were on the live shows, we were treated like we were famous. It was wild. From screaming fans waiting for us outside the studio, to the way we were treated by all the staff working backstage – there were even paparazzi trying to get pics of us and occasionally stories in the newspapers about some of the acts. For four normal girls like us, who all came from relatively humble backgrounds, it was a lot to get our heads around. For me, this was my first taste of stardom, and as overwhelming as it was, I knew I wanted more of it. Younger me was hooked. I think if the same thing were to happen to me now, as a grown-ass woman in her thirties, the idea of fame – the glitz and glamour of it all – wouldn't have appealed to me in the same way. I would have the maturity to see through it, to be a bit more wary of the downsides that can come with being famous. But me at nineteen? Well, it was everything I could have dreamed of and more.

As each week passed and we made it through, we were defying the odds. Defying the curse of *The X Factor* girl band. It was so energising to take a step closer each week; to prove more people wrong; to show them that we weren't just an anomaly; that we *did* have something special.

The homesickness was real during the live shows. We didn't get to go home at all. In fact, we barely saw our families, and our weeks were so packed with rehearsals and then the adrenaline rush of the performances at the weekends that we rarely even had the energy to speak to them on the phone. We had slipped into a kind of bubble where the only thing that mattered to us was what went on in rehearsal rooms and on the stage. Anything beyond that had kind of melted into the background. But I missed home. I missed my parents. I pined for a hug from my mum, to bicker with my sisters over Sunday lunch, to fly out to Jamaica and spend time in the sunshine with my grandad. But I had to push those feelings down. It was the only way to get through it. I had to throw myself into the moment, pretend that nothing else existed.

The only time we got to see our families was at the weekends, and even then, it was only briefly. All our parents came to watch the live shows, and for my parents, after all the messy and confusing things that went on around their separation – with Mum moving out and then getting back together with Dad and breaking up again – it felt extra special for me to see them as a unit again. I really believe that me being on *The X Factor* helped to pull my family back together. Rather than all the tension and the arguments about selling the house or figuring out who was going to live where, my parents were united with a single goal – to support me. Everyone in my family was desperate for me to go all the way. They knew how much I wanted this; they had seen me working towards my dream to be a singer since I was at school and, most importantly, they believed in my abilities. They hoped for me to win almost as much as I did, and seeing their

126

smiles beaming out at me from the darkness of the crowds every time we stepped on that stage gave me a little internal boost. I couldn't have made it through the intensity of that time without knowing that my family was behind me, every step of the way. The other girls were the same. We were all so lucky like that. Our parents all started going to the same pub opposite Wembley, where the live shows were filmed. Our mums all became close during that time too, which we thought was the most adorable thing.

I couldn't contain the homesickness all the time though. I'm too emotional. There were times when it all became too much, and I just longed for a cuddle with my mum and all my home comforts. One week, the producers took pity on me and arranged for my dog – an angel little Pug called Harvey – to come for a visit at the house. It was a surprise, and I was led outside on a brilliant sunny day, and spotted Harvey bounding across the grass towards me. I was so happy in that moment – a little flash of familiarity and home amidst all the madness. But it wasn't only missing home that was starting to get to me. Slowly but surely, the confidence that had been flowing through me easily, was starting to dry up. I was losing my self-belief, and it meant that every week, the performances were getting a little harder. I would lift the microphone to my lips and feel a jolt of that old uncertainty, that desire to hide, to let the backing music drown me out – just like I had felt as a little girl. I was going backwards, and I didn't know why.

Suddenly, something started to feel different . . . off. I couldn't quite put my finger on it. But something had shifted.

It was a change that happened inside me, like a vital part of my internal stability had been knocked out of place, making things that used to feel safe and solid feel wobbly. Things like my ability, my talent, my confidence. It unnerved me to suddenly see a question mark where I had always been so certain. No matter what ups and downs had happened on my *X Factor* journey, I had always been unshakeable on the issue of my talent. I was good. I could sing. I was born for the stage. I knew that, in some deep place. I had known it ever since I had overcome my shyness as a child and found the strength to battle through my nerves. Even when I thought I was being sent home, or was being shunted around into different groups in the early stages of Bootcamp – even then, I never questioned my ability. But now, as we got closer to the finish line, I felt that belief slipping from my grasp. The better we did, the closer we came to winning, the worse I started to feel about myself. At the time, I didn't know why.

Looking back, the causes of this inner downfall are much clearer. I had started to compare myself to the other girls in the band. Something I had never done before. The pressure of the whole situation was starting to get into my head, and I convinced myself that the other girls were better than me, that they had better voices than mine. The producers and people working on the show reinforced this idea in my mind. I began to notice that my singing parts in our performances were getting shorter and shorter. One week, we were singing 'Telephone' by Lady Gaga and Beyoncé. Prior to the show, they took my part away and gave it to one of the others. There was little communication about it, no real explanation or any attempt to solve the issue another way.

Rather than suggesting I sing it in a different way, or swap to sing a different part, they would just cut my line. That was it. That was the confirmation I needed that I wasn't as good as the others. People thought I wasn't as good. The idea of that crushed me. I was so upset, I called Sairah in tears.

'Leigh-Anne. You get out on that stage, and you dance like you have never danced before,' she said to me in her typical style of tough love. 'They might not hear you sing that line, but they are damn well going to see you.'

So that's what I did. I gave it everything in that performance. I threw all my energy into it. You never would have known that I had been in tears about it just hours before. Another week we sang 'Don't Let Go' by En Vogue. There was one part that I was desperate to sing. I knew I could do it – but I also knew that I would have to fight for it because no one was going to just give it to me. I grabbed one of the producers between rehearsals and pleaded my case. I told her I wanted that part.

'Sing it now then,' she said, her tone cold. My stomach dropped. I hadn't expected that. It didn't feel like a particularly professional way to approach the issue. I wasn't warmed up.

'Right . . . right now? Here?' I asked, looking around to see if anyone else was going to walk past.

'Yep. If you think you can do the part . . . show me.'

I had already done it in rehearsals and I couldn't believe that I was still being asked to prove myself in this way. I tried to believe that I had just as much right as any of the other members of the group to be in this position, to speak up for what I wanted, but I couldn't imagine the producers speaking to the others in this way. But I wanted it. *Fine*, I thought, *let me show her.* I took a swift deep breath and sang the part. Perfectly.

'OK, sure,' she said. 'You can do it.' She didn't say anything else. I felt ecstatic that I had convinced her and, in that moment, I didn't even think about the injustice of the fact that I had had to convince her in that way. My crisis of confidence had sunk deep into me, and I felt almost grateful to have been given the chance to show them what I could do. And at the same time, I was terrified about having to sing that part on stage.

It became a cycle – like a self-fulfilling prophecy. The more I worried about my performances, the more pressure I put on myself, and the more likely I was to mess up, leading to more worrying and more mistakes. I couldn't find a way out of this vicious circle. Now I had been given this line that I so badly wanted to sing. The fear swelled in my chest, until it was so big that I found it hard to breathe. It was inevitable that something was going to give.

The competition got even more intense as the weeks went on. There were fewer acts, which meant we all had to perform twice. So that meant more rehearsals, more early mornings and long days, more pressure. It also meant there were more opportunities for me to shine – which was what I needed at that point.

For semi-finals week we were singing a song by The Supremes. Diana Ross – there isn't a much better showcase of vocal talent out there. I was excited. I knew I would finally have more of a chance to have more lines to sing because we had two performances – so two of us would lead one of the songs, and the other two would lead the other. After weeks of feeling like I was being out of the limelight, this was my opportunity. Really, all that meant was that I had a verse to sing on my own. Two to four lines, that was it, but it meant everything. I practised harder than ever, hyped myself every chance I got. I sang the lines in the mirror; in the shower. I even began dreaming about it. I was so excited to show the producers – and the viewers at home – what I could do. It felt like this was my moment to prove them wrong, to make them realise that I *did* deserve to be there.

It was the first performance of the semi-finals, and the stakes couldn't have been higher. All we had to do was nail these performances just like we had rehearsed them, and we would sail straight through to the finals. The music started and I felt the blood pound in my ears. This was it. We were singing 'You Keep Me Hanging On', and we were styled in this adorable 1960s aesthetic – my hair was piled up in a voluminous bouffant, and I wore a frilly mini-dress with sparkly ankle boots. Jade belted out the opening lines of the song perfectly while we hit the choreography, gripping our mic stands, bouncing our hips and swinging our arms. By this point, we were used to the lights and the cameras of the studio, the mass of unidentifiable faces in the crowd, we weren't even fazed by the podiums we were dancing on, or the backing dancers who twirled in front of us. We had come this far, and we weren't about to mess up now.

Jade finished her verse. We launched into the chorus. The harmonies were smooth, we sounded amazing. Then it was my verse. Normally, when I have a microphone in front of me, I enter this calm, purposeful state. Performing is my happy place. My mind becomes clear and focused, the adrenaline pulses through me as a positive energy. But this time, nothing felt clear or focused. My heartbeat raced erratically at my temples, my head felt full and cloudy. I was panicking. I got the first line out OK, but then the words just melted out of my brain. The lyrics disappeared. I could feel the hot, panicked breath rising in my chest. I knew the words weren't there. I had no idea what I was meant to sing next. When I watch the clip back (which is rarely – I can't bear to), I can see the split-second of pure terror in my eyes. I can pinpoint the exact moment where I knew the words were gone. There is no other feeling like it. It is every performer's worst nightmare.

I mumbled something unintelligible into the microphone. They weren't words. I moved my mouth, but they were just sounds. It was clear to everyone that I had forgotten the lyrics. But the show had to go on. I had to keep performing. I strutted to the top of the stage with the other girls, hit my poses, nailed my harmonies. But all the time there was this hot, sick feeling constricting my throat. I had messed up, big time. I had been given a chance to shine, and what had I done with that chance? Thrown it down the drain. We hit the final note and the lights went down. I bit my lip hard to keep the tears from falling. I wanted to collapse in a heap and cry my heart out. Shame crawled across my skin like pins and needles. Not only had I ruined my own moment, but also – what if I had ruined all of our chances of getting to the final? I couldn't handle that. The guilt was crushing, we came off stage and I crumbled. I could barely speak I was crying so hard, I just kept saying: 'I'm sorry, I'm sorry.'

At the time I blamed myself entirely. Of course I did. How could I not? I had blown it right when it mattered.

No wonder the producers didn't want to give me the big lines to sing. No wonder they thought I wasn't as good as the others. It felt like the horrible culmination of everything that had led up to that moment – all the doubts and fears that had plagued me since the live shows started. It was all true. Every negative thought I'd had about myself, in that moment – they all felt true.

But looking back, is it any wonder that I let the pressure get to me when I had been through weeks of being demoralised and criticised at every turn? When I had been treated as invisible and overlooked? I put too much pressure on myself to try to prove my worth, and it had started to break me.

# CHAPTER ELEVEN

## The Finals

'It's all come down to this.'

As we edged closer to the big final, it was that dream that kept me going. Despite the doubts and fears, and the slow draining of my confidence, my ultimate goal never wavered. I wanted to win the show, to be a real musician, a pop star, to share my music with fans. It was the only thing I had ever wanted, and now it was within touching distance. I kept that vision in my mind. I imagined the envelope being opened during the grand final and hearing the words 'Little Mix'. I imagined the screams and the fireworks, our name up in lights, our faces on the cover of every newspaper, our singles played on the radio. I visualised it and clung to that image in the moments when everything felt too hard.

The girls got me through it, too. I wanted this for each of them as much as I wanted it for myself. There were times when I wavered, when it all felt overwhelming, and I was scared about what was happening to me, to my confidence. But whenever I had a wobble like this, Jade, Perrie and Jesy were right there to pull me out of it, to remind me that we were all in this together. It could have been so easy for the tensions of the show to come between us. We were grappling with competition over who would sing which lines, worries about who got to shine in each performance, and the constant comparison coming from everyone who interacted with us. We could have slipped into rivalries, jealousy and resentment, but we didn't. It is a great credit to our friendship, to our individual characters, and to our connections with each other, that we managed to rise above all that noise. We never forgot what was truly important to us – which was achieving this goal together, as a unit. We never stopped being a team. We never stopped looking out for each other and having each other's backs.

After our infamous semi-finals performance, where I forgot the words and pleaded internally for the stage to open up and plunge me into the basement, we got mixed feedback from the judges. Gary Barlow's main point was that he felt like Perrie should be the leader of the group. He said she had the strongest voice. I tried to imagine it – a Pussycat Dolls-style setup with Perrie as Nicole Scherzinger and the rest of us little more than glorified backing singers. It stung. Not because I didn't think Perrie was good enough – I believed in her with my whole heart and would have supported her to the ends of the earth – but we were meant to be doing this as a team. And after a performance where I knew I had messed up, the comment felt pointed. Another person with a different kind of character might have leaned in to praise like that; they might have let it get to their head or started acting differently, but that just wasn't Perrie. Even as Gary was making that comment about her, she was shaking her head. She never went along with that line of thinking, or let it boost her ego. She was in it as an equal, with the rest of us. I saw them as my sisters, and I knew they felt the same.

So, even when I got overlooked or had my parts taken away from me, I never once felt any negativity towards the other girls about it. That just wasn't how we operated. We had such a beautiful bond, right from the beginning, nothing could shake that. I truly believe it was our sisterhood, our genuine, authentic friendship and love for each other that got us to that final. A day that would change each one of our lives forever.

The day of the finals felt so surreal. How the hell did we get here? The question bounced around my mind endlessly. Although we believed in ourselves, we were the underdogs of the competition and every week we had prepared ourselves for going home. Even that week, every day up until we were physically walking through the studio doors at the finals, we thought something would stop us from going all the way. But we hadn't been sent home or been voted off. We were here – at the final hurdle. Was this actually happening?

The format of the show is designed to build tension to the point of torture. You will remember how those finals used to go. The two remaining acts take to the centre of the stage and it was up to the host to open an envelope and read out the name of the act the public had voted as the winners for that year. The lights would go down, the studio would go deathly quiet. Even the audience seemed to hold its breath. The host would then take what felt like a million years to put us out of our misery. The camera would cut to the judges, to the audience, to our faces, back to the host, the judges again, to our hands gripping on to each other with tight little fists. It felt like an eternity. I could feel my pulse throbbing in my ears, the nerves almost making me dizzy, then I heard Dermot O'Leary's voice.

'I'm about to reveal the winner of *The X Factor* 2011. From the thousands that applied, it's all come down to this.' Around the studio, the sound of a heartbeat thud-thudded from the speakers. I edged myself closer to Jade, Perrie and

Jesy. Tulisa stood with us, staring straight ahead, just like we were, all our faces etched with fear. We couldn't look at each other. We couldn't make a sound.

'I can now reveal, the winner of *The X Factor* 2011 . . . is . . .'

Time stood still. I gave up trying to control my breathing and started taking shallow little gulps of air. My eyes scanned the faces of the crowd. I was looking for my mum. I needed her tough love in that moment. I needed her strength. I looked for my dad's face. I needed him to remind me of why I was doing this, of the passion that lives like fire in my chest. I needed to see my sisters' faces. I wanted to feel their steady hands on my shoulders giving me a gentle push, believing in me no matter what. I wish I could have seen Nanny's face in that crowd. More than anything, I longed to show her how far I had come from doing karaoke in her living room, to show her how my voice had grown louder, how I had learned to speak up, to back myself. I wanted to see the kindness in her eyes, the pride in her smile. I knew she was watching me. I could feel her. I closed my eyes.

'Little Mix!'

The moment I heard that first syllable, that 'Li–' sound, everything fell away. I turned my back to the crowd, to Tulisa, to the other girls, and stared at the back of the studio for half a second, my hands flying up towards my head. *What? What?! Was this really happening?* I could barely connect a coherent thought together. Around me, the stage exploded into light and sparkles, music blared, the crowd erupted into screams. I couldn't take it all in. I turned round to face the other girls and that's when it started to hit me. This was real. We had done it. Everything we had worked so hard for had paid off. We ran towards each other and collapsed into each other's arms. We crumpled under the weight of the emotion, weeks of hard work, stress, fear, hope weighed heavy on our shoulders, and we held on to each other as we finally let ourselves feel the full force of it. What a moment! I had heard people say that they were 'on cloud nine', or 'on top of the world' before, but now I really got what they meant. We were floating above ourselves, somewhere up in the sky, watching what was happening from this place of elevated unreality. The kind of joy that levitates you.

I'm not sure how long we stayed up there, floating about in the clouds like that, but it lasted for a while. The hours, days, weeks after winning blur into something dreamlike. We had to keep taking moments to remind each other that this was truly happening, that we weren't just in some extended fantasy, about to wake up at any moment. When we came off stage I immediately called my sister Sairah. She was at home because she had just given birth to her son, my nephew Kailum. I just remember screaming at her in total disbelief. After that, we went back to the dressing room. I rested both my hands on the table and froze as everything flashed before my eyes. Every single second of the whole experience – from filling out the form for the first auditions sat on my mum's sofa, to crying our eyes out as we performed our winner's song at the end of the show – played in front of my eyes like an epic montage. It was an unbelievable feeling. We all felt it.

Straight after winning, we got the chance to see our families for – and I kid you not – no more than thirty minutes. We had barely hugged our mums, we were still crying into their shoulders, and our new manager – because all of a sudden we had a manager – was like, 'Right, come on, girls, time to go back to the hotel!'

The show finished late in the evening, and we had to be up at 4 a.m. the next day for the first of our interviews. It didn't matter that we were physically and mentally drained. It didn't matter that our bodies ached from performing, or that we missed our families and desperately needed a break. It didn't matter that we had just finished a long and arduous competition process, because the end of *The X Factor* meant the beginning of Little Mix – and we had to hit the ground running. We had a solid week of wall-to-wall promo straight after the final, and there was no time for rest, for processing what had just happened, for contemplating the future. No. We were living it.

We were delirious during that week. All I remember is being pushed in front of different cameras, different media outlets, radio microphones, photoshoots. *Lorraine*, *This Morning*, *Loose Women*, ITV, BBC – every programme you can think of, we were on it. Every radio show, every online outlet. The interviews started to merge into one. And at the end of each day, we would sink into bed and fall into a coma-like sleep, before doing it all again six hours later. We were so tired. My god, we were *so* tired. We would fall asleep while the beauticians were putting makeup on us each morning. It was our first taste of the intensity of pop-star life and, although we were exhausted beyond comprehension, we were also relishing every damn second. This was it. The dream. And we had so much fun. We were laughing every second, delighting in the excitement and the absurdity of it all. We tried to hold on to every moment, appreciate everything that was happening to us.

We became famous overnight. Well, practically overnight. While we were on the show, we had some media attention, and we had some fans who would show up outside the studio asking for autographs, but it reached a whole new level as soon as we won; as soon as we started showing up in places outside of that familiar X *Factor* format. Now people were starting to see us as pop stars in our own right. It was intense, but also incredibly exciting to feel that shift. To feel *famous*.

From early in our journey, there were a smaller amount of people who were *my* fans. There are two girls I remember who were there at the beginning, who used to come to the live shows, and then they came to everything we did after we won and started promoting ourselves. They loved Little Mix as a whole, of course, but really, they were there for me. They would always ask me for my autograph, or for a selfie. They're still fans now. They are my ride-or-dies. I can't tell you how much I needed their support early on. Every time I saw one of their faces in a crowd, or waiting outside a venue, it was like my whole body could relax a bit. Like the tension I didn't even know I was holding in my neck and shoulders would ebb away. Someone was here for *me*, someone wanted to see *me*. Even in these early moments, the very first days and weeks of being in the band, I already felt a longing for this. I already knew that I had to be grateful for the few faces that turned towards me, for the few voices that shouted my name. I noticed them because it was rare, because I was becoming conscious of the fact that the other band members had bigger followings, more fans than I did.

It had started on the live shows, this sense of inadequacy, the feeling that I was 'less than', an unequal quarter of the band. And now that we had started our real journey in the music industry, those feelings only intensified.

I tried my best to push those feelings down. I didn't vocalise them to anyone, it felt like something I had to handle on my own. In my mind, what I was feeling was my fault. I wasn't good enough. I wasn't talented enough. I couldn't find the words to tell anyone how low I was feeling. How could I? This was everything I had ever dreamed of. I had broken into the industry; I was going to get to make music and perform for a living. What a dream! How could I feel anything other than euphoric at this moment? It should have been the happiest time of my life, the world was at my feet and there wasn't any time to dwell on my feelings because everything was moving incredibly quickly. So I squashed those emotions into some dark hole deep inside me. I told myself it would get better. Surely everything would start falling into place. Surely I would start feeling like I was supposed to, like a star, like a person whose dreams had just come true.

We realised quickly that we had to be in London. We had to live there. That was where everything was happening, that was where the majority of our work was, and we couldn't all commute from where we had been living before we won the show. I was still with my parents in Wycombe, in the bedroom I had as a teenager with my posters on the walls and stuffed toys on the bed. Moving out was the first big change. I rented a penthouse apartment with Jesy, in Putney, south London. It was beautiful. One of the bedrooms had this huge dressing room attached to it – like Sarah Jessica Parker had in the *Sex and the City* movie. Jesy and I tossed a coin to decide who would get that bedroom. She won, but I didn't mind because my room was bigger anyway, and I adored the space. We had the most fun living there. Probably *too* much fun, because after six months they asked us to leave – we basically got evicted. We were still only nineteen or twenty, and we didn't know how to do anything. The dishwasher, the washing machine, the heating – we were constantly calling service people to help us. Not because anything was broken, but simply because we didn't know how to use things. Looking back, we were taking the piss. It was so stupid. Understandably, the management company who looked after the building got tired of us and we had to go.

Next, I started renting my own place in Ladbroke Grove, west London. It was such a cute little flat, but I hated being on my own. I wasn't the only one who struggled. Jesy and I were a bit older, and both pretty independent people, but Jade and Perrie found it hard at first too. They missed their families so much. They were used to their mums doing a lot for them, and moving to London was so far from what they knew. They couldn't just pop home back to the North East for an evening if they were feeling overwhelmed. The change was a lot, for both of them. For me, it wasn't the homesickness that got to me, but living on my own in London felt scary, if I'm honest. Despite my independence, I hated the nights when I was home alone – I preferred to be around people. So, eventually I ended up back at home. Back at my parents'. The old bedroom I had grown up in became mine again. I realised there was no point wasting money on rent when it wasn't *too* difficult to get in and out of London. We may have been on the path to superstardom, but in those early months, I was still waking up in my old room with my old cuddly toys, shouting down the stairs to ask Mum to make me a cuppa.

But we were barely ever at home, anyway. Home became the road, the studio, the makeup chair, different hotel beds. Home was wherever I was with the girls. We became each other's family, each other's safe space. Everything had changed, everything was moving at a speed we could barely keep up with, but at least we had each other. We were only teenagers. Still kids. But we had stepped into an incredibly adult world. There were pressures and responsibilities and we desperately needed to succeed. We reverted to what we had always done – work. Our work ethic never faltered, even in the face of all the madness, all the shiny lights and cameras pointing in our faces, all the new attention we were getting. Our focus was clear. We knew what we aimed to achieve, and how we planned to do it. Just like when we were on the show, our instinct was to get our heads down and get to work.

At some point during those early weeks of the band, Simon Cowell told us we were the 'hardest working girls in the business.' But we didn't think we were doing anything out of the ordinary. Working hard was all we knew. We came into this expecting to work our arses off. We never wanted an easy ride or to have anything handed to us on a silver platter. I think it was to do with where we came from – we all have relatively humble beginnings and high hopes for our futures – and as a result, we were never entitled or arrogant. We kept that humility at our core, always. And we never fully shook off that sense of being the underdogs. The belief that we always had to prove somebody wrong.

For me, the demands of the job were a distraction from my insecurities. I threw myself into rehearsals, promotion, writing. Every moment when I was busy, striving to achieve the next thing, and then the next thing, I wasn't thinking about those niggling doubts. I wasn't thinking about the uncertainty or the inadequacy that had plagued me since the live shows. Keeping busy helped.

We won the show on 11 December 2011, and by February 2012 we were already touring with X *Factor* Live, heading up and down the country with some of the other acts that did well in that year's competition, playing in front of crowds of thousands for the first time. On top of that, there was also the relentless promotion and media. But our focus during that time was writing the first album. Musicians from reality TV shows and competitions often get a bad rep, and get stuck with labels like 'manufactured'. The assumption is that we are just mouthpieces, given a load of tracks to memorise and perform. I can't speak for how other artists from that kind of background work, but we never operated like that. We were heavily involved in the writing process and had an enormous amount of creative input and control over our sound, our lyrics and the musical arrangements. We pushed to be involved in every single stage – that was really important to all of us.

We were so excited to create music. We intended to make music that was empowering, uplifting – songs that made people feel good. Where were the people doing that? At that time, nobody was doing that. We felt that nobody was really speaking directly to young people, specifically young girls – and we knew that we had the power to connect with them. Our main motivation was wanting to inspire. That was the word that we always returned to whenever we spoke about our vision. Obviously, I had spent my teens writing songs and recording. Jade and Perrie both had musical experience as well and had written songs before, but really this process was new for all of us. None of us had ever worked like this, with the input of all these established writers and producers – people who had had countless number-one hits with the biggest stars in the business – in the best studios London had to offer. This was a whole different ball game. We had every tool available to us to enable us to create something special, to enable us to succeed – all we had to do was use our talents and our collective vision to pull it all together.

People are always fascinated by the process of writing a song. What comes first – the lyrics or the sounds? The idea or the chords? How do you decide who sings which parts? In bands, who gets the final say over the lyrics and the har- monies? I would say that, like any creative process, there isn't one correct way to do it. Everyone has their own process and the systems and structures that work for them.

For us, the work usually started in the studio. We would gather together with a writer and a producer and we'd just start talking. We would speak about our ideas, about the things we want to say, what we want the song to sound like. Maybe at this point we would throw out a couple of references, examples of other songs or sounds that we like. Then the producers would play us something – maybe a drumbeat, or a sound they had already created that fit with the vibe we're going for. We would either choose a sound, or work with them to create a new sound from scratch.

For our first single, 'Wings', it was all from scratch. We did so much research, listening to different references, different kinds of sounds and mixes. We knew what we liked: something that was upbeat, something that would lift you out of the monotony of daily life. We wanted to remind people how much greatness they had inside themselves. The goal was for people to feel powerful, limitless, but we also wanted it to be fun. The opening was iconic – jazzy brass notes like a live band. It felt fitting for our first single to start like this, triumphant and positive. It felt like a real declaration of everything we were about. While we were writing, there was a moment when it started to come together, and it felt like magic. We looked at each other like – *oh my god*. We knew we had something special on our hands. Nothing else out there sounded like this. There was nothing on the radio like this. On the second day working on the song, a writer called Ian James came in. He went into the booth and started singing these melodies and I will never forget that moment – that's when it all just clicked. He was singing all these phenomenal riffs and we were screaming in the studio – we were so, so gassed. He was a genius and definitely helped turn 'Wings' into the final product.

Back on X *Factor*, just before I went into the Bootcamp stage, I was sitting outside, buzzing with nerves and adrenaline, when a butterfly flew right towards me and landed on the ground, less than an inch from my foot. It just sat there. I stared at it. Delicate wings trembling, a flash of orange glinting like a flame in the sunlight. I studied the intricate patterns, the swirling black against the vibrant yellows and reds. It's hard to believe a design so beautiful and precise could exist in nature. It felt like the butterfly had chosen to visit me, to bring me a moment of calm, to bring me luck. I held on to that feeling, and now here we were where, months later, our dreams had come true and we were about to launch our first single. It felt like no coincidence that we were singing about wings. It was such a special moment. I even got a tattoo of a butterfly on my back to help me remember the luck that I was granted, to help me remember that I had been blessed by something so beautiful. I believe in fate, I believe that all these tiny things came together to bring me to where I was always destined to go. I never wanted to forget that I had wings inside of me, that I had the potential to reach incredible heights. But everything that was about to happen would make me forget that I could fly. My wings withered, unused, crushed under the weight of my own doubts.

I need to pause for a moment here – I feel like I need to explain something. I can understand if you're tempted to pull out the world's tiniest violin for me at this point. Oh, poor me. I'm in a girl band, I'm living out my dream as a musician, I'm famous, I'm earning more money than I have ever earned in my life. What the hell do I have to complain about? What the hell do I have to be sad about? I asked myself these questions all the time, particularly back then. Every time I panicked that I wasn't good enough, every time I came off stage and burst into tears without knowing why, every time I came home after an interview with the crushing feeling that I was unwanted, unloved – I would ask myself what right I had to be sad about any of this.

Whenever I brought these feelings up to other people, they said varying versions of the same thing, too. My mum and dad would tell me to stop worrying. 'You're earning the same as all the other girls. You're just as much a part of the band as they are. What are you worrying about?' My manager said the same when I mentioned it to her. 'I just don't think that's what's happening, Leigh. I think it's all in your head. You're just as good, you're just as loved.' Everyone said these things with the utmost kindness. They tried to reassure me, to console me and convince me that everything was fine. They didn't want me to worry or be upset. But the result of these well-intentioned comments was to make me think I was making it all up. You might be thinking along the same lines. You might be wondering what I'm whingeing about. But what I have learned, after years of being part of the fame machine, after reaching the greatest possible heights with my career, selling millions of records, earning a significant amount of money and having a huge amount of fun in the process, is that none of these things protect you from the pain of being made to feel less-than. No number of records on my walls or amount of money in my bank account invalidates my feelings. Achieving a certain level of success doesn't mean I'm not allowed to feel what I feel. It doesn't mean people can't hurt me. It doesn't mean my existence in this world as a Black woman is miraculously simple and easy.

Yes, of course there are privileges that come with money and fame, there are doors that open more easily for me because of my position, there are resources and levels of support that are available to me that aren't available to so many other people. But does that mean I'm not allowed to share what I've experienced? Does that undermine my lived reality? In 2023, I think we all should have learned to understand that holding privilege does not exempt you from pain, it does not exempt you from going through difficult things. And for anyone reading this who questions whether they should share their suffering, whether they should speak out – your pain is valid. Your feelings are valid. No matter who you are, no matter where you are in your journey. All of us should feel empowered to speak our truth.

My truth has been difficult to confront. Hard to name. Hard to admit to myself, even. It took me the best part of a decade to figure out what that truth was. To unpick all the complicated, nuanced elements, the visible and invisible barriers, the aggressions – some micro, some not so micro. But back then, in those first days, weeks and months after joining the band, I didn't have the language for it. I wasn't able to vocalise what was happening to myself, let alone to anyone else. And without the language, there was nowhere for those emotions to go but back inside me, to some deep, unspoken place. I doubted every thought I had, questioned my own instincts, pushed back against every emotion I was feeling. Back then, in my fledgling years as a teenage, baby pop star, I swallowed it all. It's difficult to overstate the cumulative impact of so many years of avoidance. But one thing I know for certain is that I will never doubt my instincts in future. I will never let myself become so lost, for so long, ever again.

# CHAPTER TWELVE

# Losing My Identity

'Who are you, Leigh-Anne?'

Identity can be a fluid, shifting thing. It can change depending on who you're with, where you are in your life, or how you want other people to see you. You can define yourself in so many different ways. Daughter, sister, mother, singer, lover. These are just a tiny handful of the many parts of my identity, and they're important because these definitions help me to understand myself, my place in the world – where I fit. When you lose your grip on your identity, if those definitions fade or become shaky and unstable, your place in the world can feel unstable too. If you can't clearly identify who you are – even to yourself – then you're in trouble.

I began to notice I was becoming less certain of my own identity during the first year of being in Little Mix. In the world of girl bands, identity is vital. Which one are you? Sporty Spice? Baby Spice? Posh Spice? It's part of the marketing of the group. It's easier to sell us if each of our characters are neatly packaged up into something that is clearly definable, easy to understand – an identity that fans can either relate to or aspire to. It also felt important for each of us to have our own distinct identities within the group so we could feel like individuals, not just a homogeneous mass of bright white smiles, shiny hair and perky dance moves. We were more than that. Little Mix as a whole didn't work without each individual part, and we all needed to stand out on our own, as well as coming together seamlessly as a collective. But when we came off the show, it felt to me that the others had already found their identities, they all seemed to already have their own roles that they slipped into effortlessly. They all had identities that made perfect sense.

It wasn't that I was the only person struggling with new-found fame, but I felt lost in comparison. Perrie was the gorgeous, glamorous blonde with the big voice. Jade was the cute one, adorably pocket-sized, Disney-princess eyes, butter-wouldn't-melt smile, and that sweet, soft Geordie accent. Jesy was the cool one, the sick dancer with the urban style, baggy jeans and oversized tees. She had already spoken out bravely on her experiences of being bullied; she was already an inspiration for so many girls. But me . . . what did I have to offer? Nothing seemed natural. I would look in the mirror and say, 'Who are you, Leigh-Anne?' It felt like any label I tried on was fake or forced, or an overlap with one of the other girls. I couldn't figure out who I was supposed to be, who people wanted me to be. It felt like there just wasn't a place for me. I had been the one who raps, I had been the one who wears snapbacks, but something about it just wasn't working. I tried to own it, I really did, but I just couldn't make myself believe in that version of me. I went through a phase of thinking I had to be the 'sexy' one, so I started wearing tight dresses and sultry makeup on stage and at events, but that wasn't me either. This forced hyper-sexuality felt false and over-done. I desperately wanted to wipe off the layers of makeup, shake out the hairstyles, peel off the costumes, and find out who was left underneath it all, when all those external things were taken away. But I didn't know how.

This feeling bled into everything. When we were on stage, doing interviews, even during photoshoots, I didn't know the role I was expected to play, so I felt myself fading into the background. I started clamming up during interviews. I didn't say much, I didn't feel confident to make my voice heard. I felt self-conscious in our group photos, as though I was an afterthought, the piece that didn't fit. I shrank myself, I became smaller and smaller.

It wasn't all in my head, our management and producers didn't seem to know how to define my identity either. Rather than encourage me to be myself or give me the space for my own personality to shine through, instead they tried to simply copy and paste an identity from somewhere else. Notably, Rihanna. During the makeover stage on *The X Factor*, the producers gave me her iconic red hairstyle – from her *Loud* era – an exact match, shade for shade. And they shaved one side of my head. I think this was partly because they just didn't know what to do with my hair type, but also it was an attempt to give me this kind of 'punky pop' personality, which wasn't me at all. I remember the sickening buzz of the clippers, my curls dropping to the floor around my feet. I stared at this girl in the mirror, a face I barely recognised. Who was she? What did other people see when they looked at me? Did they even see me at all?

I found this period incredibly confusing. We were just starting out, getting used to our new fame. We were all under so much scrutiny, having our photos taken constantly, being thrown into new and unfamiliar situations practically every day. It was a time when I needed to have a solid grip on my sense of self. I needed that knowledge to help ground me, to provide a sense of safety in this jarring new reality of being a pop star. But I didn't have that. And that lack of stability manifested in weird ways. Tiny, irrelevant things that I would normally have been able to shrug off started to really get to me. For one of our early shows, the stylists gave me a ponytail with a voluminous quiff. I loved it. Maybe this could be my signature style, I thought. But then the next night, one of the other girls had the exact same hairstyle. The ponytail and the quiff. I got so upset. I was on the verge of tears. This tiny thing shook me. *What are you doing? How can you take this hairstyle when I'm desperately trying to find 'me'?* I thought. Which, looking back, is a pretty intense reaction to a ponytail. I know nothing bad was meant by it, and there was no intention of hurting me or 'stealing my style', but because of where I was mentally in that moment, I took it hard and blew it into something much bigger. I was struggling deeply.

My real identity in the band was 'the silly one'. Behind closed doors I was loud, I was goofy and ridiculous, I was always laughing and having jokes with the other girls. That was who I was. Sam, our manager, even said, 'You just light up the room whenever you walk in.' She would always comment on how happy and bubbly I seemed, but that was one of the most frustrating things. For some reason, this real version of myself, the happy, vibrant, fun-loving me, wasn't what anyone else was seeing. I wasn't playing a role, or trying to be anything I'm not, but it just wasn't connecting with people and I wasn't able to let this side of me shine. I kept giving myself little pep-talks. I would tell myself that I had to speak up more, I had to talk more in interviews, I had to let people see the real me. I knew that was the only way to deal with the nagging suspicion that I was being overlooked, that I wasn't getting the attention I deserved. It felt like an uphill battle, but at that time I still had hope. I still believed

# LOSING MY IDENTITY

I would settle and find my place within the band, that things would eventually start to feel better.

☆

In that first year, there wasn't much time to worry about myself, or where I fit. We had a job to do, and it was time to get our music out into the world. The debut album was going to be our first opportunity to plant our flag in the sand, to show everyone what we were about. As much as I could, I poured my energy into that. It was helpful to have a collective focus, rather than worrying about my own individual concerns all the time.

We already had our first single, 'Wings'. And I told you how that felt to write – like magic. We found our sound naturally, and when we started putting all the elements together, it was like alchemy. Although, the first time we heard it on the radio wasn't exactly the perfect start we wanted. We were all in the car, we knew they were going to play it and we were so excited. But there must have been a mix-up because for some reason they played the instrumental version of the song. Just the beat. None of our voices. We all looked at each other when we didn't hear those opening notes. What the hell?! What an anti-climax!

It didn't matter in the end. We still got the number one. Our first number one with a song that we had been involved with writing, with our own established sound as Little Mix. We had been watching the numbers roll in all week and we knew we were close to that top spot, but to get the actual announcement, that was one of the greatest moments I can remember. The euphoria was intense. One of my favourite movies is *Glitter*, which is all about Mariah Carey becoming a huge pop star, and it felt like I was mirroring that life. There was a scene where she heard her single played on the radio for the first time, and in another scene she played live at Madison Square Garden. These were moments that I had dreamed of, fantasised about, for as long as I could remember, and now they were all happening for real. It was genuinely overwhelming.

The second single was 'DNA', which was also the title of our debut album. It felt like there was a lot riding on this one. We released them in pretty quick succession – 'Wings' came out in September of 2012, and 'DNA' was released in the November – we aimed to move with the momentum, establishing ourselves as artists in our own right, not just *The X Factor* winners, but a real band, real contenders in the industry who could compete with the best. I think we all had this little fear in the back of our minds that the success of 'Wings' could be a fluke, that we would end up as one-hit-wonders and slide off into irrelevance now that the buzz of the show had started to die down. We weren't going to let that happen. So, we pushed this second single super hard.

As part of the promo, we even came back on to *The X Factor* – during the 2012 competition – to perform the single during one of the live shows. It was such a trip to be back there. They treated us like royalty. I can't lie, that perform-ance felt good. To be back on that stage, not fighting for survival or trying to earn votes from people at home, but as returning winners, as the celebrity act. It was surreal. While we were in hair and makeup, my mind wandered back to the intense anxiety I had felt in those dressing rooms, in those dark corridors that led to the studio and the stage, just a year previously. I thought back to all of the uncertainty and stress of being on the show, the times when I had had to fight to be seen, to fight for lines in a song, to hustle and graft just to show the producers that I deserved to be there. Now, we were walking back on stage as the former champions, with a number-one single and a debut album to our name. We had fans screaming our names, going wild for us. The judges gave us a standing ovation when the song was over, and we didn't have to wait nervously to hear their criticism. It felt amazing.

The single came in at number three. We didn't get the second consecutive number-one spot we had so desperately craved and we were devastated. Number three is still a spectacular result and a huge achievement, but for us, it felt like a disappointment. We had always been perfectionists – striving to be the best, to achieve the best possible results – so to fall short of that felt painful. It was our first real taste of the kind of pressure that existed in the real world. We weren't simply trying to win a competition anymore, we were trying to build a real career – and that meant selling records and having huge commercial success. We realised that *The X Factor* final had been the starting line, not the finish line. In order to make this dream a reality that lasted longer than fifteen minutes, we knew we were going to have to work harder than ever before. There were no guarantees, no promises, nothing would be handed to us. If we wanted it, we were going to have to work for it. Luckily, that hard-working mentality came naturally to us, it was threaded into our DNA.

Releasing singles, promoting them, hearing our songs on the radio – this was just one part of our new reality. The other part, the part that made us the happiest, was performing. The stage was our happy place, the place where we felt most comfortable, most at home. Our focus has always been to connect with our fans, inspire joy, create magical memories for people, and live performances are where we really came into our own. Our music was meant for the stage, it was meant for big, exciting, live shows, dance routines, crazy costumes, dazzling light shows. We wanted to create unforgettable experiences, shows that took you by the hand and transported you into another world, a world where anything was possible. Our first live show after *The X Factor* and the winner's tour was at Party in the Park. A main stage at a huge festival, outside with thousands of people watching. This was new territory for us, a huge, decisive moment. We were shitting ourselves. We were so scared. It was going to be our first live performance of 'Wings', and we could all feel just how important this moment was.

Being on a stage outside of *The X Factor* studio was such a different experience. It felt like we had popped the bubble and wandered out into the elements, exposed and unprotected. You don't know all the producers, you don't know how it's all going to work, you don't have the comfort of spotting your friends and family in the audience, of knowing there are people who love you in the crowd. This audience is real people – thousands of them. What if they hate us? What if they hate our music? What if we run on stage and are met with deathly silence, or no one claps and cheers when we finish? What if we don't hit our notes, or we forget the lyrics, or one of the microphones stops working? The imposter syndrome that we had battled with from the beginning turned up a notch, and we were suddenly faced with the possibility that the British public might not like us after all.

# LOSING MY IDENTITY

The moments before we walked out onto the stage were intense. They were some of the most violent nerves I have ever felt. My hand was trembling as we came together as a group after our vocal warm-ups, formed a tight little circle and stuck our hands together, one on top of the other. I felt the warmth of the other girls' skin, clammy with fear, the light fluttering of pulses in wrists. That skin contact calmed me. I think it calmed all of us. I looked at their faces – my new best friends, my new family – and felt so grateful that we were in this together, so grateful that we had each other. I remembered what we were capable of, what we had worked so hard to achieve together, and I knew we had so much more to give. We stepped out in front of that crowd and gave it everything. The crowd loved us. They cheered for us. They screamed for us. They went wild when we played 'Wings'. This was it. The beginning of a thrilling new chapter of our lives and it felt amazing.

It was on stage where I felt the closest to knowing who I was, who I was meant to be. The rest of it – worries about what I was supposed to be wearing, wondering what my 'thing' was, fighting not to fade into the background – it all kind of dropped away when I got to sing and dance on stage. This was my identity – the performer, the singer, the pop star. And when I was given the space to simply be her, to show our fans what I could really do with my voice, it felt like none of those other superficial stresses even mattered. Those moments of pure joy on stage allowed me to reconnect with my inner self, the self who had dreamed of this, manifested it, and was full of self-belief. But while I was desperately trying to cling to my own sense of identity, we were also working hard as a group to figure out who we were as a collective.

Who are Little Mix? What kind of band did we want to be? How were we going to make our mark, to stamp our place in history? We knew we had the makings of something special; we knew there was so much talent, so much potential, and now we had to harness all of that raw energy and convert it into something that our fans would love. We also had to figure out how to exist in this brutal, complicated industry. At first, every single day felt like the first day of school, or the first week in a new job. You know when you don't know how anything works, you don't know who to eat with at lunchtime, you don't even know where the loos are? That's how we felt, all the time. There was so much for us to learn, and we had to start standing up for ourselves.

It's wild to think of us when we were just starting out. We were young and inexperienced, and we would walk into rooms with all these people who all had opinions about what kind of band we should be, what kind of music we should be making, and how we should be selling ourselves. On *The X Factor*, it was like we had been wrapped in cotton wool, like we were just playing pretend, but now we were doing it for real, and every conversation felt loaded, every decision felt terrifyingly important. We didn't have a clue. About any of it. We had never seen a contract before, we didn't know what we were supposed to be asking for, or what protections we should have, we didn't know what to expect in any situation. At first, it felt like we were working for our management company, rather than the other way around, simply because we didn't know what we were meant to do.

We were kids, and we were essentially mothered for a while. We had to be led through so many different processes, from legals to contracts to representation. It took us a long time to realise that we were the ones who were supposed to hold the power. But how else are you meant to learn these things? You can't learn about this stuff in school, our parents didn't know any more about this stuff than we did, there was no one else we could ask for guidance. We had to learn by doing. It was a steep and intense learning curve and we had no choice but to learn the hard way.

We could so easily have been influenced or manipulated into becoming a band that we didn't recognise. We could so easily have been led down a path none of us really wanted to go down, and I'm so proud of us for not allowing that to happen. Despite our youth, our relative inexperience, the fact that there were so many things we didn't understand, the one thing we did have was solidarity as a group and that has never been in doubt for us. As a result, we stood our ground, we advocated for our demands, we pushed hard to make sure our values and principles – to inspire, to include, to empower – were at the forefront of everything we did.

We developed our own way to communicate what we wanted and, crucially, what we didn't want. While we were busy writing and recording for the first album, someone from the label said they thought we should do a country music song. It was an immediate 'no' from us. That is just so not our vibe, never had been, never will be. We heard the song and just knew that wasn't us. But it wasn't always as simple as just vetoing things we didn't like. We wanted to show we were willing and sometimes listen to the experts, so it became a bit of a balancing act. We had to learn when to compromise, when to listen to other people's opinions, but also when to trust our gut instincts.

I'm proud of us for always standing up for ourselves, but I'm also proud of our attitude, and our ability to always remain grounded and humble. There are so many big and difficult personalities within the music industry, but we always made a point to be pleasant and welcoming to everyone we encountered. We were so grateful and just happy to be there, and we found that being nice to people has a way of coming back to you. It wasn't an effort for us to be like this. We didn't have to try – it was just who we were. We were normal girls, from normal beginnings, and we weren't about to let five minutes of fame get to our heads and change our personalities. I think people saw that in us. I think they appreciated our positive attitudes, our kindness, and it helped us get by. We treated everyone with respect and gratitude, from the people serving us food to the big dogs at the record label, and it meant we always had someone in our corner looking out for us.

We needed that more than ever at the start of our journey. We needed each other, too. In those early months, I found my identity in sisterhood. I understood who I was when I was with Jade, Perrie and Jesy. I understood their friendship, and their love for me helped me keep a grip on myself. Even if I didn't quite know who I was in the eyes of our fans, I knew who I was to them. I was their friend; I was their sister. We were on this wild journey together, and our bond kept us all going, even in the wildest moments when life started to feel unrecognisable. There would always be someone within touching distance who understood what you were going through, who would hold your hand or pull you into a tight hug. Whether we needed silly jokes and distraction, or deep chats and a cuddle on the sofa, we were always there for each other. Although I had entered *The X Factor* as a solo act with no intention of sharing the stage, being in a group now felt as natural as breathing. I couldn't imagine it any other way. Our personalities slotted together so neatly, complementing each other's best traits, gelling in a genuine, solid way. Our friendship was the thing that pinned everything together, the kinetic energy that powered us forward, the spark that created something special, a warmth that permeated everything. It still astounds me that we were able to bond like this, to become so close, given that we were essentially four strangers thrown together on a reality TV show. I couldn't have got through that first year without those girls.

And yet, even with such amazing people around me, I still had times where I felt completely alone. Due to the demands of the job, the ridiculous schedule, the touring and the travel, there were parts of my old identity that I no longer had space for. The girl I was before *The X Factor* wasn't gone completely, but there were so many significant changes in my life that it was inevitable that parts of me would change along with that. My friends from school, my best friends I had known for years, I would now have to go weeks or months without seeing them. I missed so many things. I missed birthdays and break-ups, new job celebrations, graduations. So many milestones I just wasn't there for. A close friend went through a tragedy – a friend of hers took their own life. I couldn't be there for her while she was grieving because I was touring the first album. That hurt me, and I still carry that guilt. Thank god my friends stuck with me through this time. They knew what I had to sacrifice for the life I wanted to have, and I am forever grateful that my best friends never gave up on me. They never punished me or made me feel bad for missing things.

It was the same with my family. I barely got to see them. I missed my nephew being born. As someone who has always put family first, that was a real struggle. To not be there for my sister when she brought new life into the world? That just wasn't me. But life had become a relentless machine, and there was hardly any time scheduled in to do the things that existed outside of the pop-star bubble, to see the people I had loved before this wild ride had started. I went from being a person who prioritised their relationships – their oldest friendships and closest family – above all else, to being some-one whose life was entirely consumed by work, someone who only had time to say a quick hello on the phone before jumping on the next flight; someone who forgot to write birthday cards or sent last-minute flowers instead of showing up. I had been pulled out of the world I recognised, pulled away from those connections that made me feel safe, and this inevitably had a negative impact on my sense of self. No wonder I had no idea who I was, who I was meant to be. My sense of stability had been pulled out from under me, and now I had to find myself again, under the glare of spotlights and the blinding flash of paparazzi cameras. This was not going to be easy. The next thing on our to-do list was to try to crack America, our biggest challenge so far.

# CHAPTER THIRTEEN

# Is This About Race?

'The Black one'

We were in constant motion. Everything was so busy, so full-on, all the time. It was easy to get swept along by the current, to stop noticing how breathtaking all of this was. There was barely any time to reflect, to properly pause and just let it all sink in. Everything was racing by us at hyper-speed, flashes of light and colour and sound. At times it felt like I was on a bullet train, whizzing through life, desperately trying to focus on the blurred images I could just about make out through the window. Somehow, it all became normal fairly quickly. The interviews, the press, the studios, the per-formances. I never took any of it for granted, but there was so much, so fast, that I had to put all those feelings of awe and amazement to one side and just get on with it.

But when we visited other countries, they were the moments when I felt the magnitude of everything that had happened to us – to me. There was something about the way we were treated when we were abroad that made it all properly sink in. *Oh my god*, I would think. *This is real. We are actually famous pop stars. People all around the world know our names, they know our music, they're excited to see us.* It was these moments that stuck with me, that made me step back from the whirlwind for a second and appreciate everything that was happening.

We visited America to promote *DNA*, and it was one of the most wondrous experiences of my life. I loved every second of it, and we were blown away by the reaction. The first stop on the promo tour was a venue where we were set

171

to sign autographs for fans, and when we got there, there was a queue around the entire building. It was bewildering to see that huge number of people queuing just to get a glimpse of us, to get close to us, we couldn't believe it. Another time, we performed in a shopping mall and the place was heaving with people. We filled an entire mall with fans who were screaming, singing our lyrics, clamouring to get closer to the stage. It was wild. I don't think any of us really believed that our fame would travel across the Atlantic Ocean, that the power of our music would really extend that far, or would really touch this many people. It was astounding and overwhelming.

The promo tour was intense. It was really tough, we barely slept. Every day or so we would jump on another plane and then a short while later land in a new state to do the radio run. We must have been on every big radio show on the continent. The reception we got was amazing everywhere we went, so everyone was feeling quietly confident about breaking through into the American market. But it didn't work out how we hoped. America never really happened for us, and it is genuinely one of my biggest regrets about my experience with Little Mix because we came so close.

After the promotion tour, we planned to do our own proper arena tour of the first album all around the States. We pushed hard for it and our team started to make it happen, but when the venues didn't immediately sell out, they decided to cancel the whole tour. They told us to stay home and focus on finishing our second album instead. It felt like a huge mistake. It didn't feel like they had even given the venues the opportunity to sell more tickets, and we had been there on the ground doing promo, we knew how passionate our fans were out there. The first album was doing well too – it came in at number four in the Billboard charts, and was the highest-charting debut album by a girl band in the US – which meant we beat the Spice Girls. That is no small thing. I truly believe that if we had been given the opportunity to do that tour, to let the tickets sell, then we could have properly cracked America, which might have taken us to a whole different level – a different stratosphere of success.

But we didn't get to do it, and the next time we went to America, we were supporting another artist – Demi Lovato. I don't begrudge this experience in the slightest, though. It was still a taste of something that we deeply desired, and that tour was one of the happiest times of my life. They are some of my favourite memories of being in Little Mix. We were on tour in America, just like in the movies, just like in *Glitter*. We were living on an actual tour bus, sleeping, eating, rehearsing, partying, as we travelled state-to-state. Jade and I in particular had the best time on that bus. We became close with all the dancers, and we had these long nights with them, sitting up and laughing and talking, going out and having after-parties that carried on until the early hours. It was wild, it was messy, it was the most fun I have ever had. We were living our best lives, and all of that is before I've even mentioned the shows. With sell-out stadiums and arenas every night, not a single show felt like we were the support act. It almost started to feel a bit awkward because so many of the people in the crowd were there for us. We weren't a filler act, these crowds knew our songs, they knew our names, they went wild every time we stepped on stage. I loved that feeling. It was everything I have ever wanted.

# BELIEVE

There was something about being in America that allowed me to forget everything else – all the doubts and insecurities that had started to creep to the edges of my mind, all the fears about where I fit within the band, or whether I was good enough to be there. The sheer adrenaline of playing in those spectacular venues, with thousands of fans singing our lyrics back to us. I could push all those fears down, focus on all of the incredible things that were happening right in front of me. The tantalising promise of 'making it' in the USA was all I had space to think about. It wasn't like those problems disappeared when I was in America, but it felt like I could at least forget about them for a little while. At least, until we got home.

We arrived back in the UK and it was straight back to the grind. Back then, the early 2010s before Spotify and streaming had taken off, everything about the music industry was much more rigid and structured. You would write the album, release the singles, promo the singles, tour the album. Then the next year you would go again, the whole cycle starts from the beginning. We had the second album – *Salute* – to get off the ground, and we were excited. This album felt like a chance to push our capabilities. We were expanding on our signature pop sound, but adding more layers of funk, more layers of vocal ability, showing our flair and personality – with the creative range of the songs themselves, but also with our harmonies and riffs. We were developing as artists and it was imperative to show what we had learned, what we were becoming.

# IS THIS ABOUT RACE?

I was particularly excited about this album because it felt like a fresh start. My first year in the band had seemed, at times, rocky and uncertain. I had been unsure of myself, lacking in confidence, lacking in belief. But with this new album it was like I could hit the reset button. There would be new rounds of promotion, interviews and slots on prime-time TV. This was my chance to firmly establish my position in the group. I wasn't going to hold back this time. I wasn't going to doubt my place or second-guess myself. I was going to let my personality shine through, I was going to be happier. I was going to hold on to the joy I had felt in the USA. I was going to live my dream and not let myself be held back. Or so I thought. The reality was that so much of my experience was beyond my control – I just didn't know that yet.

The second album should have been a moment to settle. The mad, fluky energy of winning *The X Factor* and putting out our first album was behind us. We were no longer just some competition winners. Now we were doing this thing for real. It was time to declare our intentions to the world. We wanted to make a change; to have a huge and lasting impact on the industry, on our fans. It should have been the time when everything started to come together, when all our hard work and tenacity started to pay off. But for me, nothing was connecting. Nothing was making sense. Every time we had a performance, or an event, or an interview, I tried to convince myself things were easier, to feel better. I told myself each time – this one will be different, this one will be *good*. But it was the same thing every time: just under the surface, an unidentifiable feeling of rejection, of worthlessness. An energy that was so hard to describe, so hard to pin down. But I could feel it – I knew it was real. I just didn't know why it was happening. I didn't know why I couldn't feel part of the group; why I felt so horribly unwanted.

There are so many examples, so many instances that happened over a span of years. Some stay with me and pop up in my memory frequently. Others I barely remember; the details are smudged, but there is always the lingering memory of the feeling – the sadness and the pain. And there are many, many more that I have forgotten entirely, or repressed to some deep place for my own protection. Part of me begrudges the idea that I have to prove to people what happened. I kind of hate that I have to provide examples, 'evidence', to convince other people of what I know to be true. But at the same time, I know it's important to share the realities of what it was like for me, and for the many other Black people and people of colour who are trying to exist, to thrive, in majority white spaces. These stories will be so rec-ognisable, no matter whether you're a pop star or you work in a bank or an office or a school. The hierarchies of power and the unspoken rules that determine who gets to be seen, who gets to be successful, are the same. So if you have ever felt like this, know that you are not alone.

There are key moments that will always be easy for me to remember. We did a couple of live interviews on TV shows where we interacted with some young fans. The presenters would always ask them which member of the band was their favourite. From the moment they started asking that ques-tion, I would feel my body flooding with anxiety, because I knew how it was going to go.

'Perrie!'

'Perrie!'

'Jesy!'

'Jade!'

'Jade!'

'Perrie!'

I just had to stand there. It got more and more awkward as it became increasingly clear that none of the little girls were going to say I was their favourite. They were dressed up to look like their favourites too. The little blonde girls wanted to be Perrie, the girls with dark hair wanted to be anyone but me. We didn't have many Black fans. I wasn't the one they wanted to look like, I wasn't the one they wanted to meet and get a selfie with. The presenters made it into a joke. What could I do other than laugh along? It hurt me, deeply, and it was intensely embarrassing – let's not forget this was happening on live TV – but there was nothing to be done other than shrug it off and pretend it didn't affect me.

A similar thing happened on a popular morning TV show. We were going to meet some of our youngest super-fans. It was another group of little girls, four of them, and they were dressed up like a miniature version of the band. So far, so cute. But almost instantly it became clear that only three of the girls were actual Little Mix fans. The fourth girl was one of the others' little sisters, just there to make up the numbers. And, you guessed it, she was the 'Leigh-Anne fan'. Only, she wasn't, not really. Again, I smiled through it. But under the surface, something like hot shame bubbled in my veins.

The first time it happened was during our first radio tour. We were abroad, I can't remember where we were, but when we landed there were crowds waiting for us. We walked off the plane and had to pass all these fans. I was at the front,

177

next to our manager, and the other girls were a little bit behind us. The fans rushed towards us as we approached, and they kept going – straight past me. Every single one of them walked straight past me and went to the other girls instead. I ended up just standing and watching as the others were handing out hugs and selfies and autographs.

'Well, this is awkward,' I said to my manager with a little laugh. She brushed it off and said it didn't mean anything, that they probably just hadn't seen me. But I knew it was deeper than that.

On stage, I always felt like I got the fewest cheers. I know that sounds ridiculous, but it didn't feel ridiculous. It felt horribly real and obvious, at least to me. There were certain moments where we each got to be prominent during a performance – maybe it was speaking to the crowd, or just during one of our solo parts in a song – and whenever it was my turn, the crowd just sounded more subdued. I know it wasn't in my head, it was a noticeable difference. I felt like no one was watching me. It's difficult to describe how I could know that from my position stood on stage in front of a crowd of hundreds or thousands, but I would scan their faces and I would always notice that there weren't many pairs of eyes looking at me. I felt invisible, like I was part of the set, blending in with the lighting and the sound systems, just background decoration.

It's not as if I needed an army of fans screaming my name. I just wanted it to feel equal, to feel as loved as the others. I know it's hard to imagine feeling lonely and ignored when you're performing in front of fans, but in a way, having all those people there and knowing that they don't care about you is in some ways worse than not having a crowd at all. It simply increased the number of ways I could feel rejected – all in one go. I would dream of hearing my name chanted by the crowd, like they did for the other girls. I would hope and hope that some of the signs and banners were directed at me, that the little girls who waited at the stage door would have a photo of my face to sign, that they would reach out towards my hand, desperate for a hug and a selfie. But it was hardly ever me they aspired to be.

Another time, a fan stopped us for a photo while we were at an airport. I don't remember much about her. I think she was a teenage girl, maybe she was with her mum. She was perfectly sweet. But this fan didn't want a photo with all of us. She turned to me, holding out her phone, and asked me if I could *take* the photo. That broke something in me. I said no, turned away from them and walked away. Is that how little I meant? That I wasn't even seen as worthy of being in the picture? That they couldn't even ask a passer-by to take a photo that included me? I once noticed a comment on social media, it was comparing Perrie and me. It said, 'The white girl sounds like a Black girl, and the Black girl sounds like a white girl.' That comment hit me in a complicated way. It dug itself under my skin and burrowed into me. It felt like a criticism, not just of my voice, but of my entire identity. I started to get anxious before meeting fans. Anytime I knew we would have to interact with crowds I would feel scared that I was going to be rejected and embarrassed, that no one would want to talk to me, and that once again I would have to pretend it didn't affect me, that it didn't hurt.

Doing signings as a group was particularly excruciating for me. We would sit on these long tables, all four of us, and people would queue up – sometimes for hours – so we could sign an autograph for them and take a photo. The classic fan meet-and-greet. But for me, these events were a huge source of anxiety. I was uncomfortable being the first one on the table, or the last. I would always plead to sit in the middle because I was terrified that fans would just skip me if I was on one of the ends. I could feel it, the disinterest. The way their eyes would skip over me like I was invisible, the way they would avoid even looking at me. Sometimes they would just walk past me.

What gets to me is how much additional mental labour I had to do in order to deal with all of this. As if coming to terms with my new life, grappling with the realities of fame, struggling with being thrust into the public eye in my teens wasn't enough. On top of that, I had all these extra fears, and this desperate need to impress people. I had more to prove than everyone else. I had to work harder than every-one else just to be seen, to be noticed, to be respected. And I couldn't work out why that was. It was exhausting to feel like this all the time.

The rejection was painful and frequent. Every time something like this happened, it felt like a small blow to the head – shocking and unpleasant, but manageable in isola-tion. But when you're being hit in the head every single day, it starts to knock you off balance. I felt my knees buckling under the weight of it all. My vision was spinning, I was close to hitting the ground. All I had wanted – all I had ever wanted – was to make music and perform it for people to hear it. My drive was to use my energy to work on becoming a better singer, a better dancer, to make a game-changing album, to put on a performance that would stand out in the history books, that would live in people's memories forever.

But far too much of my energy was now being used to constantly deal with the complexity and the pain of all this rejection. I could no longer focus on reaching the heights of my potential, because all I could think about was how to survive this, how to make it better, how to feel wanted and loved. The pain was solid and heavy. I held it in my chest and it began to weigh me down, dragging me slowly under the surface.

It was coming at me from all angles. I wasn't only feeling unloved by some of our fans, I was also feeling unwanted and under-appreciated within the industry itself. It started to affect my craft and the things that I loved most about being in the band – making music. We began working with a well-known and respected songwriter. I am not going to name him, but he has worked with everyone who is anyone. We were excited to have him on our team, and I was buzzing to be working with one of the greats. What an opportunity. But the reality turned out to be different.

I used to write my own raps for our songs and I loved doing that. I did it frequently during the live shows on *The X Factor*, and it was something I knew I could bring to the group that was special, that made us stand out. It was part of our unique style, our musical identity, and I always felt proud that I was able to contribute in this way and show off this other side of my talents. It felt like it was my 'thing'. And I knew our fans loved it. We were working on a new track with this writer and when I went into the booth to record my rap, he mocked me. He made fun of me and made me feel so small. It was horrible.

# BELIEVE

'OK . . . let's do it again . . . but without the *"rap"* this time,' he said, with this horrible smirk on his face. His tone of voice was so dismissive, so belittling. I wanted the ground to swallow me up. How dare he make me feel so awful for simply expressing my creativity? How dare he erase my voice with such casual callousness? I was livid, but I was also mortified. He was the one with the influence, he was the one with all the industry experience and connections, and he was a white man, so he held all of the power. I have never been afraid of criticism, and I would happily have sat down with him to work on my rap or talk about how he thought he could improve it, or even if we ultimately decided not to include it that would have been OK if it had been a discussion. But it was the way he spoke to me as though I was nothing, as though my contribution was meaningless. That was what hurt so bad. With my confidence where it was in that moment – hanging by a thread – I simply didn't have it in me to stand up for myself. So I accepted it. I accepted the erasure, I accepted it when my lines were cut down again and again until you could barely hear my voice in the chorus. I started to believe it was what I deserved, that I wasn't worthy of being given the big notes to hit, or the fun solos in the opening verse. It started to sink in – this idea that I wasn't as good. The idea lodged itself deep in my brain and started to grow.

Every tiny thing became a big issue. This is what happens when insecurity starts to take over, you obsess and worry about everything. When you are one of four in a band, your opportunities to prove yourself can be limited. Think about a song, for example. With four of us, there might only be a couple of lines in the whole song that you get to sing on your own. So every line, every riff, every harmony, started to feel incredibly pressurised. On top of that, there was always the looming threat that they would take your line off you if you couldn't deliver – they would just give it to one of the other girls to sing. It made the process feel intense. For 'Woman Like Me', I was given the chance to sing the second half of the first verse. It was too low for my voice. But it just so happened that I was ill with a cold on the day we were recording, so I managed to get down to hit those notes and it came out sounding so good. Everyone was happy, and I was happy because of that. Until it dawned on me that I was going to have to sing those notes live, and that without my gravelly sick voice, I wouldn't be able to get down there. I didn't want that part in the song. I knew it didn't suit my voice, and the idea of having to sing it live filled me with so much anxiety. But it didn't matter how stressed it made me, how panicked I was, no one listened. My feelings about the matter were at the bottom of the pile. To me, every line I got to sing felt *so* important. It felt like I had this one moment to show everyone what I could do, what I was made of. It reminded me of the time I forgot my lyrics during the live X *Factor* performance. The pressure of the moment sent me spiralling. I was overthinking everything, and it was impacting my ability and my joy – it was a vicious cycle.

I came off stage after so many performances and cried. I would fall into the arms of my manager, or my sister, and sometimes even the dancers, and it would all flood out of me. All the emotions I'd had to hold back while I was on stage, while I could feel the shift in energy, the lack of attention from the crowd when it was my turn to sing. I would look out in to the audience and not see any signs with my name on; I wouldn't hear the crowd chanting my name. It was a lot to take and it made me afraid. It made me hold back. I thought that if I could blend into the background then the pain of not being recognised wouldn't sting so bad. In the studio, I didn't push my voice to the limits of what I knew I could do. In interviews, I sat quietly and smiled sweetly. At live events and performances, I focused on getting through it; I didn't allow my personality to shine through. I went into 'self-protection' mode. I could feel myself slipping back to that little girl who had hidden behind her dad's legs, who was too scared to sing louder than the backing track. After so many years of pushing to rid myself of those insecurities, the old fear was back. I could feel its icy grip on my shoulder every time I stepped on stage. I hated it.

Maybe I was right to be afraid. One time, during a festival performance, someone in the crowd launched a bottle at the stage and it whistled past me, centimetres from my face, smashing noisily somewhere behind my right shoulder. I think my heart stopped in that moment. It could have knocked me out. It could have killed me. Obviously, there is no way to know if someone had thrown a bottle at me specifically. Maybe it was an accident. Maybe it was just some drunk idiot who had forgotten there were real people up on that stage. But given how I was feeling at the time, how much I had struggled with feeling unloved, the bottle felt targeted. We were performing our song 'How You Doin'?', and immediately after this bottle incident, it was time for my verse. I could have stopped the performance; I could have walked off. I could have shrunk into my shell and then cried when I came off stage like I had done so many times before.

But I didn't want to, I wasn't going to let them chase me off stage or make me feel like shit. Not this time. I launched into my verse, giving it everything. I was eager to show everyone in the crowd, including the person who threw that bottle, that I wasn't afraid. I wasn't going to let them tear me down. I have always been resilient. It takes a lot to shake me or bring me down. And in that moment, I realised I wasn't beaten yet. I still had so much more to give, and I was going to show everyone. It was a small rebellion, a tiny 'fuck you' to the millions of voices in my head that were telling me I wasn't good enough.

The hardest thing about all of this was not understanding *why* it was happening. I didn't see myself as any different to the other members of the group. I hadn't ever considered the possibility that things might be different for me because I was Black. Even in the early stages of my journey, some people tried to warn me. Older Black people who had experience with the industry told me I would have to work harder, that it would be different for me, that it would be more difficult, that I would face hostility. I didn't believe them. And back then, as a society, we simply were not speaking about these things.

Race and racism were just not on the agenda. Conversations that feel so normal now, about white privilege, microaggressions, unconscious bias – all those terms that have slowly filtered into our collective understanding – weren't happening. Nobody else had spoken out about going through anything similar, there were no hashtags, no anti-racism reading lists, nobody was pledging to educate themselves or 'do the work'. I couldn't relate what I was feeling to my experience as a Black woman existing in a white world. The dots were not connecting. And so I intern-alised it. All that shame and sadness and rejection – there was nowhere else to put it but back into myself. I couldn't name what was happening to me. I couldn't define it and I couldn't blame anyone else. So I blamed myself. I put it all on my shoulders and tried my hardest not to let it crush me.

# CHAPTER FOURTEEN

*Beauty*

'Remembering
how to love myself'

It was around this time that I started to become obsessed with the idea of getting a nose job. Every time I saw a photo of myself, it was all I could see. My nose. It was wrong. It was too big; I was certain of it. And it was impossible to avoid – I saw so many photos of myself.

Millennials like me, and a lot of our Little Mix fans, are the Instagram generation. We're the ones who came up with the concept of the 'selfie', for god's sake. Everything we do is documented online, perfectly curated, filtered with soft light, tweaked and tinted for perfection. It didn't happen if we didn't post it, right? In the early–mid 2010s, this obsession with a constant, perfect online presence was peaking; Instagram was at the height of its powers, which was tough on everyone, but for women in particular. In the weird world of celebrity, that pressure was only intensified, it felt like there was little escape from it. Everything we did, everywhere we went, there were cameras, paparazzi, photo ops, endless posting on our official Instagram page, which would then be picked up (and picked apart) by the tabloid press. You'll likely be familiar with the *Daily Mail's* 'sidebar of shame'. Well, once you've made it on there a few times, with horrible comments about your body or your face or your makeup or your outfit, it becomes almost impossible not to develop a bit of a complex about it all. For me, already feeling unloved, rejected, left out in so many areas of my professional life, those feelings began to turn inwards towards myself. They started to manifest as deep physical

189

insecurities about things I had never even thought to worry about in the past.

Sometimes the paparazzi would do it on purpose. They would try to get a bad picture of you – looking tired or hung-over or bloated. But other times, I would just happen to pull a weird face, or there would be an unflattering light, and that was it, that bad photo of you was out there in the world for everyone to see, and there was nothing you could do about it. That thought used to give me genuine anxiety. In every photo, there was the opportunity for comparison.

More often than not, I would be in pictures with Jade, Perrie and Jesy. We are all beautiful, and we are all different, entirely unique in our beauty – but it was easy to forget that. It was easy to start comparing yourself, your body shape, the size of your bum, the quality of your skin, to the girls stood beside you. I tried to fight it. I tried to hold on to my inner confidence, the part of me that knew I was beautiful, the part of me that didn't attach so much of my self-worth to external things like the way I looked or the size of my boobs, but it was difficult, and those negative thoughts frequently took over. And there I was again, obsessing about my nose.

We did a photoshoot for a major magazine, which I really enjoyed. They dressed us in gorgeous outfits, we all had our own unique style, the hair and makeup were on point. I was so excited to see the final shots. But when we saw them, I realised they had significantly altered my face. I barely recognised myself. Jade noticed it too as her face looked different as well. They had chiselled our cheekbones, slimmed out our cheeks, tweaked our eyes. But the thing that stuck out to me the most, the change that stung like a knife twisting into my abdomen, was my nose. They had made it smaller – a lot smaller. They had given me the nose that I internally desired at the time, a nose that looked much more like my bandmates' noses, looked much more like a white woman's nose. I felt sick, it was the confirmation of my worst fears. My nose was too big, it stood out, it needed changing, and everybody else could see it too – it was no longer just my own private insecurity, people at the magazine had also identified my nose as a problem and had taken it upon themselves to change it, to 'improve' me. It was an awful moment, but not an isolated one. Things like this would happen all the time. Being in the public eye makes you public property. Your appearance is fair game for anyone to comment on, to dissect, to criticise. Those experiences cut deep and lingered in my psyche. Was I less beautiful than the other girls? Was there something wrong with my appearance? Did I need to change something? I hated how much space these thoughts were occupying in my brain, and yet it was almost impossible to stop them.

My motto when I was younger was 'I love me.' I had it in my MSN Messenger username and scrawled it on my diaries and school notebooks. I had this intense, irrefutable love for myself, including the way I looked. I never really went through that teenage phase of feeling bad about my body, or wishing I looked like someone else. I had this unquench-able confidence that originated somewhere deep inside of me and shone out of me like sunbeams. I would positively reinforce myself with statements like this, affirmations, all the time. Of course, I had moments of doubt, I dealt with insecurities and all the people who didn't believe in me while I was growing up, but throughout all of that, I always backed myself so hard. I love that for young me. What a legend. But it's so sad to see how all that positive energy slowly fizzled out of me. The belief I had in myself, in my beauty, dimmed and faltered, until everything went dark.

I have always been slim and naturally petite, and there are certain privileges that come with that. And yet, there are also ways in which I deviate from conventional beauty standards, things that complicate how I am perceived, and therefore how I have been able to perceive myself. I'm referring to the impact of being racialised, of being a Black woman, a Black woman in a famous girl group. My Blackness had a direct impact on perceptions of my beauty because in the majority of the media we consume, beauty standards are Eurocentric and closely linked to whiteness. So, the closer to whiteness you are, the more beautiful you are allowed to be – according to our societal standards. So for me, a Black woman with some white heritage, lighter skin, looser curls and more Eurocentric features than many Black women, the idea of my attractiveness felt complicated and changeable depending on where I was and who I was with.

The spaces that we moved in during that time, the mid 2010s, were incredibly white. Pop music, and the music industry as a whole in the UK, was dominated by white faces, both on the talent side and on the management side. I became used to being one of the only Black women in the room, no matter what room we happened to be in. Whether that was a room full of our fans, a room full of executives, producers and managers, or a room full of other pop stars and mainstream artists, it was rare to see other Black faces. At the time, this was so normal to me that I didn't think

192

much of it. I became used to blending in, to assimilating to whatever the majority crowd demanded at the time. I didn't think about the fact that I was the 'only one'; I was too busy working, too busy navigating the complexities of our newfound fame. Too busy trying to fit in, trying to be successful – we all were. The only thing that I noticed was that I never felt desirable.

Desirability is an elusive, intangible thing. It's hard to describe, but everybody knows the feeling of walking into a room and feeling desired, of feeling attractive. It's a subtle shift in energy, eyes swivelling towards you as you pass. You feel it in the way people speak to you – maybe they lean a fraction closer than they need to, maybe they watch your lips as you talk. It's usually a tantilising feeling. It isn't a feeling I have ever needed or expected. I don't need to feel validated and desired whenever I walk into a room, and I never expected to be treated any differently, but it was hard not to notice that I was the only one in the group who wasn't treated like this. Over and over again. It didn't seem to matter how good I felt in the mirror before I left for an event. It didn't seem to matter what I did with my hair, or my makeup, or what I wore. I was noticeably less desirable than the others, in a way that you couldn't quantify with stats or numbers or specific examples – it was just something I felt. I know so many people will relate to that feeling. It's like an instant deflation. Every time it happened, I felt a little more air seep out of my lungs, I felt myself shrink just a touch more; I felt the edges of my confidence being eroded and chipped away.

A popular radio station used to run an annual competition where they ranked female musicians by order of attractiveness. By today's standards, it's pretty gross, but back in the mid 2010s, it felt normal. I became aware of it the first year we were together, back in 2012. I'm pretty sure all the other girls made the list, but I was never on it. And it wasn't a public vote. Listeners would vote for the winner, but they didn't decide who made the list in the first place – that was people at the radio station. And for whatever reason, I was never a consideration. Between 2012 and 2017, every member of Little Mix made the list, apart from me. It made me feel awful. It felt like a public declaration that I was officially the least attractive member of the band, the least desirable.It's not as if I wanted to be considered more attractive than the others, but being left out of the running entirely was a confirmation of my insecurities.

Looking back, I can see that this was, at least in part, because of race. Black women have the worst results on dating apps, we are consistently rated as the 'least attractive', we get the fewest matches, the fewest romantic interactions. It correlates with what the media – from the newspapers to magazines, TV shows, movies and advertising – tell us is attractive, and what is not. Growing up in the nineties and noughties, we were taught – relentlessly – that white women are the ideal image of beauty. A specific type of white woman: always thin, usually blonde. Those ideals are pervasive, it takes years, decades, for those widespread images of the 'ideal female' to shift. When we first became famous, there was nothing about my image that was considered particularly 'desirable' by mainstream standards – especially when in direct comparison to the other members of the band. I spent years in the pop industry moving almost exclusively within predominantly white spaces, spaces that deemed me less worthy, less valuable, less beautiful. That's going to have an impact. I still struggle with these feelings.

Some years ago, I made the decision to unfollow lots of Instagram accounts. These accounts focused on body image and beauty, all the external, superficial stuff that we are told is so important. I realised that consuming content like that, every day, wasn't making me feel good about myself. Seeing all these women, all conforming to the same kind of image, having work done to their bodies to look like *Love Island* stars, was making me feel anxious. It was making me worry that my body and my face wouldn't be good enough unless I looked like this exact social-media blueprint. It is yet another unattainable beauty ideal that piles pressure on women. And thankfully, I have come to a point in my life where I refuse to give in to that pressure. I refuse to let it warp my own sense of worth. But it takes work – I have to consciously push back against it. Being careful with my social media interaction is part of that, but I also work on my confidence with affirmations and positive self-talk, and ensure that I surround myself with people who build me up rather than tear me down.

This is not to say that I am completely against cosmetic surgery, we should all be able to do whatever we want in order to feel at our best, of course. But what I don't like is the incessant pressure, the idea that there is one single body type, or one kind of face that we should all be aiming for. Our beauty is in our individuality, in the things that make us unique, that set us apart. The desire to alter our appearances doesn't exist in a vacuum, apps like Instagram seek to homogenise us, to make us all look the same and conform to exclusionary beauty standards. When we aspire to conformity, it breeds the idea that anyone who doesn't meet this specific set of criteria is an outsider and can't see themselves as beautiful. I know this because it is how I felt, for years, despite the ethos of Little Mix being to embrace difference, to empower individuality, to celebrate the endless ways you can be beautiful and brilliant and talented. The industry, the pressures of the media, the microaggressions and racism that I experienced without being able to name it, made me forget this. I forgot that my power lies within what makes me stand out, not what allows me to 'fit in' with everyone else. I forgot about the little girl who wrote 'I love me' on all her notebooks. I forgot how to love myself.

I'm so glad I never got that nose job. Today, I love my nose! I adore it. I can't believe I ever thought I needed to change it. But I haven't waved some magic wand and now I never worry about my body or my appearance anymore. I am a woman, living in the world, which means there will always be pressures, there will always be voices telling me that I am not good enough, that I am not slim enough, not curvy enough, too old, too short, too frumpy, too slutty. The challenge is remembering how to love yourself despite all of these voices. The challenge is letting your voice be the loudest one in the room, the one you listen to the most.

I still look at myself sometimes and worry. I worry that I look like a child, that my figure isn't 'womanly' enough. I worry about how my body has changed since having children. I worry how my body and face have changed since I turned thirty, how I will continue to change as I age. Being in the public eye and existing under a ridiculous level of scrutiny can make these worries seem huge and unmanageable. Do I need to look a certain way in order to be successful? Do I need a certain kind of sex appeal in order to sell records? I can't pretend these thoughts don't cross my mind. But I make sure the other voice is louder. The voice that tells me that I am worthy, just the way I am. The voice that tells me not to change, not for anyone. The voice that tells me to love myself, the way I am now, the way I will be in ten years, in twenty years. I want to use that voice to tell you the same thing – you are beautiful, just as you are. You don't need to conform to the images you see on the internet, or try to look like somebody else. Your beauty comes from your confidence, from your self-belief, from the kindness you put into the world. These are the beautiful things about you, not the plumpness of your lips or the size of your bum. It took me too long to accept this for myself. I hope you can listen to this voice, let it drown out the others.

When Little Mix was first created, the whole idea was to represent our fans. We weren't these unattainable, pin-up women who people were supposed to fantasise about. We were normal girls, like your friends at school, who loved performing and loved making music. We aimed to be relatable and inspirational for other girls in a way that felt realistic and truly authentic. That meant the focus was never on our looks, not for us anyway. That pressure came from external factors, from the competitions that rated us on our looks, from the nasty comments in the press and on social media, from the pervasive cultural pressures that make women pick apart every element of themselves. There will have been times when every member of the band worried about their looks, worried that they weren't 'enough'.

For me, the racialised element of these worries created a different dynamic. It is one thing to worry that you might not be beautiful enough, but it is another thing to be deemed less beautiful because of your race. It's only looking back that I can piece together how my Blackness played a part in this, how being perceived as 'other' directly influenced the feeling that I was less desirable than the other girls, that it may have been my race that kept me off those 'most beautiful women' lists that the others were featured on. It is a hard pill to swallow. No one should feel this way. I think things are getting better. At least, I hope they are. I feel hopeful when I see greater representation of Black and mixed-race women in the music industry, in mainstream media, in movies, on billboards. It sends a message that there is not one singular way to be beautiful. It feels inclusive and encouraging. But representation is always just the starting point. Black faces are not just a trend to be cast aside when a cultural moment moves on. We are not simply a box-ticking exercise to give a company diversity points. Our beauty has value; we deserve to be seen and celebrated in all of our glory.

In 2018, the radio station finally put me on their list of nominees for their attractiveness ranking – I only went and won the whole thing! But it didn't feel like an achievement of any kind, I don't think women should be ranked by their attractiveness. I don't think we should be objectifying women or pitting them against each other in this way. I'll admit there was a tiny vindication in winning. Not that I needed it anymore, as I know now all those years of not being included, of letting myself believe that I wasn't beautiful – none of it

# BEAUTY

was true; none of those things I felt were real. As much as I hate the concept of winning a prize for my perceived 'beauty', this moment flipped something for me. It made me start questioning all of it: the ways I had been treated, the things I had been conditioned to believe about myself. It was all a fallacy. I didn't have to believe it. I could choose to believe in myself instead.

# CHAPTER FIFTEEN

# Racial Gaslighting

'Am I losing my mind?'

Around 2013, I went to therapy for the first time. I needed help. I knew it. My family and friends knew it. It was my management team who suggested it and encouraged me to go. They knew I wasn't coping well, crying after every show, feeling anxious and stressed all the time. I knew I needed to do something about this pain that was sitting heavy in my chest, dragging the air out of my lungs. I didn't know what was wrong with me, but maybe someone else would be able to figure it out.

My therapist was lovely. She was kind, empathetic, warm, analytical, objective, clear and a great communicator – all the attributes you would want from a therapist. She was also white. Which, back then, I didn't think anything of. But now, I would always insist on a Black therapist. As helpful as it was to discuss how I was feeling with my therapist – and it was cathartic and soothing in a way, and she provided tips around stress and anxiety – there were certain things about what I was going through that she would never be able to understand. I don't blame her for that. How could she understand? But what makes me sad is looking back and realising that I didn't understand what I was going through either. It didn't occur to me to seek out a Black therapist because I didn't even understand that the root of my sadness was inextricably tied to racial trauma. I had no language for that back then, I thought I was sad because I wasn't good enough, because I wasn't anyone's 'favourite', because I wasn't able to shine in the way I knew that I should.

# BELIEVE

I wonder if a Black therapist would have spotted this. I wonder if they would have opened up these questions for me, if they would have identified the racial element in all of this. Maybe they would have talked to me about microaggressions, about the impact of Eurocentric beauty standards, about the difficulties of existing in majority-white spaces as a Black woman. I wonder if having a Black therapist would have helped me get there a lot faster. Maybe I could have figured all of this out almost a decade sooner. But I didn't have a Black therapist, and I can't beat myself up about not getting there by a certain point. It was going to take as long as it was going to take.

My stint at therapy didn't last long. It helped me, but more so to address the symptoms rather than the root cause of why I was feeling like I was. Instead, I coped how I always coped, by throwing myself into my work. Despite all the stresses and the feelings of inadequacy that were plaguing me, I never lost my love for the work itself. I loved being in the band, I adored performing, touring, writing songs, creating music. It was everything for me and as perfectionists, we never lost that intense work ethic we had from the start of our journey. We had a thirst to get better and better, there was no limit for how good we could be, and we were willing to put everything into it to make it a reality, to push the limits of our potential. I loved it. The constant work was the perfect distraction from all the drama that was going on inside my head. Even on my lowest days, I could still lose myself in the rehearsal room, drilling choreography until my lungs burned and my feet felt bruised, working with our vocal coaches to improve my tone, to practise those trickier runs. Work was my haven, and I hid there for as long as I could. But denial could only take me so far, I couldn't ignore these feelings forever. They kept coming back.

I *was* being treated differently. I was unloved, unwanted, rejected. These things were irrefutable, undeniable facts to me. Yet everyone was determined to tell me that it wasn't happening, that it was all in my head. It made me feel as though I was losing my mind.

Outside of my head, and the pain I was dealing with privately, things for the band as a whole were getting better and better. Little Mix were going from strength to strength. We had been through a shaky period after cancelling our tour of America. The second album did well, but not as well as the first. It didn't sell as well in America. It was such a shame because it was a great album and we loved it. But looking back, maybe it wasn't the right time for a more R&B-focused record. It just didn't land like we wanted it to. We were feeling nervous, like we were losing momentum, we weren't living up to what we had hoped, or hitting the levels we knew we could. There were even rumblings that we could be dropped by our label. That petrified us and seriously turned the pressure up. We were right at the beginning of writing our third album, and we knew everything was riding on this. If this album didn't land . . . well, that could have been the end of us.

We finished the album, and I think we all knew in our hearts that it wasn't good enough. We knew we could do better. We were all at Perrie's house, listening to it together, and we just looked at each other and shook our heads. It wasn't right, so we scrapped it. The whole thing. Months of work, writing, recording, rehearsing – straight in the bin. It was so painful to do that, but we had no choice. We had to get this next move *exactly* right, or our dream could be over. It was perfect or nothing. We got back in the writing room and started again from scratch. We worked with an incredible writer called Kamille – she was like our sister and worked with us on all our biggest hits – and she brought in a song called 'Black Magic'. The moment we heard that song we knew we had something special on our hands. The energy was so perfectly *us*, and there was nothing else out there like it at that time. It became the basis of our new and improved third album, and it was a huge hit for us. Enormous. Everyone at the label was behind it, and they all had renewed faith in Little Mix. There was no more talk of dropping us, we were smashing it.

We shot the video for 'Black Magic' and the single that came after it – 'Love Me Like You' – in America. We used experienced, renowned directors who came up with these wonderful, narrative-driven concepts that felt like mini-movies. They had ridiculous production values, and they looked so slick, so professional. It was a great vibe being in America to produce those visuals. We felt like we were in among the action, properly living it. Everyone was so on board with the new campaign, everyone was on the same page trying to help us achieve our goals, and the results started to show. We were flying. The new record was flying off the shelves, the singles were flying up the charts. It was a great feeling.

The cycle continued. We finished the campaign for *Get Weird* with a whirlwind of an arena tour. That's the part we live for, the live shows, bringing all that hard work together in a culmination of lights, choreography and music blasting out across a sea of thousands of fans. But you blinked and it was over. We were back home, and straight back at it. Album number four: *Glory Days*. The title of that album couldn't have been any more right. These were our most glorious days. We came out with 'Shout Out to My Ex' followed by 'Touch', and everything went up to the next level. We didn't even know there were more levels left to climb to, but there were, and we were reaching them. It was a surreal time, everybody was talking about these singles. We were on top of the world, at the height of our powers, the height of our fame. We were also settled in ourselves. We had been on this journey for years now and were no longer the nervous teenagers who had won a competition and were just grateful to be there, we were women in our mid-twenties who knew what we wanted and had the confidence and experience to navigate this industry with more certainty than we ever had before.

We promoted *Glory Days* in America, toured Europe, Australia and Japan before going on tour with Ariana Grande. It was another three months of travelling around the US, performing our songs to crowds who loved us, screamed for us, sang our lyrics word-for-word. It was an unbelievable experience. Ariana is the sweetest person, she was always so lovely to us and it was amazing to be able to hang out with her. We all went to an escape room together once, which was adorable. This tour wasn't as hectic as when we supported Demi Lovato. We were older, slightly more sensible. I had moved away from being that wild party girl who was going out all the time. So, we still had a lot of fun, but we weren't as feral as last time. That's growing up for you. I had also fallen in love. A lot of my memories of that tour are wrapped up in pining for him – Andre. As is my way, I fell for him so hard. I'm all in or nothing, baby. I was utterly obsessed with him and being away from him was painfully difficult at times, but it was also good to have a distraction. Back home, I had also bought my first house. Nestled in the picturesque countryside of Bucks, it was amazing to have a base that was all my own, and so out of the way. Whenever I wasn't touring or promoting, I was here, shielded from the madness of the city, shielded from the intensity of our new levels of fame. Whenever I was there it felt like I had space to breathe. I needed my little haven, another world I could disappear into when it all got too much, because I was still struggling.

No matter how famous we got, no matter how much success we managed to achieve, it didn't change my own personal reality. Underneath all the glitz and glamour, the star-studded launch parties, the stratospheric growth of our fan base, I was still being plagued by the feeling that I didn't belong. Somehow, this wonderful world that we had built for ourselves and worked so hard for, still felt out of reach. I still felt excluded from it but it was hard to explain how. Wasn't I up there on that stage with the others? Wasn't I getting paid the same? Wasn't my name there printed in the credits next to my bandmates? Yes, this was all true. But what I was feeling was less tangible than that. It was something you couldn't measure in column inches, or album sales. It was something I could feel in my heart, something I knew to be true. But I was frequently made to question that truth, and it shook my grip on reality. It wasn't until much later on that I realised this was a form of gaslighting.

The UK charity Relate defines gaslighting as 'a form of psychological abuse where a person manipulates information to make you question your own reality, thoughts, feelings, and memories.' It is often used in the context of romantic relationships, but is not limited to such. It's a tactic used to assert power over someone. Gaslighting sows seeds of doubt in your mind, making you question what you thought was a concrete fact. It makes you question your memories, and what is real and what isn't. I know how this feels because I felt it anytime I brought up the issue of race.

'It's not about that.'

'Everyone sees you as an equal.'

'You're not treated any differently.'

I heard every single version of this sentence . . . The people who said these things didn't wish me any harm, they all intended the best for me. But by denying my truth in this way, I felt like I was being silenced. I also started to believe that maybe it wasn't happening. Maybe it was all in my mind. I couldn't reconcile what I was feeling with what everyone else was telling me. If it really had nothing to do with race, if I wasn't being treated differently because I was Black, then what the hell was going on? Why did I feel like this?

This was compounded by the fact that I didn't want it to be true. I didn't want to be the victim or to be treated differently for something that had nothing to do with my talent, my ability, my personality, for something that was entirely out of my control. It was an awful, disempowering feeling. A feeling that anyone who has experienced racism will recognise – the lack of control, the frustration at not being able to change people's minds, to change how you are perceived. The unfairness of it all. The injustice. It made me want to sob and scream in anger every time I thought about it. So, instead of confronting reality, I told myself that I was the problem. I made myself believe that I didn't feel good enough because I *wasn't* good enough. I wasn't talented enough, sexy enough, loud enough or likeable enough. It was all my fault. Looking back, I can see that this is textbook gaslighting, though there was no one individual who was the culprit. This is how people so frequently feel when they are made to question their reality; when they are disbelieved over and over again. They blame themselves; they turn all of that pain and fear inwards. But it was eating away at me.

For so much of my career, I had become used to being one of the only Black people in the room. It was such a normal thing that I didn't even realise how much it was affecting me. The small ways in which always being a minority chips away at you, the little moments where you can't fully relate to a conversation, or something racially insensitive is said and no one understands why that isn't OK. Even things like taking out the raps that I had written for songs, cutting down my lines, moving us away from our R&B influences. All these moments piled up, higher and higher, until I was facing a mountain of opposition and isolation – without even realising it was happening. I wonder a lot about how this all would have felt if there had been more diversity in those rooms, if there had been other Black people in those spaces who could recognise what I was going through. Who could have acknowledged it and reassured me that what I was feeling was valid. That what was happening was real, and that it was because of the colour of my skin. How powerful that would have been. How much heartache and confusion that could have saved me.

It was the loneliness that was the hardest part. All these complicated thoughts, emotions and fears, spiralling round and round in my mind, with no outlet, nowhere to go. I didn't have anyone to talk to. Not about this. I couldn't. The girls in the band were my soul sisters and we shared almost everything, but I couldn't burden them with this. It wasn't their fault and I didn't want to make them feel bad about what I was going through. And, if I am honest with myself, I just didn't think they would understand. My parents and my sisters were always there for me, no matter what, but when it came to this issue, their particular brand of tough love meant they would always tell me to stop worrying, to hold my head high, to keep going. There was part of me that felt guilty about it all, for feeling so low when I should have been on top of the world. Anyone else would have been living their best lives in my circumstances, I told myself. So why wasn't I? Maybe I was just ungrateful. Maybe I was just weak. Shouldn't I be able to handle this?

The thought of speaking out publicly about any of this felt impossible. How could I? How could I tell my fans they were treating me differently because I was Black? How would I ever put that thought into words? Even now, after all the progress that has been made and after all the conversations that have been had about race and inequality, accusations of racism are still frequently met with defensiveness and denial. But back then, in the mid 2010s, that conversation would have been even harder. Nobody was talking about this stuff. There weren't as many books or podcasts, there weren't TV shows and news articles exposing the realities of racism. Celebrities weren't sharing their stories. It was happening everywhere, in every industry, in every walk of life, but it all existed under the surface. It was unspoken, tacitly accepted as the norm. Speaking out wasn't an option, it would have rocked the boat too aggressively. I had no idea where I would have stood if I had tried to vocalise my suspicions about what was really going on. I had no idea if people would turn against me, if I would be ostracised even further, if I would lose the dream I had been working for my whole life.

Every time I tried speaking up, to tell someone about what was going on, to detail how I was being undervalued and treated differently, I would be told it wasn't that. It wasn't about race. Of course it wasn't about that. *You're just anxious, Leigh-Anne. You're too insecure, Leigh-Anne. It's all in your head, Leigh-Anne. You've got nothing to worry about, Leigh-Anne.* And so the cycle continued. I felt like I was giving so much and getting nothing in response. But I squashed it down, that cold, empty sadness. I ignored it. I told myself it wasn't because of my race, I pushed through it, again and again, because I didn't know what else to do. If no one else could see what I could see, then I couldn't trust how I felt about anything.

There was a certain dance routine that we performed as part of the *Glory Days* arena tour that always filled my heart with joy. The stage was full of dancers, the lights were dazzling, the heat was rising from the crowd as we hit the steps uniform with one another. We moved as one, perfectly in sync. The song sounded amazing, our vocals were as smooth as honey after weeks of meticulous practice and rehearsals. This is what we lived for, what I lived for.

A moment in the song positioned us towards the back of the stage with the dancers in front of us. We stood still for a couple of seconds. It wasn't my line so I could let myself catch my breath, ready myself for the next beat. The dancers in front of us turned back and walked towards us. The two dancers in front of me were my good friends, King and Lorenzo – two Black guys I had a real bond with and had become close to over the years of performing together. As they walked towards me, they both raised their hands just above their heads, palms facing inwards, as though they were lifting a crown onto their heads. King caught my eye and mouthed the word 'queen' at me. They were both grinning, I could feel the love radiating from them, bathing me in their light. My eyes filled with tears and my breath caught in my throat. That wasn't part of the choreography. The other dancers didn't make crown symbols. Just my dancers. Because they knew I needed that reminder. They did the same thing every night for the rest of the tour. So every time we performed that song I would get a little reminder to hold my head high and remember who I am and what I am capable of. It was such a tiny gesture, but it meant the world to me.

The night before, I had come off stage and burst into tears once again. King had spotted me sobbing my heart out in one of the backstage rooms, and he held on to my arms and asked me what was wrong. He didn't tell me I was imagining it. He didn't tell me it was all in my head, or that I wasn't being treated differently. There was something in his eyes that told me he got it. Really got it. He understood the feeling I was describing, the thing that was so hard for me to even put into words. He recognised that feeling and he had felt it too. I can't tell you how reassuring it felt to have that acknowledgement. To have someone tell me that they hear me, they understand me, rather than simply batting it away. It felt like a deep sigh of relief. He came back to me in the morning with a book that had a Black woman on the front with affirmations coming from her hair, and he wrote me a letter filled with encouragement and inspirational messages. I kept it with me so I could read it at my lowest moments. King told me never to forget about my crown. I tried hard to keep that sentiment in my heart, to lift my chin. It wasn't easy, but it helped knowing I at least had somebody in my corner who wasn't going to deny my experience.

King and Lorenzo weren't the only people who got it. They were few and far between in the industry, but I did encounter some people who implicitly understood what it was like to be a Black woman in this industry. Frank Gatson is a giant in the music business. He has worked with Beyoncé, Rihanna, JLo. Anyone who is anyone has worked with Frank, and we were lucky enough to work with him on 'Wings'. As a seasoned director and choreographer, he was an invaluable resource for all of us. We couldn't believe we got to work with someone like him. We learned so much from him. He pushed us, helped us hone our craft. We had a lot of sessions with him, particularly early on in our journey with the band. There was one interaction I had with Frank that will always stay with me. We had been working together as a group, perfecting the choreography for the single, when he took me aside to speak to me on my own. As a Black man in the industry, he wanted to warn me of what was to come.

'You're the Black girl, you'll have to work ten times harder. You know that, right?' he said to me. I looked at him, confused. His words hung in the air. I heard them, but I couldn't understand them in relation to my own experience. This didn't sound right. Why would I have to work ten times harder than the others?

I was taken aback. I misunderstood and thought he was saying I would have to work harder because I wasn't as good as the other girls. I bristled and shook my head. I knew I was just as good, I knew I had just as much right to be on that stage, to share the limelight equally. I didn't want to hear anything that suggested otherwise. This was before the crying backstage, the weird encounters with fans, and the hostile treatment from certain sections of the press. None of that had happened yet, but Frank predicted that it would. He predicted – almost to the letter – how I would feel, how hard it would be for me. I didn't listen to him because I wasn't ready to hear it. I think I mumbled something in reply and shrugged his warning off. I didn't want to believe what he was saying was true. I still believed that my talent, my ability, my personality, would be all I needed to carry me to success. I still believed that it was all within my control. I put it down to Frank being American. They have different experiences over there, I thought. That might be the case for them, but it wouldn't be the case for me. I naively believed that none of those things could touch me. I had grown up relatively sheltered. I'd had a diverse group of friends at school, I had never really experienced any kind of overt, obvious racism. I was brought up to be acutely aware of racism – I knew it existed, it wasn't a surprise or something I had to learn about. But in terms of my career, and my success as a musician, I didn't initially believe racism could touch that. It couldn't happen. Not to me. I wouldn't be treated differently.

I wish I could go back and tell my younger self to listen to Frank's warning. I wish I could tell her that it was all true, that she would have to work harder, that she wouldn't be seen as equal to her bandmates. I didn't want to hear it at the time, but I think understanding this reality earlier could have helped me process the pain. Because to process something, you *have* to understand it, and I spent years – almost a decade – completely confused about why I felt the way I did. Knowing that this was about race wouldn't have changed much, wouldn't have removed the challenges I faced. But if I had a name for it, if I had the language to talk about it, I would have been much more equipped to deal with the emotional fallout, the legacies of trauma that still sit in my body, that still burst out as tears in unexpected moments, or make me quiet and insular in moments when I should feel happy. I wish I could go back and wipe the tears from my younger self's cheeks, straighten the invisible crown on her head and tell her that it's OK. I would tell her that I believe her and that she will come through this even stronger than before.

A promo shot for the *Race, Pop and Power* documentary. I am so proud of what Natasha and I achieved and part of the reason for that is because it went so far beyond simply telling my own story.

Filming for the documentary gave me the opportunity to speak to so many amazing women and highlight their stories. My struggle in the industry is one of many.

Speaking at the One Young World Summit with Ebinehita Iyere, founder of Milk Honey Bees. She is a phenomenal leader and a wonderful and selfless person.

(*above*) My family. Forever grateful for the sacrifices my parents made.

(*below*) In 2021, we made history as the first-ever girl group to win the BRIT Award for Best British Group.

Pregnancy felt like the longest wait of my life to meet my babies. It was so tough, but all worth it.

We spent weeks living in pyjamas, having endless cuddles on the sofa, getting to grips with breastfeeding. We have been so lucky in that these babies love their food.

Everything I do is for them. The most precious things in the world.

(*left*) Cuddles with my bubbas are my favourite thing.

(*below, left*) At the premiere of the Christmas movie *Boxing Day*. I loved acting and the whole experience.

(*below, right*) Boxing Day but this time at home – our first family Christmas, so of course we had to have matching pyjamas. The family tradition has begun!

Having support from Jamaica fills me with such pride and joy. With every visit, my connection to my heritage got stronger, and I can't wait for my children to feel the same way.

(*below*) A group of my girlfriends. People ask me how I have managed to keep such a solid group of friends. I think the only explanation is that I have been incredibly lucky.

(*above*) Our final tour before our break. *Confetti* was the perfect name for it because everything had an air of celebration.

(*below*) Visiting Spotify in New York and feeling dazzled by this sign. There I was. They were expecting me. They were waiting for me.

Surrounded by love. Celebrating one of the happiest days of my life with the people who mean the world to me. I will always cherish this memory.

I couldn't think of anywhere more beautiful to get married; the white sand, the crystal blue ocean, and the warmth of the Caribbean breeze on our cheeks.

What Andre and I have now, the life we have built for ourselves, the bond
we have with each other, with our families, our beautiful babies – it is everything
both of us dreamed of. And we are still so young. I can't wait to see where
this great love will take us.

# CHAPTER SIXTEEN

## The Love of My Life

'I deserve a love
that builds me up'

I met Andre during a slightly strange phase of my life. So much of it was brilliant, and so much of it was hard. My career was booming, and alongside it, so were my fears and insecurities. As much as I was loving the promotion and tour of our fourth album, *Glory Days*, I was also struggling with a lack of belonging, my confidence was crumbling around me, and I felt lost and overwhelmed. At the same time, the boyfriend I was with at that point had just told me he was having 'doubts'. He said he had looked at his future and he wasn't sure he saw me in it. I was devastated. Our relationship wasn't perfect, but I loved him, and getting dumped was the last thing I needed in that moment. My self-worth was already on the floor, and now another person in my life was no longer sure if they wanted me. It pushed me to the brink.

So, I did something outrageous. Something I had never done before. I hired a private jet and flew out to Marbella with my mum, my sister Sairah and some of my friends. There were no commercial flights available, but I knew I needed to get out of the country. It was one of the most extravagant things I have ever done. But in that moment, when I felt like so many things were falling apart in my life, I thought, *Fuck it*, and I booked the jet. In my experience, there aren't many things in life that can't be made better with some quality time with the women who love you the most. A girly holiday was just the ticket – time away from the stresses of my love life, away from the constant scrutiny of the media, away from the pain of rejection I was feeling in my professional life. I yearned for an escape to the sunshine, drinking cocktails on the beach, dancing into the small hours of the morning. I wanted to feel normal, happy, free, to just be a young, carefree woman, even if only for a couple of days.

It was just the tonic I needed. The Spanish sunshine poured down on me giving my skin a rich glow. I swam every morning, ate fresh fruit and walked on the beach with my girls, putting the world to rights. At night, we let loose. I felt unleashed. All the pent-up emotion I had been grappling with for months, years at this point, seemed to dissipate. I felt lighter, as though something had lifted. It was like having a holiday from my own brain. We partied hard, and I knew I deserved every second of it. I didn't speak to my then-boyfriend the entire time I was away, I didn't know what was going on between us, and I didn't really care. I just needed space from the whole situation.

One night, we were in a club right on the harbour. The music was great, the drinks were flowing, and the vibes were just right. We were having the time of our lives. My mum was certainly having the time of her life. I left her for half a minute to go and get a drink at the bar. By the time I turned around, she had managed to go flying into one of the fancy tables at the edge of the dance floor. It was carnage – drinks everywhere, girls dabbing napkins against their soaking-wet dresses, glasses and bottles on the floor. And there was Mum in the middle of it all, laughing her head off. When I got closer, I realised whose table it was – Alex Oxlade-Chamberlain's. He hadn't even got together with

Perrie yet, so that made the whole thing even more hilarious and random.

After shaking off that particularly mortifying moment, I managed to regain some composure. We met this lovely guy, a football agent who asked us if we wanted to go to another club with him. He said it was good, so we agreed and headed over there. The agent had a table at the back of the club, and we were all hanging out in that area. That's when I spotted someone on the other side of the table next to us.

'That guy is nice,' my sister yelled into my ear, battling to be heard against the heavy baseline of the music. I turned to look at the table and saw him for the first time. My heart did a little flip. *Oh my god.* I was so attracted to him. It was an immediate force that seemed to pull me towards him. He had these beautiful eyes. His clothes fit him so nicely – and don't even get me started on his lips. I kept making eyes at him, I couldn't help myself. As I was dancing in front of his table he leaned forward and grabbed my hand. I instantly liked his energy, he seemed calm and confident. We introduced ourselves, and then I asked him what he did.

'I'm a man of leisure,' he said with a mischievous grin. I did not like that.

'Oh whatever,' I said. And I stalked off. Whoever he was, whatever he did, he couldn't be a serious person with an answer like that. I asked Dwayne, the football agent, if he was someone dodgy and he laughed and told me he was a professional footballer, that he had just been promoted to the Premier League. I walked back over to him.

'So you're a footballer,' I said.

'No. No, I'm a man of leisure,' he said again, that annoying smile still on his face. I rolled my eyes so hard it hurt.

'Stop,' I said. 'Just tell me!' Eventually, I got the truth out of him. He tried to avoid admitting he was a footballer. He thought it would put me off. I guess footballers historically have a bit of a bad reputation. But I didn't care, I could feel the connection between us. This was less a spark, more a lightning bolt striking us both in the chest. It wasn't just physical (although that was definitely part of it). There was something about his aura that sucked me in like a gravitational force. And with the unlikely circumstances of how we had met, it felt like fate, like an inevitability. Something was pulling the two of us together, a kind of cosmic energy that neither of us could resist. But the start of our relationship was anything but neat and tidy. In fact, it was very messy.

It was a holiday whirlwind. I saw Andre again the next day. We had this kind of weird date at my villa. As we were having dinner I just turned to him and said, 'You've got a girlfriend.' It wasn't a question. It was a statement. I just knew it. It was something in the vibe he was giving off.

'Well, you've got a boyfriend,' he shot back at me. He must have googled me. We just looked at each other like – what the hell are we going to do about any of this?

Nothing about this situation was simple, except for the way I was feeling about Andre. I was falling for this man already. I hardly knew him, and yet I was certain we were going to be together. I could feel it. So we had this strange, imperfect holiday romance, getting to know each other even though neither of us was available. Then we both went home. Back to reality and to our partners. Soon after I got home, my boyfriend officially ended things with me. But things weren't so simple on Andre's side.

He had been with his girlfriend since they were young, they lived together and even had a dog. The next six months were challenging for us both, Andre was unsure whether to end his relationship and he went back and forth on his decision. I was in love, I was completely in it, I wanted to be with him, he wasn't sure if he could do it. He didn't want to hurt his girlfriend, and I understood how difficult that was for him. But at the same time, he had to decide. The longer things continued in this impossible limbo, the more pain it was causing to both his girlfriend and to me. The whole situation wasn't fair on any of us, and I don't think anyone handled it perfectly. But sometimes our decisions are messy, complex and driven more by emotion than by logic.

One part of me understood why it was taking Andre so long to decide, but the other part was fuming. How could there be so much deliberation? How could he leave me hanging like this? Why hadn't he chosen me, without a second thought? It hurt me deeply that he hadn't jumped in headfirst like I had. But I was in love with him, I couldn't walk away. All I could do was wait and hope that he would figure this mess out quickly. He asked his girlfriend to move out while he was trying to make sense of it all. He hadn't properly broken up with her, but the fact they were no longer living under the same roof gave me hope. He told me he was in love with me, and that he wasn't in love with her anymore. The problem was that he still cared about her and didn't want to hurt her. It is these situations where you have to be cruel to be kind; you have to cut ties and allow people to heal and move on – but he didn't. He was young; he had never been in a situation like this before, and he didn't know what he was meant to do.

I watched all of this play out from a distance. I was on tour, flying around the world, spending weeks living on buses, performing every night, and grappling with my own career issues. We spoke constantly, FaceTiming and voice-noting each other into the small hours, whispering under the covers while everyone else slept, our own private little universe of hopes and dreams and plans for our future. I wondered what I would be coming home to after the tour. Would we finally be able to be together properly? I wished for nothing else. I could talk to him about everything. I told him how I felt about being in the band. I told him about crying after the shows, about shrinking myself day by day to fit into other people's expectations. He didn't tell me it was all in my head. He listened. He understood. He got it. I loved him all the more for his ability to truly see me, and to see my potential. After months of holding on and hoping and praying we could make it work, he finally said, 'Let's do this. Let's be together.'

I was over the moon. I couldn't wait to get home from tour.

Then one night, I was on the bus on my way to Italy for a show, and I received this long message from Andre. He had changed his mind. He said he couldn't do it. He told me his football was suffering because his head wasn't in the right place, and that he needed some time on his own to figure it all out. Not with his girlfriend, but not with me either. I was *crushed*. I was so in love with this boy, and I felt like he was playing with my heart. I spent the whole night crying.

But then I had to pack all those emotions up and put them in a little box inside me, because the next day we were performing on Italian *X Factor*. Before the show, I stared in the mirror and gulped down huge breaths, trying to calm myself down. I couldn't stop crying.

'You're beautiful. You're amazing. Stop crying. Stop it,' I muttered to myself over and over. Somehow, I managed to hold the emotions back long enough to walk out on that stage. And of course, we were performing 'Shout Out to My Ex'. I sang the shit out of that song. I channelled all that raw pain into that performance, and it did make me feel a little bit better to sing some of the hurt out of my body. I gave myself a little talking to. I changed my WhatsApp picture to something really sexy. Because that's what you do when you're heartbroken.

'Nice thirst trap,' Andre sent, later that night. I shrugged it off, pretended the sexy pic wasn't entirely for his benefit. But eventually, we started talking again. That gravitational pull made it impossible for either of us to walk away. Everything had got so messy and so complicated, but underneath all of that, was the simple fact that we had fallen for each other. I knew in my heart we were perfect for one another. Andre knew it, too. It just took him a little longer to come to terms with it. It was coming up to Christmas when I received another long message from him.

'I love you. I'm in love with you. Let's do whatever we need to do to make this work. We have to be together.' It was the message I had been waiting for. They were the words I had been so desperate to hear. The rest is history. Almost a decade later, we have our beautiful babies, our house, and a full life together. All because of one moment in a club in

Marbella. We never could have known that it would lead to this. But that doesn't mean everything was easy from that moment on. Far from it.

Remember when we first met, Andre hadn't been coy in telling me he was a footballer? He'd thought it would put me off getting to know him because of the negative associations many people have around footballers and their personal lives. In the early years of our relationship, there were those moments when I began to understand that sometimes footballers have a bad reputation for a reason. Before I tell you about the bumps though, let me tell you why I fell for this man – the reasons I loved him, and love him still.

I knew from the start that he wasn't bothered about materialistic things. He was a real person and cared about real things that mattered. In the past, I had been with people who operated at a surface level – everything was for show. It was all about how it looked to other people. Andre wasn't like that, he was a family person. Family was his first concern, always. That is something pivotal to me, too, someone who could be my family, someone I could be real with, someone I didn't have to dress up with or show off with, someone who wasn't obsessed with the glitz and glamour. He felt solid and stable; he made me laugh until I couldn't breathe. I could be my true self around him – the silly girl who doesn't take anything seriously, the girl who cries easily and loves hard, the girl who is soft and sensitive, the girl who likes to spend her days off walking the dogs in the countryside. He loved that girl. Not just the girl on stage in all the makeup and glittery outfits. He loved the person who existed underneath all of that. I never had to pretend to be anyone else with him. Like me, Andre wanted a life, not a lifestyle.

But, as much as we both cared about the simple things in life, neither of our lives were simple. I was touring the world in one of the biggest-ever girl bands, and he was adjusting to his new life as a footballer in the Premier League – and all of the madness, money and mania that comes with that. It was a huge life shift for him. In the initial stage of us deciding to be together, he was still living up north, playing for Burnley. But then we had an amazing stroke of luck and he got signed to Watford, just down the road. So he moved in with me, quicker than we would have done it if it wasn't for the circumstances, but it felt right for us. But relationships take work, and we have certainly had to work through our fair share of shit.

No relationship is perfect. They all have their hard moments, difficult patches, struggles and challenges to overcome. I have always been a romantic. I love *love*. Giving it, receiving it and showing it in a million different ways. But part of my growing-up journey has been the realisation that real love, mature love, doesn't always look like it does in the movies. It isn't this idealised string of perfect moments filled with roses and candlelight. Love shifts and changes, love adapts to circumstances, love makes compromises that you don't necessarily want to make, love – when it is worth it – endures the hardships that we humans can put each other through. Building a life together with another person, buying a house, getting married, starting a family, is about choosing to make it work. Over and over again. Every single year, month, week, you have to decide that you want this, and you have to work for it. Love might spring from nothing, appearing magically when you first lay eyes on someone, but it doesn't stick around unless you put the graft in. And, at times, we have had to graft. My relationship with Andre is the light of my life. Now, we are strong; we are happier than ever. We know each other inside out; there is so much mutual respect and admiration. Our relationship is everything I have ever wished for. He put a ring on my finger and I couldn't be happier or more secure about my decision to spend the rest of my life with him. But I think it's so important to be honest about what it took to get to this point, because too often we only see the sugar-coated, rose-tinted version of love. But that isn't real.

What's real is falling for someone at a stage in life when he still had a lot of growing up to do. He was young and his life was changing faster than he could ever have imagined. He was all ego and bravado, and the environments he was existing in – the world of professional football, young men with too much money and status – felt toxic in many ways. He got himself into all sorts of situations that didn't put him in a great light; situations that hurt me. He never cheated on me to the point of being intimate with someone else – it was never that – but in relationships there are other things that can happen that can cause a whole lot of damage before you get to that point.

It was especially painful to go through rocky patches because my self-esteem during those years was already so fragile. For Andre to put me in situations where I was forced, once again, to question whether or not I was good enough – it was almost too much to bear. It made me feel unsexy, unlovable, as though I deserved to be treated badly.

One time when we had argued earlier in the week, I was due to go to the BRIT Awards. I told him that he still had to come with me. It didn't matter that we were in this awful moment of uncertainty. What mattered to me most back then was how it would look to everyone else. How would it look if he didn't turn up? What would everyone else think? This same fear kept me silent about some of the hardest things we had been through. I was so scared that people would judge me for staying with him, for not kicking him out or punishing him. But now, I don't care what anyone has to say about our relationship. I chose to stay; I chose to work through it. And I am so happy that I did.

Now, I can look back on those turbulent times with a new kind of distance and clarity. Andre has been having therapy to work through certain difficult elements of his childhood that made it hard for him to commit to a relationship. He has stopped drinking as much and he doesn't party like he used to. We are in such a good, secure, strong place. And I honestly don't know if we would be where we are today if we hadn't been through all the shit we went through at the beginning. I'm not exactly grateful, but I can appreciate that everything that happened between Andre and me happened for a reason.

I don't share these stories lightly. None of these anecdotes paint either of us in a particularly glowing light. But I also think it's so important to be honest about the realities of grown-up relationships, the challenges that come alongside the highs of love. We are so often only presented with the curated, Insta-perfect, idealised versions of relationships and love, and that can create so much dissatisfaction and an unattainable goal to aim for. Life isn't a Disney movie. The person you fall in love with isn't going to be a flawless prince. There will be arguments, there will be compromises, there will be hard days. Maybe hard weeks or months. But at the end of it, if you both decide that what you have is worth it, worth the effort, worth the heartache, then you will be left with something so special, and so strong.

What Andre and I have now, the life we have built for ourselves, the bond we have with each other, with our families, our beautiful babies – it is everything both of us dreamed of. It has been a privilege to grow up alongside Andre, to watch him become the man I always knew was inside of him, and the dad I always knew he could be. And for me to become the woman I knew I was destined to be, the mother I always hoped I would be, with my husband by my side. I couldn't ask for much more out of this life. And we are still so young. I can't wait to see where this great love will take us.

# CHAPTER SEVENTEEN

*Black Lives Matter*

'I can no longer keep quiet about injustice'

In March 2020, I returned from our festival performance in Brazil with a new feeling of strength. The way the fans out there had welcomed me, specifically the Black fans, had shifted something in my brain chemistry. At night I lay in bed, and I could hear the crowd chanting my name. I closed my eyes and let the feeling wash over me. I pictured the banners with my name painted in block capitals, I replayed conversations with the fans who were there for me, who wanted photos with me, wanted to tell me that I had inspired them, that I had made them feel as though they could achieve anything they dreamed of.

The memories were like a soothing balm, spreading cool and comforting over all the hurt that had built up inside of me. I felt my confidence stabilising, growing ever so slightly. I felt more like myself than I had in years. I wanted to bottle this feeling so I could sip from it whenever I was doubting myself or feeling unloved. It meant there were people out there who understood me, who valued me. Knowing this felt like a secret new superpower. Nothing could take that knowledge away from me. Nothing could erase those memories from Brazil. And yet, at the same time – having this knowledge also made me feel strangely helpless. OK, I now knew that what I had been feeling for so long was due to racism . . . but that didn't mean I could change it. It felt impossible to change. If I had been the problem, if I was simply not good enough or not likeable enough, that was one thing, but if the problem was a systemic issue with society, with humanity as a whole . . . how could I fight back against that? I felt small in the face of something so enormous and overwhelming.

But in March 2020, I suddenly found myself facing another giant problem. We all did. Covid-19 hit and everything changed overnight. There wouldn't be another tour, we wouldn't perform for a live crowd again for years. We wouldn't see our fans, or go to TV studios, or photoshoots, or award ceremonies. Little Mix, along with everything else in the world, was about to grind to a halt. The pandemic crashed into our lives, ripping away our sense of stability, routine and normality. Everything changed, even a simple trip to the shops felt like a post-apocalyptic mission. The masks, the sanitiser, queuing in single file outside the supermarket, decontaminating our groceries and parcels. I find it hard to believe that it actually happened. That collectively, as a society, we all went through that trauma together. Large parts of it feel surreal now. There are times when I randomly remember moments of madness during lockdown – clapping and banging pans out the bedroom window in support of the brave NHS workers, celebrities tunelessly singing 'Imagine' on the timeline, that period where we all obsessed over *Tiger King* – and I'll ask myself, *Was that real? Did it really happen?*

At the height of the pandemic, I was cocooned in a privilege that so many people weren't fortunate enough to have during that time. I was blessed to have a comfortable home, a loving family, financial security, and little need to put myself at risk. I was miles away from the front lines of this global disaster, and the only thing I had to worry about was my career, and my music. What happened to pop stars during a government-mandated lockdown? Well, the same thing that happened to a lot of people. We stayed at home and watched on. There was no touring, no time in the studio, no endless promo. The four of us were all thrown into our own little bubbles of isolation. We went from being in each other's pockets 24/7, to suddenly being without each other.

I missed the girls so much. We were coming off the back of a hugely successful tour, an album that was flying, we were at the height of our popularity. It felt like the world was at our feet, and it was frustrating to have to stop that momentum and just go home and sit on our sofas. We understood why it was necessary, of course, and that we had it lucky. But we didn't really know how to slow down, the concept of a break was unfamiliar to us. Rest? Don't know her. We had been working – relentlessly – since winning *The X Factor* in 2011. Almost a decade of intense, hard graft. Album after album, tour after tour; interview, photoshoot, award ceremony, repeat.

At first, it felt like the wind had been taken out of my sails. I felt deflated, unsure what to do with myself. I was fizzing with all this pent-up energy left over from that pivotal show in Brazil, but I had nowhere to put it. But soon, this new quiet, still life – at home with family, not travelling, not constantly adjusting to different time zones, not partying and out late, not being pushed from one venue to the next with no time to even take a breath – it became my new normal. Holed up in the beautiful home I had recently bought, I spent my time walking in the country, cooking extravagant meals, writing songs, spending quality time with the people I love. I hadn't realised how much I needed this. In both my body and mind. A break from the endless cycle of pop-stardom, the wheel I had been turning on since

# BELIEVE

I was just eighteen years old, it started to become just the thing I needed.

☆

One morning, towards the end of May 2020 – two months into lockdown – I woke up and watched a video that was circulating on social media. It was unavoidable. It was all over my Twitter feed, all over Instagram. I hit play. I watched a white police officer kneel on a Black man's neck for eight minutes and forty-six seconds, until the man was dead. I watched as people stood by, helpless. I watched as the other police officers at the scene did nothing. I heard the man on the floor scream for help, scream for his mother. The horror of what I was watching turned my blood to ice. I started shivering and crying. My reaction was the same as many Black people who watched or even heard about that horrific murder – visceral disgust followed by a choking rage. I was angry. So angry. And so exhausted. George Floyd was not the first person to be murdered at the hands of the police, and he would not be the last. This was a seminal moment, a seismic moment – but it was also a continuum of the relentless brutality and racist violence that we have been forced to witness and experience for decades, for generations.

Alongside my anger, I also felt a kind of soul-sucking helplessness. It was compounded by the weird intensity of being in lockdown, the fact that everything in life felt so desperately sad, difficult, and insurmountable. I just couldn't see anything hopeful. I felt overwhelmed by the awfulness of it, and with everything I had been feeling for years, the many different ways I had seen racism and discrimination played down and ignored. I felt hollow.

But then that started to shift. It began to feel like something new was happening. That there might be a reaction that could genuinely improve things. Was this the tipping point the world needed to finally say, 'enough is enough'? Were we about to experience a racial reckoning? I held on to that hope. I needed to believe something good could come out of something so unbearable. It had to.

There was a different energy about this atrocity. It felt like people weren't just going to let their anger dissipate, like we so often had before. Maybe it was because we were in lockdown. The world had stopped, there was finally the time and the space to properly examine what had happened, to consider how we felt about it and to do something about it, collectively. And people did. They took to the streets. They protested. They ripped down statues and monuments to racist historical figures and tossed them in the river. People taped banners in their windows, made pledges on social media, went to anti-racism talks, read anti-racist books and articles, companies promised to make structural changes to increase diversity. It was galvanising. People wanted to be part of it, to say something, to do something, to show the world that they were on the right side of history. It felt hopeful. We screamed it into the sky: *Black lives matter*. Our lives *matter*.

People started speaking out about their experiences. Across every industry, from every walk of life, there were stories of racism, inequality, discrimination. People were sharing stories of feeling less worthy, of being held back from their potential, of experiencing racial abuse and violence, but also of the more subtle elements of racism that are so frequently brushed under the carpet or explained away.

They were stories I recognised. People were articulating the feelings I had struggled with for almost ten years. I was no longer alone with these thoughts. I no longer believed I was imagining it, or worried that I was blowing things out of proportion. It wasn't only happening to me – the things I had been through, the unequal treatment that had chipped away at my sense of self, at my confidence, at my happiness – these things were *real*, and people were calling them out.

I found the speed of it all difficult to comprehend. How did we go from one day – no one giving a shit about racism or wanting to hear our stories, to overnight – everyone is talking about it? It was the top story on the news every evening, for weeks. There were documentaries, podcasts, new books about it, people were talking about it online, or over dinner with family members who have never spoken about this stuff in their lives. All the things I had been trying to grapple with almost entirely on my own, things I had been trying to hide or had no idea how to talk about, were now acceptable topics of conversation. It was a lot to get my head around. I needed to decide what I was going to do about it, and how I was going to do it. But I knew this was my moment to do *something*. I knew I had to speak my truth, now was the moment to be brave because it felt like it could have a real impact.

'More than ever, I felt like it was time that I was com-pletely open and honest with you all because finally, the world is awake and people want to listen, help and under-stand,' I wrote in the Instagram caption. It was a post I had been thinking about writing for a long time. It was time to tell the world everything I had been through, and why it needed to change. 'I'm not doing this video for sympathy or for you to watch and then go about normal life. I'm doing it because enough is enough and hopefully from sharing this we can all do more to understand the racism that takes place. In doing this, we are able to approach the bigger issue and break down systemic racism. All we want is equality and justice for our Black community.'

I sat in my dressing room, my phone set up on a mini-tripod in front of me. I was wearing my lockdown 'uniform' of casual sweats, no makeup, my hair chucked in a ponytail. I took a long, steadying breath and hit record. You can hear the slight tremor in my voice as I start to speak. I wrote down the words I intended to say because I knew I would be overcome with emotion, but even with the script in front of me it was a fight to get it all out without breaking down into tears.

'Growing up, me and my sisters never saw race as being a limitation on what we wanted to achieve. Because if our grandparents could raise mixed-race children in the sixties, we could do anything.' My eyes flicked between the camera and the paper lying on the desk in front of me. My hoody slipped off one of my shoulders and I fiddled with the fabric nervously.

'Too often, Black people are reminded how far we have come as opposed to how far we can go. Think about it, do you ever hear white people having to be thankful about how far they have come as a race?

'There comes a point in every Black human's life – no matter how much money you have, or what you have achieved – where you realise racism does not exclude you. Nine years ago, after joining Little Mix, I had the biggest awakening of my life. I learned that the dream of being in the biggest girl band in the world, came with its flaws and consequences.

'You can't be seen to be "too loud" or "too opinionated", otherwise you're deemed a diva, or aggressive. You learn that by walking into a room you are deemed unapproachable or "offish" before anyone has even approached you. You learn that voicing your opinion about the lack of diversity in the industry is like smashing your head against a brick wall.'

I spoke about all of the things that had weighed so heavily on my heart for the longest time. I spoke about myself, about the people who have it worse than I do – specifically, dark-skinned Black women who face colourism too. I spoke about the ways in which racism pervades every element of our society, from sport and the creative indus-tries to the corporate world and political policies. I made a desperate plea for this to be more than a moment, for it to be treated like a movement. There were too many things I could no longer hold inside of myself for fear of upsetting people, or making people feel awkward. I could no longer sit silently with my lived experiences of racism just so other people didn't have to feel bad. I couldn't be quiet any longer.

'My reality was feeling lonely while touring predomin-antly white countries. I sing to fans who don't see me, or hear me, or cheer me on.' My voice broke with emotion, and I started to cry. I wasn't about to stop, though. I took a deep breath and kept going. 'My reality is feeling anxious before fan events and signings because I always feel like I'm the least favoured. My reality is feeling like I have to work ten times harder and longer to mark my place in the group because my talent alone isn't enough.'

240

I leaned forward and pressed my phone screen to stop recording. There. It was done. I sat perfectly still for a couple of seconds. Then I grabbed my phone and hit post before I could change my mind. The likes and comments started pouring in. I flipped my phone over, so the screen was face-down on the desk. I needed to take a second. I needed to breathe before opening myself up to the rest of the world, to their opinions and judgements. I wasn't fearful of seeing the reaction – I had already made my decision to speak out and that was more important to me than any criticism anyone could throw at me – but this was a huge moment for me. A moment that had been a long time coming.

My body buzzed with adrenaline and emotion, but I felt a lightness in my bones, as though I could float up towards the sky. Everything I had been carrying for so long, the fears and the doubts that had weighed me down and threatened to drag me under the surface, it all felt lighter. By speaking it, by sharing it with everyone, I had taken it out of my own head and turned it into something more manageable. I no longer had to carry it all on my own. I felt a smile spread across my face. I hugged my arms tightly around my body. I realised in that moment that sharing my truth, the darkest, hardest parts of my experiences, was the most profound act of self-love I had ever performed.

My phone was still buzzing. The vibrations rattled ominously against the desk. Slowly, I picked up my phone and swiped it open. My notifications were popping off. The little red number in the corner went up and up, demanding my attention. I couldn't ignore them any longer. I didn't know what I was about to see, whether it would be torrents of hate, or people calling me a liar. I didn't know if they would think I was exaggerating or 'playing the victim', or if they simply wouldn't care about what I had to say. But it was out there now. Whether people believed me or not, supported me or not, I was finally ready to face it. I opened the app and started scrolling.

Wow. The response nearly knocked me off my seat. The support was overwhelming. Hundreds and hundreds of comments of sympathy, of empathy, of empowerment. Heart emojis popped out at me. They were everywhere.

'We're so proud of you!'

'You are so brave.'

'We love you, Leigh!'

'We love you!'

'We love you.'

Tears blurred my vision as I read. There wasn't only support for me, there were people who were sharing their own stories, Black fans who told me they could relate to what I was saying, that my video had made them feel seen, or had made them feel less alone. I couldn't express what that meant to me. I started to truly understand the power of sharing my story. With the platform I have, expressing the realities of my experiences with racism could shine a light on the issue in a new way, and I had the potential to reach a huge amount of people. I felt like I had a responsibility to do everything in my power to push back against the systems of oppression and discrimination that pervade not only the music industry but every institution and facet of society.

For so long, I had thought that strength was about endurance. I had struggled in silence because I thought I had to just take it on the chin and quietly accept that things were harder for me. To push through the pain and work harder than everyone else just to be treated as an equal. I thought that was strength. But real strength comes from refusing to accept this reality. Strength is using your voice to illuminate injustice – wherever you see it. Strength is calling people out on problematic behaviour, even if it makes things uncomfortable, even if it risks putting you in an awkward position.

Yes, I took a risk when I posted that video. I knew that. There was a risk I would be ostracised in the industry, labelled a troublemaker. I knew there would be people who would put a little mark next to my name, who would want to avoid working with me because of the things I'd said. I knew there was a risk to my career, to my reputation, and that what I'd shared was going to make a lot of people feel incredibly uneasy. If I felt the way I did, having been part of one of the biggest girl bands in the world, in my privileged position of financial security, fame and power – how must everyone else feel when they try to speak out against racism? Calling out racism is a difficult conversation, no matter who you are. For me, I knew the risk was worth it and entirely necessary. I had got to the point where I had no choice but to use my platform to make a positive difference. And after posting that video, I felt the drive to take it even further.

# CHAPTER EIGHTEEN

# Listening, Learning, Growing

'Our shared experiences are so powerful'

I needed to take this beyond my bedroom. Beyond my social media accounts. There was only so much that could be done by staying at home and interacting through a screen. This was bigger than my personal struggle. What I was going through was part of a much larger picture of injustice. The things I had felt, the inequality that had impacted me so deeply for so long, was happening everywhere. In every walk of life, in every profession, in every institution, in every realm of society. And finally, we were able to say that we had had enough, that we weren't going to take it anymore, that something big had to change. This was a global movement, and I needed to do whatever I could to help. I had never felt an urge so strong. It was like a compulsion. I couldn't *not* get involved. The anger that I was feeling, that so many people were feeling, had hit boiling point, bubbled over and spilled out into the streets. It was inspiring and beautiful, I felt hopeful and ready for action.

I watched on the news as thousands of protestors hit the streets all over America. Their signs held proud above their heads, their voices loud and clear. We matter. Our lives matter. I felt it in some deep place in my chest – it was in my soul. Those words echoed on a repeated loop. They became an unspoken mantra, powering me forward, giving me the confidence to share my story, giving me the strength to fight for what I knew was right. When those protests started happening here in the UK, I didn't hesitate for even a moment. I knew I had to be there.

# BELIEVE

The country was still in lockdown at the time, those surreal months in the spring and summer of 2020, so we all had to make a call. Being around crowds and taking part in a protest obviously didn't come without risk. But for me, having weighed it up and taken into account my own personal circumstances and living arrangements – I knew what I needed to do. I made sure I was as safe as possible, I masked up and went to the protest in Hyde Park. As soon as I arrived, I could feel something powerful. It was a collective and shared energy, as though we were all feeling as one. There was anger, yes, but there was also so much determination and purpose. There was a single-mindedness; we were all heading in the same direction, wanting the same things. That unity felt incredibly special, and I knew we would be able to channel all this strength of feeling into something real – real change.

During the march, I bumped into a group of young Black women and got chatting to them. We connected instantly. They had such a cool and dynamic vibe, they spoke with such confidence and belief that I felt empowered just from being in their presence. One of the group was a woman called Aries, and I had so much time for her and what she had to say. She told me about how she had struggled at work, just like I had; how she had felt alienated and left out, and had struggled to progress through her career. Like me, she was angry and exhausted. Like me, she was sick of feeling like no one was listening to her, that no one would believe her. The more I spoke to Aries and her friends, the more I realised that so many Black people in this country will have felt like this at some point. They will have experienced racism and discrimination in some form. And, as much as

248

these conversations were heavy and painful, they were also necessary. I felt safe in being able to talk so openly and hear other people talk about things that were so similar to what I had experienced, too. I felt a strong sense of belonging, not just through the shared trauma but also through the shared resilience – how much we had all been through, and yet we were still standing, we were still holding our heads high and pushing for change.

Aries and her friends have a podcast called The Trilly Trio. I found them on Instagram, and I was inspired to continue our conversation, so I messaged them and told them I would love to be a guest on their show. It was a remarkable conversation; no stone was left unturned, no topic was off limits. We spoke about my experiences in the band, the feelings I had struggled with silently for years, the insecurities that plagued me whenever I stepped on the stage. We spoke about the impacts of the Black Lives Matter (BLM) movement, and where we hope it will go from here. We spoke about our hopes for the future, our dreams for a better world. I'm so grateful I met these girls at the march. I'm so grateful I had the chance to hear them speak and to share in their wisdom.

I learned so much during this period. I learned that I was more powerful than I had ever given myself credit for. I learned that embracing who I am – rather than running from it, or desperately trying to fit in with everyone else – was the most powerful thing I could do. I also learned that there are different kinds of racism, from unconscious bias, to microaggressions, to systemic and institutional racism. It felt empowering to build my knowledge in this area, to give myself the tools to talk about the nuances of this situation with authority and real understanding. I learned that just because I'm Black, it doesn't mean I'm born knowing everything about race and inequality. It doesn't mean I have an inbuilt understanding of all the ways racism intersects with the realities of lived experience. I still had work to do. I still had lots to learn – and I was so willing and eager to do that.

The Trilly Trio are three beautiful dark-skinned Black women. Inevitably, we also spoke about colourism. Colourism is defined by the Cambridge Dictionary as 'dislike and unfair treatment of the members of a particular racial group who have a darker skin colour than others in the same group.' It is a form of discrimination and another symptom of white supremacy, but it can also happen within Black and other ethnic minority communities. It's the idea that the closer you are to whiteness, the better you will be treated. It means that Black people with lighter skin, or people like me who are mixed-race with white heritage, are treated differently – often better – than Black people with darker skin. There is privilege that comes with having lighter skin and Eurocentric features (such as looser curl texture, or certain facial features). This is true. This happens. I have seen it, I have felt it, I have benefitted from it. You see it everywhere. It's the reason why light-skinned Black people are more prominent in advertising, on TV and in films, in magazines. It's the reason why dark-skinned Black women have the least success on dating apps, why they are excluded from the hierarchies of beauty. It's probably part of the reason why I am where I am today. I honestly believe I would not have had the success I have had if I was a dark-skinned Black woman. I'm not sure if I would have been chosen to be part of Little Mix all those years ago on *The X Factor*, if I was a dark-skinned Black woman. I can't say this with certainty because I just don't know, but I strongly suspect that my lighter skin grants me a certain amount of palatability that producers knew would work for a broader market. Thanks to the colour of my skin, I can tick that diversity box while also being close enough to whiteness. That is a hard thing to acknowledge, but it is the sad reality. I already knew I had privilege because of the colour of my skin, and I had some understanding of colourism, but speaking to Aries and her friends helped me get my head around the realities even more, and how it impacts dark-skinned people.

It makes me so angry when I think about it. How ridiculous it all is. That something as superficial, as incidental as the colour of your skin can have such a huge impact on your life. That it can make your life harder, that it can hinder your chances of success, or even put you in physical danger. Speaking to the girls on the podcast about all of this felt like a release of some of that anger. Just knowing that I was speaking to people who understood what I was talking about, who had been through so much of what I had been through, felt safe. It was the same sense of community and belonging that I had felt at the march. This unspoken understanding, where you know that everybody around you just *gets it*, that they're on the same page and they support you – it made me feel proud. Proud of myself, proud of our community, proud of Black women specifically. I have seen how resilient Black women are, how much we have to go through, how much shit we have to take simply for existing. And yet we rise up to face it, to fight back, again and again and again. I hate that we have to. I hate that there are still so many battles to fight, but I am proud of our ability to keep showing up, ready to fight, no matter how exhausted or demoralised we might be.

Now that I had started to speak out, there was no way I was going to stop. The floodgates would never be closed again, and I was never going back to a place where I had to keep these thoughts in, to second-guess myself, or suppress my feelings. I was in a new moment, a new headspace, and now that I had found my voice, people were going to hear me. It felt powerful. I felt stronger and more confident than I had in years. I was no longer hiding a huge part of who I was. I was no longer grappling with the secret shame of feeling unworthy and unloved. There is so much power in vocalising your experiences. There is so much power in radical honesty and unapologetic openness. And finally, we were in a place where people were listening, *really* listening – for the first time in my life. The momentum was building, and it felt like a spiralling vortex of positive energy. I had never felt so empowered to speak out.

But even though I had so much certainty in what I was doing, and we now had the societal green light to talk about these things, that didn't always mean it was easy. Every time I spoke out about the racism I had experienced and the racism that plagued the entire industry, I was anxious. I was anxious about how it would be received; I was anxious that nobody would ever want to work with me again. I was anxious about the response. It was impossible not to be. And I did lose friends. There were some people who didn't like what I had to say. Maybe they weren't ready to hear it, maybe they felt defensive in some way. I don't know what it was.

One person – a white woman who is now a former friend – simply did not get it. She couldn't support me. Any time I tried to speak to her about these issues, she closed up on me, changed the subject, or even told me that what she was going through in her life at that time was 'worse'. I hated that she was trying to make it a competition, as though she couldn't acknowledge the inequalities I was highlighting simply because she also had her own problems. She was missing the point. None of this is about competition, or who has it 'worse'. This is about supporting people to speak their truth, supporting a friend in the expression of their lived experience. She didn't want to hear it; she didn't want to believe it. In that moment she showed me her true colours, and as a result we don't speak anymore. I'm OK with that, I no longer have the capacity for people in my life who are wilfully ignorant to the realities of racism. Not understanding is one thing, but being unwilling to listen and learn is what I can't accept, especially not from a friend.

There was always going to be some backlash, I expected it. But that didn't mean I was ready for it. It still hurt to see some people saying that I was lying or exaggerating, or that I was only saying these things for attention. Some people questioned why I was speaking out now, why hadn't I spoken about these things earlier. That was a particularly painful criticism, because I *had* spoken out about these things. Before George Floyd and BLM, before my Instagram video, I had tried to share my experiences, I had tried to get people to listen to me – on several occasions. But it was always dismissed.

In one interview for *ASOS* magazine, back in 2018, each member of the band had a page dedicated to our portion of the interview. I used my space to talk about feeling 'invisible'. I told them I felt like I had fewer fans than the other girls. I told them that I felt like I had to work harder because of my race. It's all there, in black and white, years before it became acceptable to talk about these things. I was terrified to share it. I didn't even say it during the interview because it was that difficult to talk about it, I ended up calling the magazine after the interview to ask them to include those points. But everything I said was overlooked. There was no big reaction, there were no calls for change. There was practically zero acknowledgement of what I had said. It was horrible to put myself out there like that, to share the most painful realities of my experiences, only to have it pretty much ignored. And then to be asked why I have never spoken about this stuff before . . . I have! But had anyone been willing to listen?

What I loved about this time was the fact that the majority of my white friends were unbelievably supportive. They threw themselves into the conversation with open ears and open hearts. They were willing to listen, to share and be vulnerable, to be honest about the things they didn't know, and they showed me so much kindness in the moments where I was hurting, or when it all felt too much. I was and am incredibly grateful to have the friends that I have. I loved seeing them coming to marches and protests, sharing insightful information about anti-racism on their social media accounts, instigating the difficult conversations. I loved how brave they were about discussing these issues, how they didn't shy away from them or make me feel like I was being too much, or too intense. They just got it.

When I spoke to my friends about my experiences, it felt like we had always spoken about this stuff. It was incredibly natural. I can't tell you how much it helped to have them in my corner, backing me in this moment. That is what true allyship looks like. It looks like showing up, shouldering the burden whenever you can, doing the work to learn and educate yourself. Sometimes, as in the case of many of my friends, it's as simple as letting me know they were there for me, and always would be.

The love and support I received during this time kept me going. My friends and family were amazing, but my fans were a huge part of it as well. I received so many messages from young Black girls who had been moved and inspired by what I had shared. I was doing this for them. I wanted to show them that being a Black girl was a strength, a superpower, that there was nothing that could hold them back from achieving their dreams. It's important that I can help create a world where that is true, where Black girls are celebrated and loved, not held back and limited. I was doing this for the little girl who lives inside me, the one who had the world at her feet and wanted nothing more than to sing and perform. I could feel myself returning to her, the girl I was before I had the confidence stamped out of me, before I was made to question my talent and my beauty and my worth. She was still in there – the girl who believed in herself. I was getting close to finding her again, and it was a beautiful feeling.

# CHAPTER NINETEEN

## The Documentary

# 'Race, Pop
# & Power'

After the murder of George Floyd and the global protests that followed, many new platforms talking about racism and discrimination were given the green light. Out of something so horrible, so tragic, so unjust, people got to work, creating brilliant, important things. Books were written, podcasts were started, TV shows and documentaries were commissioned. It's awful that it took the traumatic loss of life for these things to happen – but the fact that they could now exist, that people were finally listening, was a positive thing.

Most people assume that my documentary was part of this post-BLM wave, that it was a reaction to the wider conversations that were happening about racism in all areas of society. But that isn't how it happened. I was already working on this documentary, already planning to speak my truth about racism in the industry. It was a need that had been building inside me for many years, a need to share this story, a need to speak out about the realities of what I had been through. It had taken me a long time to figure it out for myself, and then an even longer time to feel ready to speak about it, but this documentary felt like a huge and important first step. The wheels were first set in motion while I was halfway up Mount Kilimanjaro, talking to Ed Balls – the former MP. Random, I know.

I was climbing the mountain for Sport Relief. The celebrity group I was part of included Jade and me, Alexander Armstrong, Osi Umenyiora, Dan Walker, Ed Balls, Shirley Ballas, Anita Rani and Dani Dyer. None of us had ever done anything like this, and it was a truly amazing experience. The scenery was stunning, and I loved being so immersed in nature. The physical challenge was also incredible. Every night we slept in these tiny little tents, and during the days we faced hours and hours of walking and climbing uphill. It was so tough, my leg muscles were burning every night when I tried to fall asleep. On the final day, making it to the summit involved a nine-hour trek in the dark in sub-zero temperatures. Needless to say, we had a lot of time on our hands to talk – all we were doing was walking – and some of our conversations got pretty deep. I think it was something about where we were, the majesty of the landscapes, it knocked down some of our barriers and I felt like I could be open in that environment.

I found myself in a deep conversation with Ed and Anita. Anita and I spoke a lot about ideas of beauty, about the standards we are all held to, the complexities of being a Black or Asian woman and how that impacts how you are perceived, how it impacts your self-worth. I spoke about the added pressures of being in a girl band, of feeling inadequate and 'less than' my bandmates – less worthy, less beautiful. At that time, back in 2019, I still found it so difficult to talk about race directly. So I tended to talk about the issues around it, ideas that were linked to racism without explicitly using those words. This was partly because I hadn't made those connections for myself at that time, and also partly out of fear of how it would be received. But up on that mountain, with the freezing air whipping at our faces and the crunch of gravel under our boots, Anita heard me, she understood, she had her own stories to share. Ed Balls listened with interest, and he was the one who suggested I should make a documentary about it. He sowed the initial seeds, and I sat with that idea for a little while. I tried to imagine what it would feel like to speak publicly about these issues, to lay it all out bare for my friends, family and fans to see. The thought was scary, but I also felt the overwhelming urge to make it happen. I knew it was the right thing to do. I knew this was a vitally important conversation. But I also knew it had to be done in the right way.

As soon as I got home from the climb, I met up with my friend Natasha who is a TV director. I have known her since school, and I would trust her with my life. I knew she was the only person I could work with on something like this. It had to be someone who knew me, someone who understood what I was about, someone I could trust wholeheartedly to tell this story with the utmost compassion and empathy. I don't think I could have even imagined going ahead with this project if Natasha hadn't been at the helm. When we spoke, she understood my vision, but she also gave me the space and the time to work out what I wanted to say and how I wanted to say it. This was going to be a labour of love, not some rushed, reactive project. I knew how important it was to get this right and give it the time it deserved.

I told my mum about what Natasha and I were working on. I told her I was finally going to lay it all out in public, expose the bullshit I had been through, as well as the more endemic problems with racism that exist within the music industry. She was happy for me, and encouraging as she always is with whatever I do, but she didn't have much hope in how it would be received.

'That's great, Leigh-Anne, but no one's going to care,' she said. She didn't mean it in a horrible way, and she wasn't trying to undermine my efforts, she was just being real with me. And the worst thing is that part of me knew she was right. Did anyone care that racism existed in the music industry? Did anyone care that I had been treated differently because I was the Black member of the group? The sad reality is that back then, before the BLM movement, so many people didn't care. I knew this because I had spoken about my experiences in the past and no one had reacted. No one had said anything and nothing had changed. My *ASOS* interview the year before couldn't have been more explicit about my experiences as the Black member of the band . . . and what was the reaction to that? Tumbleweed. Why would the reaction to a new documentary be any different? But I still had to try. I was getting to the point where I didn't care if no one was listening, I was still going to speak my truth because I knew it needed to be said. So what if people weren't listening? My job was to try to make them pay attention. So, Natasha and I got to work in development. We started filming, we started doing interviews. We were going to make this documentary work no matter what. Fast-forward to 2020 and the aftermath of the BLM protests, with the new willingess for people to engage and learn, I knew I had a real opportunity here to make a change.

The excitement about announcing the documentary was short-lived because the backlash hit almost immediately. People were pissed. Really pissed. And they were not afraid to be vocal about it. Twitter was full of angry messages about the doc, about me. Talking about race is always contentious, and I knew some people would not be ready to have a conversation about racism in the music industry, but that wasn't where the backlash came from. It was overwhelmingly Black people on Twitter who were angry and upset, and that crushed me.

Essentially, it was all a big misunderstanding. The promo blurb that went out in the press read: 'Little Mix star Leigh-Anne Pinnock explores her own personal experiences of racism and colourism as a Black woman in the UK.' This was where we went wrong. It gave the inaccurate impression that I – a mixed-race Black woman with white heritage and light skin – would be talking about the ways in which colourism had hindered my life. People on Twitter were livid that I was the face of this documentary. They asked why it wasn't a dark-skinned Black woman raising this issue. People were outraged that I would dare to talk about colourism when I had clearly benefitted from this horrible form of inequality through having lighter skin. All these criticisms would have been completely valid, but that wasn't what the documentary was actually about. I wanted to talk about colourism, yes, but from the perspective of how it impacted darker-skinned Black women. I was interviewing many darker-skinned Black women for the programme. Colourism was only one part of what the documentary was about, but the fact that no one had seen the documentary yet, that it hadn't even been released, didn't stop people writing scathing Twitter threads and think-pieces about me, about why this documentary was wrong and flawed. I couldn't believe how much anger and hatred people had towards the project – before they had even seen a single second of it.

It's a perfect example of how outrage on social media can work, people jumping into an argument before they know all the facts. Even if it's based on something that isn't true. I know this is how Twitter works, and that in many ways, it isn't real. But it still hurt. To see that kind of negative reaction to something I had poured my heart and soul into, something I was so incredibly nervous about sharing, was difficult. It was during this time when I had to hold on to what I knew to be true. I knew I was contributing something positive to the conversation, I knew my intentions were about sharing lived experiences and holding space for other people's pain as well as my own. This was nothing to do with pitting people against each other, or creating a hierarchy of who has had it worse. I knew that when the documentary came out, people would see how I never shied away from my own privilege, how I hand the microphone over to dark-skinned Black women to speak on colourism because I know they are better placed to do that than I am, how I am honest about what I don't know and what I need to learn. I just had to hold on until people saw it. And when they did, the response was overwhelmingly positive. I was floored by the responses, the messages. People stopped me in the street to tell me they had seen the documentary, that they had been moved by it. And this wasn't only my Little Mix fans, or Black and mixed-race women, this was white people, older people, people I never would have expected to watch the documentary or feel any kind of way about these issues. It was astonishing. Mum had been wrong about this. People did care, all kinds of people cared. They were finally listening to me, and that was such an empowering feeling.

☆

# THE DOCUMENTARY

During the making of the documentary, there were also some difficult conversations that I had to have closer to home. I had to talk to Andre about some of the things he had said in the past. Nasty, childish, colourist comments that he had tweeted when he was a lot younger, which had resurfaced and been picked up in the press years before. When this all first came to light, Andre had scored in a couple of big games and was making a bit of a name for himself. As a result, people started digging up some dirt on him and they found it. I knew we had to address it; it didn't make sense for me to produce a whole film about racism and colourism without confronting his past remarks, but this also was important to me beyond the scope of making the film. I knew Andre was a different person now to who he was when he tweeted those horrible things. I knew he had overcome his difficult upbringing and challenged and changed lots of elements of his character, but I needed to hear it from him.

When I first heard about the tweets, I couldn't believe it. I was honestly so disappointed. It was 2016 and I was away working, performing at V Festival. It was a warm mid-summer's day, and we were preparing to go on stage, sorting our costumes and having finishing touches applied to our makeup, when my assistant came up to me and brandished her phone in my face.

'Have you seen this?' she asked, her face twisted up in concern. I squinted at the screen and read the list of incriminating tweets. My heart sank.

'What? That's not . . . that's not Andre? You're joking, right?' I couldn't comprehend what I was reading. That wasn't the Andre I knew. That wasn't the man I had fallen in love with. It just didn't make any sense. There wasn't time to think any more about it. I had to go on stage. I pushed it to the back of my mind and got on with my job. But as soon as I got home, I brought it up with Andre.

'What the hell are these tweets? What were you thinking?' He looked mortified. He didn't even remember tweeting those things; it had been so long ago. If he had known they were there he would have gone back and deleted them because he no longer thought like that. But that wasn't a defence, and he knew it. His defence was immaturity. He was a dumb kid, tweeting things he thought were funny at the time, things that he and his friends would say to each other and would use to take the piss out of each other. His target had been dark-skinned Black women. He made jokes about the colour of their skin. That was unacceptable. It didn't matter that he has Black heritage, his comments were colourist and discriminatory, and just plain horrible. He knew that and he admitted as such. He apologised unreservedly and wished he could take it back. He wasn't that person anymore. I knew that in my heart, and that was why I was able to accept his explanation and move forward. I also admired his courage for addressing it publicly on the documentary. That was the biggest proof of his growth as a person. He was willing to hold his hands up and admit his mistakes. He didn't shirk the responsibility or make excuses. He knew it was wrong, he admitted it, and now he is working hard to make positive changes. I respect him for that.

I'm so proud of what Natasha and I achieved with the documentary and part of the reason for that is because it went so far beyond simply telling my own story. Of course, that was a big part of it – I needed to share the sense of inadequacy I had struggled with, the injustices I had faced, the different treatment, the toxic stereotypes I had been forced to fight against for so many years. I shared my exhaustion, my helplessness, the ways in which racism and discrimination had robbed me of my confidence, of my self-worth, how it had transformed me into a shell of the person I used to be. And yet, this story was so much bigger than just my own narrative. My story was one of hundreds, thousands, of other people in the music industry who had suffered, struggled and been unable to fulfil their potential simply because of the colour of their skin. I needed to tell that story too. So I started making some calls.

I needed to speak to other Black women in pop. I knew these women would be able to understand what I was saying on the deepest possible level. I was also desperate to hear how they coped, how they managed, what strategies they used to deal with all of the shit that was thrown in their direction. I wanted to hear how they were doing now, how – if at all – they had managed to process all of that negativity. I needed to hear their stories to give me hope. I needed to know it was possible to survive it, that it was possible to come through the other side of it all. And I knew their voices were vital to this documentary. This story was not only mine to tell: it was all of ours.

Everyone I spoke to jumped at the chance to be involved. There was no deliberation, hardly any back-and-forth, people wanted to use this platform to talk about their experiences. I knew why. I recognised that feeling of needing to be heard. For some of the people I was talking to, this might have been the first time they were going to speak publicly about their experiences of racism. If they were in the industry earlier than I was, I knew they would have faced a huge amount of hostility and push-back if they tried to bring it up. People were only just about ready to start having this conversation now, but for everyone who came before me, I knew it would have been an individual burden they would have carried throughout their entire career.

There was so much beauty and power in the room when we finally got everyone together. I was a little bit over-whelmed by it all. These were women who I had looked up to and admired, some I had even modelled my own career on. And now we were working together on something so important. I could feel the energy when they walked into the room, slightly nervous, but purposeful. Alexandra Burke, Keisha Buchanan, Raye and Nao. Alexandra was obviously an *X Factor* alumni like myself, so I knew there would be a deep connection between us. But some of the things she told us shocked me to the core: she was told to bleach her skin. After winning *The X Factor* in 2008, Alexandra was told her skin was 'too dark' to sell records. She was told the only way she could be successful was if she had lighter skin, and the answer to that was bleach. I felt sick, hearing that. Physically nauseous. Alexandra told us that she had refused to bleach her skin, but the damage was already done.

'That's what is so fucked up about this industry and that is what makes me feel, at times, where I go: "I don't want to be in this industry". They took my confidence away so much that I couldn't be me.' Alexandra had tears pouring down her face while she said this. So did I, I could see the pain in her face, hear it in her voice. I could feel her pain, because her pain was all of our pain. What she said about losing her confidence struck me right in the heart. It was exactly what I had felt. The relentless stripping away of who I was, endlessly being told that who I was was not enough, was not right, could never be successful, I felt that. As I looked around the room and saw the other women nodding slowly in recognition, it filled me with sadness. There was so much talent in that room. So much creativity, boundless potential, so much musical ability and star quality. Why wasn't that enough? Why did we have to change things about ourselves, make ourselves smaller, quieter, lighter, in order to be marketable in this industry? I remember hearing Alexandra's voice on *The X Factor* for the first time and sitting up to take notice of that voice. A talent like that was a rare thing to find. An objectively beautiful voice, unbelievable levels of skill, the power she had over her breath control. She was a born star. And yet, even after winning, even after showing everybody what she was capable of, she was still treated like she was unworthy because of the colour of her skin.

Keisha's story was different to mine. She was victim to the racist stereotypes that are used to vilify and punish Black women. She was given the label of 'angry Black woman', made out to be unreasonable, unapproachable, hostile. She was called a bully. She explained the risks that come with being outspoken, how for Black women it can be impossible to stand up for yourself without being accused of being 'aggressive'. She told us that people in the industry essentially forced her out of her group, the Sugababes, without her even being told. It was disgusting the way they handled things with her. She lived with these unfair and inaccurate definitions of her character for years, people made all the wrong assumptions about her, and the more you defend yourself, the harder it can be to rid yourself of these labels. It's such a trap.

Raye's story was all too familiar. She was told by her label that she couldn't release R&B music, that it wouldn't sell. At the same time, white artists on the same label were being promoted with R&B records. It wasn't the genre the label didn't think would sell, it was Raye. They wanted that music, but only if it was fronted with a white face. She said her label refused to release her album. They held her back, suppressed her talent, forced her into this long, convoluted argument, when she should have been spending her time focusing on her art, her music. But I was so inspired by the way Raye fought for what she believed. She didn't roll over and accept what they told her. She knew she could succeed on her own terms. She believed in herself. She spoke out; she refused to be silenced. Now, she's independent, her music is out in the world and she is thriving. I felt such pride hearing that story. What a woman. What bravery. What strength. She stepped into her power and trusted in her own ability. She is living proof of what we can achieve when we have the courage to believe in ourselves, even when nobody around us believes in us.

That was one of the strongest emotions I took away from the experience of the documentary. An overwhelming sense of pride, and inspiration. Sitting in that room surrounded by powerful Black women, Black creatives and artists like me, was such a beautiful experience. Something I hadn't had the privilege of experiencing much over the course of my career up to that point. I'd never been in spaces where Black people formed the majority. I was so frequently the only one, or one of a small number. It felt amazing to be part of the majority for once.

The energy I felt in that room was nothing short of magical. I could feel how much we have collectively faced, how much hardship, how many hurdles and barriers have littered our paths. I could feel our collective exhaustion, the tears that smeared our cheeks as we bared our truths to each other and revealed the pain and heaviness in our hearts. And yet, despite how much we carry, despite the weight of it all, we were still pushing for what we believed, we still had the strength to keep going, no matter what. I loved that for us. We would not be crushed by all of the bullshit, we refused to be defeated by it. No matter how many times we were torn down, told we were worthless, told we would never succeed, we would dust ourselves off and go again. That resilience is a superpower.

But it was also a heavy experience. When we set out to make the film, we didn't know where it would go, we didn't know what we would uncover. I wanted to tell my own story, but I never expected to dig so deep into the wider, systemic problems that exist throughout the industry. I never expected to meet Black women from all walks of life and hear their stories that were both so like my own, and so very different. And as we sunk deeper and heard more and more stories, collected more and more pain, I took so much of that into myself. It was a lot to carry, and at times, it felt really hard.

There were racist trolls in my DMs on Twitter and Instagram. There was backlash, anger and hostility at every turn. Talking about racism is not an easy thing to do, and you inevitably expose yourself to a lot of hatred and a lot of negative opinions. I realised there were always going to be some minds that you simply cannot change. There will always be people who believe what they believe, who can't be argued with or reasoned with. There will always be people who believe that I am less worthy because of the colour of my skin. There will always be people who will deny and deny and deny that racism exists, who will gaslight me and tell me it's all in my head, or tell me that I'm a liar or an attention-seeker. I have struggled with the knowledge that some things are unchangeable, no matter how articulate, reasonable or factual my argument is. It's in these moments when it feels hard to have pride in the country I live in, the country I was born in. How can I be proud to be British when there are people in this country who don't want me here, people who tell me I will never belong here?

Yet, there is also so much hope. So much beauty came out of the documentary. Our stories reached people who never would have engaged with these issues. I *was* able to change minds, to open some people's eyes to the realities of racism. I saw that in the reactions, in the messages of love and support, in the people who stopped me on the street to tell me they had seen it, that they empathised, that they had learned something new from watching it. That was why I did it. I did it for myself, I did it for other Black women in the industry, I did it for my babies, for my niece and nephews, for my Black fans, for the next generation.

I had been ready to tell this story from the moment I posted my video on Instagram and finally told the world a tiny snippet of what I had been struggling with for years. The documentary, in many ways, was the natural next step.

# THE DOCUMENTARY

I was ready to spill it all, to share everything. And I hoped people would see that this was real. I had spent so many years wondering if it was all in my mind, worrying that I was imagining it. But putting it out in public like this was my way of finally ridding myself of this fear. It was real, and it runs so much deeper than simply worrying about having fewer followers than my bandmates. After almost a decade, I had found a way to articulate the vague and horrible feelings of inadequacy that had plagued me. I had finally given it a name. Racism. These experiences had happened to me because I am Black. Saying this, finally spelling it out, was empowering and incredibly freeing. It was all out there now, unavoidable and honest. I was laid bare, and it felt like an opportunity for renewal, a fresh start. It felt like a new level of potential had been unlocked. This was a chance for me to tell a new story, one in which I wasn't sidelined or pushed to the margins. This time I was going to be the version of myself without the insecurities, without the little voices of doubt whispering in my ear. This time I was going to be the version of myself I was always meant to be. The real me.

# CHAPTER TWENTY

## The Work Continues

'I want to be the change'

My management team is still majority white. That is, unfortunately, still normal within the music industry. My team is more diverse than it was, because I have insisted on it, but ultimately there is a lot of work to be done to improve opportunities within the industry. Over the last few years, I have realised it is in these spaces where the changes really need to happen. It is the management, the boardrooms and the bosses that need diversifying, shaking up. These are the people with the power and the money. These are the people who make the decisions, decisions about what music we can release, who gets more money and backing in their campaigns, who is marketed as the 'lead singer' of a band. Essentially, they get to decide who gets to be a star, or at least they decide who is going to get the best chance. So, no matter how many Black and Brown faces you see on stage or on the covers of albums and magazines, nothing will change until that same diversity is reflected all the way up through the hierarchies of power. Things are improving, and I believe there will continue to be more opportunities for the industry to keep getting better, for different voices and perspectives to be able to access positions of power. But I know that part of my job is to continue to push for that change, not only within the music industry, but wherever I can.

The last few years have taught me a lot about myself, not only about my character and my ability to find strength in the most difficult of circumstances, but also about my purpose. I truly believe I am here for a bigger reason. I am supposed to make a positive change. I know it. My dream as a little girl was to be on stage, to spread joy with my music and with my ability to perform for a crowd. It was all I wanted, more than anything else. I still want that. I still love creating music and performing and it still brings me so much joy, but now I know I can offer more. It has always been in my nature to stand up for what I believe in. As a young girl, I stood up for my friends, I stood up against bullying or injustice wherever I saw it. It didn't matter if I was the smallest girl in the room and was about to end up scrapping in a toilet cubicle, or if I was the only one to speak up when a teacher said something problematic. I have always felt that my role is to be a voice for those who are less able to speak up for themselves. My voice was robbed for a time. I lost it, and with it I lost all my power. But now it was coming back. This was the moment for me to speak up again, not only for myself, but for everyone else who had been crushed and diminished by an unfair system.

I feel passionately that I am supposed to use my time here for something good, and the platform I have provides the most amazing opportunity to impact people's lives and inspire something positive. It feels like a duty, or a responsibility, and I am determined to ensure that the steps forward we have made since the protests in 2020 are not quietly washed away or forgotten about. The job is far from finished, and I will do everything in my power to keep the conversation going. But this also has to be more than words. For me, this is about action. I will be the change I want to see in the world. I will put my money where my mouth is and spend not only my money but also my time and my energy in helping improve things within my communities, providing opportunities, and working towards ensuring the people that come after me don't have to go through anything like what I went through.

☆

This wasn't just talk. This was real, and I wanted to create something that would have a real, tangible impact. So I started a charity foundation, The Black Fund. The purpose of the foundation was simple: to build a pot of resources that I could award to Black-led community groups who were making a positive impact and needed funding. With the help of Jay Blades who is a trustee, my sister Sairah and my partner Andre, who came on board as co-founders, we set out our vision and a strategy for how we would achieve it. We used our own money to get it going; I couldn't think of any better way to use the wealth I had built up over my years in the band. This was the perfect way for me to convert my own personal success into a win that the entire community could benefit from. It just made sense to me and I was so inspired by everyone I encountered through our work with the fund. There were so many people doing such valuable, important work in so many different fields – I felt humbled to be speaking to them, and so grateful to be in a position to be able to help them to reach even greater heights.

I see The Black Fund as a helping hand. There are so many businesses and organisations out there doing the most awe-inspiring work in the community, and my motivation was to help them to continue and expand on their amazing work. There is so much power in helping each other, in coming together and providing people with the tools they need to succeed and thrive. The fund was never about me; it wasn't about Little Mix, it wasn't about my fame or my influence. In fact, it was imperative to de-centre myself entirely. This was about celebrating and supporting the people who are doing the hard graft at grassroots level, working to improve the lives of young Black people in this country, offering support to teenage girls, providing resources for mental health. These are the people I look up to with endless admiration, the people who inspire me every day. If I can use my platform, and the privileges of my wealth and status to help those people achieve even more, I'm going to do everything I can to make that happen.

I'm so proud of what we have done already. In our first year we supported eleven organisations and charities, offering each one up to £5,000 through our Give Back Grant. Each one has a special place in my heart, and I hope beyond anything that we can continue to make a difference in this way. My dream is for The Black Fund to become a name people trust, especially young people, to offer opportunities, access, work and experience in fields they are interested in. Inevitably, we will have a focus on the creative industry. I know what it's like to feel alone as a Black girl in the arts. I know what it's like to feel as though people want to use your face and your heritage and your culture for clout, while simultaneously silencing you and edging you out. I see it, again and again, how the people who hold the power cherry-pick the most marketable elements from Black creatives, without ever offering them a seat at the table. It's exploitative, discriminatory, and simply wrong. Black creatives have so much to offer. Infinite talent, infinite beauty, joy and passion, and yet we are still kept in a little box, expected to earn the money for the people who sit on boards and make decisions, and often treated as though we are worthless in the process. I have had enough of it. We need a change. This foundation feels like a small, but determined step towards a fairer, more equitable industry.

One of the successful applicants for the funding in 2022 was Ebinehita Iyere, the founder of an organisation called Milk Honey Bees, which is a beautiful organisation for young Black women and girls. The youth group provides an expressive space for girls to flourish, express themselves creatively and access opportunities – all within a safe space. Ebinehita is their phenomenal leader, and the moment I heard about her mission and what she has already done to improve the lives and prospects of so many young Black girls, I knew I had to help support her journey. She is the most wonderful, selfless person. She gives so much back and seems to have a limitless resource for doing good. We helped to fund her in a scholarship for further study to help take her work to the next level, but it was crucial to make sure the support went beyond simply handing out a cheque. Ebinehita and the girls at Milk Honey Bees wrote and published a book called *Girlhood Unfiltered*. It is the kind of book I wish had existed when I was a teenager, when I was first experiencing the stressful, conflicting realities of growing into Black womanhood, trying to exist in spaces that were not built for us to thrive. The book is an anthology of essays, letters and creative work reflecting on the experience of Black girlhood, written by the most inspiring group of teenage girls. I was so lucky to get to meet them and witness their energy and potential first-hand. I attended the launch party for the book and promoted it all over our social media pages. The event was sheer joy, I felt endlessly inspired by these powerful young women. They had everything ahead of them, and were so full of life, so full of hope. Just as I had been when I started my career. All I want is for them to be able to keep hold of that hope, to keep their power and their confidence, to keep believing in themselves.

Up on the stage, the girls shone with pride as they read out extracts from their essays and letters. They wore black T-shirts emblazoned with bright pink letters that read 'Girlhood Unfiltered'. They wore their hair in intricate cornrows, or braids that cascaded down their backs. Their laughter and excited whispered conversations were like music in the air around us – totally infectious. I couldn't keep the smile off my face as I watched them. They bubbled with that special magic unique to teenage girls, that shimmering nervousness and insecurity, somehow unsure of themselves and entirely certain at the same time. Everything was hilarious, and everything was mortifying. They hid their faces when a camera pointed in their direction. They collapsed into giggles when it was their turn to read, but underneath all of that I could see their dreams, their limitless ability to conjure their futures in a million different ways.

I want their dreams to come true: all of them. I want all young Black girls to know they can be anything they want, that nothing is out of reach. I want a world that won't crush them, that won't break them down until they have nothing left to believe in. I want a world that will hold them up and give them what they need to succeed, a world that will remind them of their power and give them the space to be whoever they want to be. I want them to have a world that I didn't have. They deserve everything. My hope is that with our work dedicated to investing in equality, we will help to create a world like this.

☆

My work with charities and activists over recent years has instilled a new set of principles within me. This work will impact everything I do going forwards. These aspects of my life and my work can't be compartmentalised. I'm not a pop star three days a week, and then an equalities campaigner on the other four days. That's not how it works. This has to be a holistic, fully integrated approach. I want to use my music, my performances and the support of my fanbase in a way that works in harmony with my equality work – they are simply different sides of the same coin.

So now, whenever I am approached to work with a new brand or partnership, I ask them – how can you help? If people want to work with me, use my name, my face, my music, then they will have to be explicit about how they are willing to help the cause. Will they donate to The Black Fund? Will they promote our work and our partners on their channels? Will they provide access or work experience to diverse communities? We can no longer be OK with companies ticking diversity boxes without doing any of the difficult, meaningful work to back it up. We need these huge institutions to use their money and power for something good. And if you're not willing to do that, then I'm not willing to work with you.

I now have the confidence to step into a room, and if I don't feel like it's diverse, I will ask them why. I have no qualms in saying, 'This is what my team needs to look like.'

It needs to be 70 per cent Black, because why not? Black people have an overwhelming influence on music – sound, rhythm, culture, expression and creativity – yet, this isn't reflected in the industry at decision-making levels. It's important to me to, at the very least, have that reflected in my team as much as I can control. I'm never going back to that feeling of being the only one in the room. My hope is that by other individuals taking a similar approach, Black artists and creatives receive greater opportunities to work with representative teams, and diverse management talent becomes the norm rather than the exception.

I am now more than willing to ask the awkward questions of everyone I work and interact with. How diverse is your team? Do you have diversity at board level, or is it just lower down the ladder? What are you doing to address inequality within your institutions? We need to keep asking, keep pushing, keep demanding change, and I am in a position to be listened to – so I need to use that power. I think back to how I used to move through the industry back when I was starting out, when I was a naive teenager, fresh out of the X *Factor* machine. How grateful I felt to even be in those rooms, how small my voice was, diluted not only by being one of four band members, but also by being a woman, by being young, and by being Black. I think back to those early songwriting and recording sessions. How white all our teams were, how they ridiculed me for writing my own raps. I felt I couldn't speak out to defend myself, I couldn't back myself or call anyone out for the way I was being treated. But now, ten years later, *everything* is different. The world is awake and the conversations I had held inside of me for a decade are finally occurring. They can no longer ignore me, or all the other

Black creatives who have taken so much shit for so long. But we aren't going to take it anymore. Change is coming. We will make sure of that.

☆

In the aftermath of the documentary and all the press I did around that time to highlight my experiences, I began to receive an influx of messages. There were so many supportive comments, from people who had watched the documentary and felt moved by it or recognised some of their own struggle in what I had said. But there was another kind of message, too. People began sharing their struggles, or the issues with racism that their friends, or classmates, or children were going through. I have had so many people approach me with stories of young Black girls being bullied or racially abused in predominantly white schools. These stories tell me that lots of little Black girls are coming home from school every day in tears, or they don't feel safe at school, or they don't feel as though they can be themselves. The messages outlined the sadness they felt, the isolation and the sense of injustice. It made me feel sick to think that this was still happening to so many people, that a new generation of Black girls was being taught that they are unwanted, that they don't belong.

A friend of my sister told me his niece had experienced overt racism at primary school. The bullying he described to me was relentless. Everywhere she goes, there is a situation, someone will say something horrible to her, or she is left out and ostracised by the other children. Once, one of her classmates was taunting her and told her that her skin 'looks like Coca-Cola', and everybody started laughing while this poor little girl was crying her eyes out. She doesn't even understand what racism is, she doesn't know why she's being targeted or called names like this. It doesn't make sense to her. It is just sickening to think that she is carrying all this pain, and taking all this abuse, for a reason she can't even comprehend. Because of the sheer pointlessness of racism. That's what gets me about it the most, that it is pointless and meaningless. And people don't even know that this is happening.

A lot of people don't realise that racism is still rife, that this sort of horrible bullying still goes on in our schools, in our workplaces, in public spaces. In the UK, we like to tell ourselves that we are past all of that, that things have improved, that people of colour have all the same opportunities as white people and that racism is a thing of the past. But that just isn't true. And the more we look away, close our eyes to the realities of what is going on, the worse it gets. We have to, all of us, be better at recognising racism, acknowledging that it is still a pervasive and damaging problem in our society, and calling it out whenever we get the opportunity. That responsibility falls on every single one of us.

Every time a message like this came through, or someone stopped me at an event to share their experience, it broke my heart. I couldn't help but imagine my babies, and the struggles they might face growing up in the predominantly white area where we live. It made me realise that despite all the progress we have made, despite all the protests and the boycotts, the pledges and promises, there is still so much more work to be done. Black girls in this country are still treated with contempt for no reason other than the colour of their skin. And those attitudes carry over far beyond school, those attitudes will follow them into the careers they choose, into the different professions they enter into. The impact that will have on their self-esteem, on their confidence and sense of who they are, will be devastating. I know this because I have lived it. We can't let this continue.

The music industry is a space that is still in dire need of change. Things have got better – I have seen that over the last ten years, but there is still so far to go. Diversity is a problem, but it's not just about that. As I've already said, it's also about where the power lies. It's about Black artists, and Black women especially, not being given equal opportunities to succeed. Labels and management – who are, let's face it, overwhelmingly made up of middle-aged white men – don't invest in us, they don't give us the same opportunities as white artists. An R&B song by a white artist will likely receive more marketing support and industry backing because of the palatability of white artists for Western audiences, comparative to a similar song by a Black artist. The change needs to come from the top, it needs to come from the people who hold the power. They need to trust in the talents and the abilities of their Black artists; they need to give us the same shot at succeeding. That's all we want, an equal chance.

For Black women, there are two fights. There's the fight against misogyny and the fight against racism. It's a double whammy. And you can't eliminate one without eliminating the other – they intersect. For Black women in the music industry, these two forces hinder our progress, push us down, and make us question our worth. All too often, the burden of speaking out, campaigning and advocating for change falls to the very people who are most affected by discrimination and

287

racism. But it can't always be on their shoulders. It is up to the people who benefit from an unequal system to take on some of this labour. Use your voices to change things for the better, to help open up this elitist, privileged world to a more diverse range of artists who deserve recognition.

At this point in my career, I can no longer sit back and let these things slide. I am determined to use my voice, my platform, and my resources, to help make this industry a more inclusive place. I want to continue to use my music to inspire, to show young Black girls that they can be anything they want to be, that they should never let anyone dull their shine. I hope to be able to create environments for other Black artists to thrive, to create opportunities, and push for change every single day. Even if that's simply asking the question: could this team be more diverse? Someone has to ask the uncomfortable questions. And after all I've been through, I'm not afraid of a bit of discomfort.

# CHAPTER TWENTY-ONE

# Taking a Break

'The pain of saying goodbye'

Since the spring of 2020, my life had undergone a pretty radical transformation. After posting my video on Instagram and finally confronting how racism had impacted my career and my life, I went on a journey of discovery, of renewal. I uncovered inner strengths, I stepped into a new, more powerful version of myself. And around me the world was changing, too. The lingering impacts of the pandemic continued to limit our ability to travel and perform and there were new anxieties and fears around group events. The world felt different; society felt different. We had all lived through an unprecedented historical event that had shifted the fabric of our existence and made us question so much about how we live . . . it's inevitable that things were going to feel different.

My life in the band was different too. In 2020, Jesy left. It wasn't the easiest time. Change is always hard, and we grieved the loss. It felt incredibly sad to no longer be a foursome, and it shook the dynamic we had maintained for nine years at this point. It also put a question mark over our future. Was it time to walk away? We came to the decision almost immediately: we weren't ready for that. As a trio, our core values remained; Perrie, Jade and I still had the same goals: we still had that beautiful, sister-like connection we had forged all those years ago when we first met as teenagers. We wanted to carry on. We still had more to give.

We had just released *Confetti* and were determined to see that campaign through. So the three of us embarked on a national arena tour, selling-out enormous venues all over the country. During lockdown we released 'Break Up Song', which had a positive reception, and then we released our final song as a foursome, 'Sweet Melody' – which went to number one. That was a stunning feeling. To know that after a decade we were still able to reach those heights, that we still had fans who would show up for us like this. It meant the world and it showed us just how far we had come and how much we had achieved. I think that number one reinvigorated us as well.

After lockdown, it could have been easy for us to all slip away into new lives, new projects, to become disconnected from each other. But the success from those songs refocused us, and reminded us that we still had more in the tank. And we were ready to unleash all of that energy out into the world.

That tour was one of the most extraordinary experiences we had had together. It felt like we had returned to something, some magic element of our early years as a group, and we appreciated the experience of being on stage, of performing and doing what we loved more than anything else. After more than a year of being confined to our homes, separated from each other, unable to see our fans, a return to touring and shows felt truly tremendous. We relished every second of it. I loved it, all of it: the travelling, the rehearsals, the costumes, the dance routines. We loved that album and it had some of our biggest hits to-date, so it was such a joy to be able to share that live with the audiences, hear them singing along and screaming our lyrics back at us as we held our microphones out towards them. I loved the sheer joy of being in a crowd and realising that all those people, thousands of them, had made the effort to come and see us, to hear our music. After nine years of it, I still hadn't got used to that, and I never took it for granted – not for one second. Every time I heard the crowd chanting for Little Mix, screaming for us to come on stage or for one more song, it still thrilled me. I still felt incredibly lucky to be in that position, to be living my dream.

It was still there, of course – the insecurity. The hollow, empty feelings that gnawed at the edges of my consciousness. I still worried that I was less appreciated than the other girls, that I didn't have as many fans. I still felt that awful feeling of being on stage and yet not being seen. The feeling that people didn't want to watch me, or at least, not as much as they enjoyed watching the others. I still battled with it. It hadn't magically dissipated overnight. But now, since speaking out about it, I felt better equipped to deal with it. No matter how bad it felt, at least I now knew it wasn't all in my head. At least if I brought it up with someone after a show, or pointed out the fact that I wasn't being treated the same, people wouldn't be able to tell me they didn't know what I was talking about, or that it was all in my head. No, it was out there now. Unavoidable. Undeniable.

That knowledge didn't fix the issue, or make it go away, but it did make me feel less alone. Now, I knew there were people in my corner, people who understood what I was going through, people who were at least willing to listen to me. It was freeing. I felt stronger and more powerful. It was as though speaking my truth had formed an invisible layer of armour around me. It wasn't impermeable and things could still hurt me, but not as much as before. It meant I was able to enjoy the moment more, appreciate my time with the group, and throw myself into the tour.

We had made the decision to take an indefinite hiatus the year before, in December 2021. We announced that *Confetti* would be our final tour. It just felt like the right time. It was nothing to do with lockdown, or the pandemic, or Perrie's and my pregnancies. The decision came before any of that. We were ten years into our Little Mix journey, longer than most other bands stay together, and collectively we all felt that it was getting close to a moment where we would want to try something new, something different. There were no bust-ups between us, no dramatic arguments between the three of us, nothing like that. We hadn't even grown apart – we were as close as ever. But after such a long time, it was understandable that we were craving change. The band was never meant to be forever. But then, our ending isn't forever either. We haven't broken up – we're on a break. What we have built will always be there, and there will always be the possibility of a return when it works for all of us.

I think that made it easier to be excited about trying something new, the fact that we weren't ending – not properly. It gave us the freedom to think about other things without feeling too sad about what we were losing. We could feel good about it. And I think, on some level, all of us were excited about trying something new. We were driven to push ourselves, to see what this music industry might feel like on an individual level. What would it feel like to step out on stage on our own? We were all curious, and we all knew there were different things we wanted to pursue. We couldn't help but feel energised by that fact.

But I'm getting ahead of myself. Before we were due to go our separate ways for a while, we had our final tour, and it was joyful. *Confetti* was the perfect name for that tour because everything had an air of celebration. Every show felt like one giant party. It was the perfect encapsulation of everything we are about as a band. Freedom, enjoyment, inspiration, and at the heart of everything – fun. Now that we knew things were coming to an end, it gave a new significance to every moment. We clung to each other and pushed ourselves with every performance. I felt like we almost unlocked a new level with that tour. We were really showing off everything we had learned over the last ten years, how we had developed, both as a group and as individuals. We had all progressed so much. We had grown up together, and we had helped each other become the best performers we could be.

All too soon it was over. The final show was upon us. Tours have this weird way of feeling endless, and also as though they pass in the blink of an eye. It's this strange sensation of time both stretching out and condensing as we exist in these liminal non-spaces – tour buses, backstage, constant motion. It's always a blur. Finally, it was time to walk out on that stage together, hand in hand, one last time. Suddenly it all felt impossible. How could this be finishing? How could this reality, the only reality I had known since I was nineteen, be ending? I held on to Jade's and Perrie's hands. These girls are my sisters. I'm not going to see them every day anymore? I'm not going to be on this journey with them anymore? It broke my heart. I held on to their hands tighter. But at the same time, I knew it felt right. We all needed to spread our wings. But if we were going out, we were going out on a high. As the lights hit us for the final time, I lifted my face towards them and felt the swell of the crowd's voices hitting me as one. I felt an overwhelming sense of pride for everything we had achieved, for the phenomenal legacy we had created. I also knew we would always come back together at some point, for our wonderful fan base, but also for ourselves because we love it so much.

At the end of everything, I couldn't help but find myself reflecting once more on where it all began. It's inevitable, isn't it, that we think of things in cycles? The beginning and end of monumental moments in our lives hold so much meaning and significance. In those final days of the tour, my mind wandered back to our early days. Those precious experiences that will live in my mind forever – so clear in my memory. The feeling of it, the excitement, the sense that we were on the precipice of something unbelievable. I think back to our hunger, our tenacity and our determination. I'm so proud of those young girls and the way we managed to hold our own, despite having so little experience. We always knew what we wanted, we knew who we were as a band and the kind of music we wanted to make – and we weren't afraid to fight for it, even in spaces where we felt intimidated or overwhelmed. It was because of our unity, that deep bond that pulled us tightly together, that beautiful friendship that underpinned everything we did, and reminded us why we were working so hard – we were doing it for each other. And boy, did we work hard. We never lost that drive, that same drive that saw us rehearsing and rehearsing and rehearsing while the other acts were chilling or having fun at Bootcamp and the judges' houses. It was our humility that made it possible. The fame, the success, the fans – none of it ever went to our heads. At our core, we were always those same normal girls who had a dream and a clear vision of the path in front of them.

I still marvel at the luck that brought us together, like a cosmic force that ensured we were the ones in the right place at the right time, with the right talent and the right personalities. Us, not another combination of girls. This is why I will always believe that everything happens for a reason. We were thrown together to create something beautiful, to touch the lives of our fans, to share something truly special with the world – and I will be eternally grateful that we were given the opportunity to do that. What a privilege to get to do this as a job. Despite all the things I have struggled with, despite all the hardships and difficulties I faced along the way, I would still choose to do this again if I had the opportunity to go back – I would choose it every time. And those struggles made me who I am. They brought me to the place I am today. They solidified my determination to use my power to make a difference, to actively help the Black community in any way that I can.

It was our bond, our friendships, that pulled me through and made it all feel worth it. For every hard day where I came off stage and cried, there were also the countless moments of joy. The way I would laugh more than I ever have in my life, the jokes and stories we built up over the years, the strong hugs and shoulders to cry on, the hands ready to wipe away tears and pull me onto the dance floor, the intense conversations that stretched into the early hours. Ours was a bond like no other. I will always love the girls who became my sisters.

☆

I've been to therapy during the course of my career, as I've already mentioned. When we decided to pause Little Mix, I felt compelled to go back. We all did. In fact, it happened a little earlier than our hiatus. We were a family, the four of us were like sisters, and we had been that way since we were teenagers, so it's not an over-exaggeration to say that losing a member was a traumatic experience for us. It was a complex and painful thing to come to terms with. We all felt it, that pain and sadness. The whole thing felt like a weird break-up, and I wasn't prepared for it, I wasn't prepared for the intensity of those emotions. When you have felt so much love and support with another person over such a long time, and then that suddenly disappears and you never fully get to understand why, it hurts. The whole thing was abrupt and sad, and then it was messy, which made it even more painful. But now, I can see that none of what has happened since the split takes anything away from what we had. That love we felt for each other was valid and real, no matter what came afterwards. Those memories I hold so dear are true. Those experiences helped build me into the person I am today, and none of that will ever be erased.

Therapy helped me, helped all of us, process what had happened and manage the emotions that came with it. All of that messiness is now so far behind me that it's not even worth commenting on. We have moved forward into something even brighter and stronger, and I'm so incredibly proud of everything we achieved in that final year before we finished our last shows. The experience pulled the three of us even closer together. We clung to each other in those last months. Jade and Perrie were the only other people who really knew what it felt like, who knew what we had been through. They just got it, implicitly. And it was so valuable to have that around me, particularly when things got hard. It bonded us tighter than ever. We are so freaking lucky to have each other.

Now that Little Mix is on a break, I look back in sheer awe of us all. The remarkable things that we have achieved, the records we have broken, the unshakeable legacy that we have left behind us. Look how far we have come. Look how far I have come. I'm proud of myself, too. I'm proud of the kind of artist I have become, I'm proud of my integrity and my honesty. I'm proud of what I stand for, both as a musician and as a person. Little Mix shaped so much of that for me. I wouldn't be the artist I am today if it wasn't for the band. I wouldn't be the person I am today. I learned so much about the industry, about how to navigate this tumultuous, contradictory world, I learned how to stand up for myself, how to pick my battles, when to compromise and negotiate – and when not to. I learned how to be brave, how to be fearless in my creative pursuits. I learned that boldness and risks make magic, and that you shouldn't always stick to the safe choice – no matter how much it scares you. But I can only do so much looking back. My focus now is the path that lies in front of me. My eyes are set firmly towards the horizon. It's time to take those steps forward.

# CHAPTER TWENTY-TWO

## Motherhood

'Everything I do
is for them'

How do you know when you're ready to be a mother? Is it some biological urge that surges through your body? Or maybe it's just a calm sense of knowing. Knowing that you're capable, knowing that you have enough love to give. For me, I had always known I wanted children, a family. It wasn't really a question of 'if', but 'when'. The timing was never going to be perfect. I was busy, busy, busy – all the time. Travelling all over the world for work, performing, recording, shooting videos. I barely had time to catch my breath, let alone think about making a decision that would change my life forever.

But it was there, in the back of my mind. This knowledge that I wanted children. Andre wanted it too – a lot. He kept bringing it up. Every time I would say, no, not yet, I have to think about my career. It was hard for me to imagine a world where I could do both, I was scared that pausing could jeopardise what I had built. I was scared that I wouldn't be able to juggle motherhood with my ambitions and goals. I worried that I would have to take a step backwards, and I might never get back to where I was. The idea nagged at me and started to grow in my mind . . . maybe it *was* possible . . . but I was still firmly in work mode. The pandemic hadn't yet hit us and we had all these tours and shows booked in. I couldn't take my foot off the gas in that moment. It was beginning to feel like a bit of a battle in my head.

To be safe, I decided to freeze my eggs. This isn't a decision to make lightly because the process is gruelling, and there are no guarantees that it will result in a pregnancy. But I was cautious in giving myself the best shot when the time was right for me. I had been to see a doctor and they'd told me that I had a relatively low egg count. That panicked me a little bit. I didn't want to miss out. The egg-freezing process is far more intense and invasive than I had imagined, but it felt like the best compromise between not missing my chance at motherhood, and not missing out on my career goals.

But then I changed my mind. It happened randomly, while I was filming the Christmas movie *Boxing Day*. It was my first time acting and I was loving it. One morning, before I had to go on set, I was getting my makeup done and chatting to my makeup artist. I told her about my thoughts on children, how my partner was keen to get started but I was uncertain about the timing and thought I should focus on my work. She looked me dead in the eye and said, 'Don't wait.'

She pointed her blusher brush towards me with a serious expression on her face: 'If I can give you one piece of advice, it is to always choose family. Always. Your career isn't going to hold you at night.'

Her words seemed to switch a light on in my head, and everything suddenly became clear. I needed to put my family first. I needed to create the life I imagined for myself, and for Andre, and that life included children. I felt suddenly like I knew I could have it all. I could balance it. It would be hard, but I knew I was capable of it. Family has always been my world. My family – my sisters, my parents, my grandparents – they are my rocks, they are my inspirations and the reasons I am where I am today. It was time for me to create more of that, to pass that love and strength on to the next generation. That love has always been more important to me than any other ambition, so I knew what I had to do.

That was it. Decision made. We decided to let nature take its course and just see what happened. I stopped the process of freezing my eggs and instead just came off the pill. We were so lucky because we didn't have to try for too long. I knew something was different in my body; I could feel it. I had missed my period, which was the big clue, but I also felt different in some other way that's hard to define. It's stunning how you can just feel it like that. But I didn't really believe it. It was too quick. It couldn't have happened already, surely. So I did a test really casually, not expecting anything. I was on my own. I didn't even get Andre to come and look at the result with me – that's how unconvinced I was that I could have been pregnant.

When I looked down and saw those two lines I screamed. Like, full-on screamed. Andre came running into the bathroom. He thought I must have seen a bug or something.

'Look at this,' I said. I showed him the test. I watched his face pass through confusion, to disbelief, to joy, in the space of about two seconds.

'No way. No way!' he said. He couldn't stop staring at those two little lines. Neither could I. We couldn't believe it. We were shocked. How could this have happened already? How could I be pregnant? It was so unexpected, but completely wonderful. We were so happy. Underneath that thick layer of shock there was an ocean of joy. This was everything we wanted. I felt so privileged and blessed to be able to do this, to bring life into this world. What a thing!

# BELIEVE

I had always pictured having my own children, but I had never really seen myself as a maternal person. Even when I had nieces and nephews in the family, I was never hugely involved in the caring side of things. I don't think I ever changed a nappy. I loved them so much and I loved spending time with them, but I wasn't the auntie that looked after them; I didn't babysit. I think this was because I was the youngest in the family. I was still the baby myself. I would be anxious when people would bring their little kids to my house. I worried about silly things like mess and noise and doors being slammed. But when it was my turn, all of those feelings melted away, and I knew it was what I wanted. *Yes,* I thought, *I am ready for this.* And a voice in my mind just told me that I would be able to do it all, that this didn't mean the end of my career. Far from it. It was simply a brand-new chapter – and that felt incredibly exciting to me.

Pregnancy was hard. Really hard. I started off fine. I didn't have much sickness or anything like that, but as time went on, I got so heavy. I spent the majority of the time feeling horribly uncomfortable. I've always had a small frame, so I think carrying one baby would have felt hard for me, let alone two. I visited Tulum, Mexico, while I was heavily pregnant, and I was so hot and heavy. Even my feet were swelling up. The doctors told me at one point that my ribs were bruised, and I was getting pains in places I didn't even know I had.

We found out that it was twins at an early scan. The doctor took ages while she was doing the sonogram. I was lying there on the bed, my stomach smeared with that cold jelly while she whisked the device back and forth across my skin. Andre stood next to me, holding my hand tightly. I stared at her intently, and the longer she kept looking silently at the screen, the more convinced I became that something was wrong. It shouldn't take this long. There must be something wrong. We were still kind of in shock that I was even pregnant. Maybe we had imagined it all. Maybe there was nothing in there. I felt my heartbeat start to speed up. Finally, she spoke.

'Is there a history of twins in either of your families?' she said. We just looked at each other.

'Um . . . yeah?' I said, not quite understanding what she was saying.

'Well, that makes sense, because there's two heartbeats in here.' She gestured towards the screen and my mouth dropped open.

Andre and I turned to each other and just started laughing. We were fully cracking up. I don't think we knew what else to do. The whole thing still felt so unbelievable, and now we had twins on our hands. We couldn't wrap our heads around it. What else could we do but laugh?

Two babies. Wow! What a blessing! Double the joy, double the love. We were deliriously happy. It was hard to contain it. We had to tell everyone. I called my sister Sairah first. That was a special call, because she had told me that she was pregnant just weeks before. We were going to be pregnant at the same time. That was such a special connection between us. And in the end, we ended up giving birth just two days apart, so our babies almost have the same birthdays. It was truly a wonderful thing to go through this experience at the same time as Sairah, and her support was such a help.

I had so much support from everyone else in my life, too. My parents were overjoyed. Mum had initially been reticent when I told her Andre and I were trying. She encouraged me to focus on my career, but when I told her I was expecting, she was delighted for us. I told all my friends in a mass Zoom call. I kind of tricked everyone and told them I needed to talk to them because I was having a hard time, so they all looked a bit concerned when they jumped on the call. But then I held up the tiny little sonograph to the camera and they all erupted in joy and screams. Then I got to surprise them again by telling them it was twins. It was such a beautiful moment.

I was the first in my friendship group to have a baby. Well, at this age anyway. One of our close friends got pregnant for the first time when she was nineteen. She's a couple of years older than us, and we were all seventeen, and we were pretty rubbish at supporting her. We were kids, and we just didn't get it. Now that I've been through pregnancy and birth and have babies of my own, I look back and regret that I wasn't able to properly be there for her at that time. She was a teenage mum and the baby's dad wasn't much use, so she must have felt incredibly alone. I wish I had had the maturity to understand that at the time, particularly now I know first-hand just how hard it all is, and how much you have to sacrifice. But she never held it against us, and she is the most amazing mother. She inspires me a lot.

Since having my twins, it seems to have caused a bit of a domino effect on my friendship group. It's partly because we're all now in our early thirties, and that's what people do, but I do think these things happen with friend groups. Once the first person takes the plunge, everyone else starts getting similar ideas. It has been so lovely to witness my amazing friends go on this life-changing journey and become strong, capable, inspirational mothers. I love hanging out with all of our children and the beautiful little families we have created. I am so proud of every single one of them, and I adore this stage of our lives.

Being one of the first in my group to become a mother meant that I wasn't hugely prepared for the realities of pregnancy. I didn't know what to expect. And there is no guidebook, not really, because everybody's journey is so different. I didn't think about, for instance, how difficult it would be to sleep, how it would be impossible to find a comfy position – especially as someone who likes to lie on her front. I didn't think about the tiredness, how exhausted I would feel – all the time. And the heaviness. I was carrying two babies, and by the third trimester, even the simplest tasks became a challenge. Tying my shoelaces, getting up from a chair. It was a lot. But there were also times when I could feel the magic of it, the beauty of what my body was doing, what it was capable of. It made me feel strong, and womanly, and in love with my body in a completely new way.

I had a C-section with the babies because I was advised that this was the safest thing for me and them, and that was what I cared about above all else. We were incredibly lucky that there were no complications. We pretty much stuck to the plan, and everything went how it was supposed to go. One minute they were in, and the next minute they were out. That's how it felt anyway, like a blur. It's such an odd and unpleasant sensation. Obviously, I couldn't feel any pain while the babies were coming out because of the anaesthesia, but I could feel *something*. It was like a tugging and pulling from somewhere inside of me. It felt like the inside of my belly was a dishwasher. It was horrible, but all I could think was, *Please let these babies be OK. Please let these babies be OK.* The thought ran through my mind over and over. Andre was by my side. We were squeezing each other's hands and just staring so intensely at each other. I could practically hear his thoughts. It was that same desperate hope and it was all that mattered to both of us in that moment, that these two little lives that I had carried for nine months would come out into the world healthy and safe. Silently, we begged the universe to do what it needed to do, to grant us this gift.

Then twin one was out. They placed the crying baby directly on my chest. That sound jolted something like an electric current through my heart. I was aware that the tugging and pulling in my belly was still happening. It felt like an eternity passed, but really it was only four minutes. Then twin two was out and was placed on the other side of my chest. Two little heads resting against each side of my neck. They were both here. They were both crying. They were both OK.

I started sobbing with happiness. I couldn't believe what was happening. Andre was crying too; he was a mess. But he pulled himself together enough to cut the cords. Then we were taken to this little room so we could have a moment with them, and I started breastfeeding. I suddenly realised that my entire world, my whole reason for being, was in that little room with me in that moment. I knew in my heart that I would never need anything else as long as they were safe, as long as we were together. It truly felt like a dream. My head was spinning with a rush of overwhelming love that was almost making me dizzy. I could think of nothing other than protecting these babies at any cost. It was the only thing that mattered to me.

I was obsessed with them. They were the most perfect babies I had ever seen. One was 4lbs 11, and the other was 5lbs 6, so they were just little dots. They wore these tiny knitted hats, and seeing them in those physically melted my heart. I could not cope with the level of cuteness! And they were mine. I got to take them home and look after them and love them and watch every single thing that they did. I was deliriously happy.

As we drove home from the hospital, I looked back and saw them both sitting in their car seats. It was something I had been imagining for weeks, and now it was real. There's a lot of recovery needed after a C-section. I couldn't lift the babies up on my own for a few weeks. Moving around was tough. I had a lot of pain, and I had to take it slowly. But none of that mattered too much because we were in our newborn bubble, and it was bliss. We spent weeks living in pyjamas, having endless cuddles on the sofa, getting to grips with breastfeeding. We have been so lucky in that these babies love their food. They have since day one, and I feel so privileged to have been able to breastfeed as I know it isn't always possible. I also quickly realised how tiring it is feeding two babies. It takes a lot out of you. And the twins didn't let me get much in the way of rest. They were good babies. They settled so quickly and went into their own rooms at seven or eight months, and they were sleeping through the night by ten months. So I know I'm lucky. But those first few weeks, wow, it was challenging. I was so physically exhausted that I started getting sleep paralysis, and I even had sleep hallucinations a few times. Once I woke up screaming, and I was convinced there was a giant spider crawling all over my body and I couldn't get it off.

The sleep thing was so tricky because there were two of them. So, one would wake up and need feeding, and then just as I would head back to bed, the other one would wake up and I would have to do it again. There were some nights when I got up to feed every hour, on the hour. I don't think I slept for a single minute that night. It was pretty rough. But we got through it, because that's what you do. It's all part of parenting. We were also so privileged to be able to hire a nanny to offer me some extra support, which was a game-changer for us. Parents, and mothers especially, are such warriors. When you are looking after little lives, there is no time for you. There is no time for rest, no time to cook or clean or run errands. But at the same time, it is the most fulfilling job I have ever taken on.

I ended up going back to work pretty quickly after having the babies. We had banked a lot of stuff that we had recorded and filmed while both Perrie and I were pregnant so that we could have some time off, but it wasn't long until we had to go back on tour. I had around three months off work. When the babies were around seven months old, we had six weeks of tour rehearsals to get into, and before that I was busy working on different bits for my solo career. It felt like I blinked, and it was back to the grind. It really feels like it passed in such a blur. And to be back on tour while the babies were so little was tough, both mentally and physically. I missed them to the point of a physical ache in my body. And the mum guilt I felt then, and still feel now, is incredibly real. Every time I have to leave them with the nanny while I'm working, or when I have to go away on tour, I feel awful about it. Particularly because Andre is currently living in Greece, and we split our time between our home in the UK and staying with him out there. It feels as though we never get enough time to be together, to be a family. But I know in my heart that everything we are doing now, all this work and travel and guilt, has a bigger purpose. Everything we are doing, everything we are working towards, is for them. And that's how I deal with the guilt and the pain of missing them.

I tried my best to stay as fit as possible while I was pregnant. I kept working out in a safe way, not because I was worried about my body changing, but because I have always loved fitness. Working out and feeling strong and healthy is important to me, and that didn't change while I was pregnant. I got back to it as soon as it was safe after my C-section. I knew I had to get my fitness back in order to go on tour – because that is always incredibly physically demanding, but I also needed it for my own mental well-being. It helped me to feel like myself again.

Pregnancy and birth have changed my body in fundamental ways. I can still feel the changes. My body is not the same as it was, and no amount of PT sessions or special diets will reverse those changes. My boobs are minute now. They were small to begin with, but now, after breastfeeding, they are tiny. It's something I have always been self-conscious about, and part of me dreams of having bigger boobs. But I don't want to have a boob job. I don't want to change that part of me. Because, as much as they aren't objectively 'perfect', these little boobs have given sustenance to my children. How can I hate a part of my body when it is so powerful and so vital for life? Having children has changed my relationship with my body. I no longer see it purely in terms of the aesthetics and how it looks. Now, I see it in terms of its power. My body is different, but I feel like Superwoman. I love that I have a new understanding of my own strength.

Soon after giving birth to my twins, I found myself caught up in a horrific online row. It was one of the most difficult moments I can remember throughout my career. I was a new mum, dealing with the mental and physical aftermath of pregnancy and birth, flooded with hormones and emotion, severely sleep-deprived, and on top of all that, I also had to deal with this. It's a familiar story. The specific details of the drama aren't worth rehashing. There are some things that are simply not worth giving more oxygen to, and this is certainly one of those circumstances. The storm has passed; the drama is over, and I have made my peace with what happened and everything that was said about me. But in the moment, it felt truly awful. As much as I tried to avoid Instagram and Twitter, I kept seeing the comments and the debates that were taking place on every platform, and the headlines that seemed to be relishing the drama. Even when I put my phone away and refused to look at it, there was still this underlying anxiety about what was happening online. It kept invading my mind.

But then something so beautiful pulled me out of that horrible spiral – one of my babies smiled at me for the first time. If you're a mum, you will know how this feels. It was like fireworks going off in my heart. I had never seen anything more beautiful on this earth. This tiny, beautiful being that I had created and given life to had looked into my eyes and offered me a smile. It felt like a precious gift that I wanted to hold in my hands and pull close to my chest. I had never felt a love like this, and everything else paled in comparison. How could I care about what people were saying about me on Instagram, or nasty headlines in the tabloids, when something as rare and magical as my baby's smile existed in the world? It didn't matter. None of it. I let it wash over me. All of that noise and stress and anxiety faded into something small and insignificant.

None of that other stuff mattered because now I was a mother; I had lives that depended on me, two babies who needed my love and my sustenance in order to live. My heart was so full of love for them, and my head was so full of all of these new responsibilities and fears for their safety, their happiness, their security, that there was no space for all the old stuff I used to worry about. It was a perspective shift on a monumental scale. I felt the very chemistry of my being shift in that moment. I was still me, but my priorities were different. The things I cared about were different. It was the most unbelievable feeling.

The trivial things no longer matter to me in the same way. Those little, everyday issues that used to take up so much space in my brain seem to have melted away to make space for the bigger things. Whether it's comments on social media or thinking about how successful my solo career is going to be, I find that I just don't worry anywhere near as much as I used to, which is a comforting feeling. I feel more settled and balanced. I know that I am where I need to be, and my focus for both my life and my future is clearer than ever.

This fresh perspective will follow me into the new era of my career. Inevitably, I am thinking differently about everything now. I still have that same fire, that passion and drive to succeed, and the same love for performance that I have always had, but now my reasons are different. I already had a new focus on using my platform to speak out against injustice and racism, and now my approach to my career is shifting even further to take into account my new responsibilities as a mother. I've realised quickly that there can be no more burning the candle at both ends. Throughout my career, I have always had a work-hard-play-hard mentality, pushing myself to the extreme in all directions because I have always been so driven and focused on my goals. That doesn't work for me now. It can't. I can't allow myself to be spread too thin, to have nothing left in the tank for my family. As much as I am still dedicated to putting as much as I can into my career, I also know how vital it is to give myself breaks and to find time to prioritise family. That is a non-negotiable for me now. It's about finding balance, and that is a continual journey. Some weeks I get the balance right, and some weeks I don't. But the point is that I am always working towards it, and my family and my children are always at the forefront of my mind.

As a mother, it's important for me to continue to work hard to try to fulfil my dreams. Not only so that I can provide the best possible life for my children, but also because I want them to learn from watching me. They will see Andre and me working and sacrificing to build something special to achieve our dreams, and they will know that anything is possible. They will also know how much work it takes. I want them to take that determination from me. I want them to take on my ethos of never doing anything with half a heart.

I am a Black mother to two Black babies, and I can't help but worry about the world they are entering into. I think about the things that I went through, the struggles I faced as a Black woman in my career, and I fear that they might experience some of the same things. It breaks my heart to picture a world in which they feel less worthy, less loved or less valuable simply because of the colour of their skin. I will do everything in my power to protect them, but my power as their mother can only go so far.

I have seen this play out with friends and family members. My beautiful niece experienced bullying so bad that she has had to move schools. She was the only Black girl in her group of 'friends' and it's hard to believe that there wasn't a racial element to the way she was treated. And this is happening now. It isn't some issue that only happened in the past. This stuff still goes on. As much as I want to feel hopeful about the progress that has been made since 2020 and the Black Lives Matter movement, when I see my twelve-year-old niece crying in my sister's arms because she has been isolated and left out, I realise how much work we still have left to do. The battle is far from over.

I worry particularly because of where we have chosen to buy our home and settle as a family. It's a predominantly white area. And my children will be attending schools that are majority white. That scares me, for sure. I look back at my own time at school – secondary school at least – and feel incredibly grateful that I was exposed to so much diversity. There were children who looked like me, there were children of all ethnicities, and as a result, I never felt like the odd one out. Instead, I was empowered to be my full self, to celebrate my heritage, my looks, my family, without shame or fear. I don't want my children to be denied that freedom or be made to feel as though they have to hide parts of themselves or dim their light. I want them to shine so brightly in safe, encouraging spaces.

I know I have to be proactive in this. If this is what I want for my children, then I have to make it happen. I will make a conscious effort to make sure they go to extra-curricular activities where they get to interact with diverse groups, where they get to hang out with other Black kids. I think this is so important. I want them to have a better, deeper understanding of race and how it impacts their place in the world, and I will have those conversations with them at an early point in their development. They will celebrate our food, our culture, they will learn our history. I want them to know where they have come from and know where they fit in. I never, ever want them to feel alone.

I think about my own journey with race, and it makes me so sad to think of what I had to go through at such a late stage in my life. I was still figuring out what racism looked like, what it felt like, in my late twenties. I was still questioning myself, blaming myself. I know now that part of the reason I went through that was so I would have the tools to pass on to my children. My babies won't have to feel like I felt because I will be able to teach them and guide them in a way I might not have been equipped to if I hadn't been through all of that. I take comfort in the fact that the conversations that were not being had when I was struggling are now socially acceptable. We can speak about racism and call it out with freedom, to an extent that didn't exist even just a few years ago. This gives me hope. Progress might feel slow, but we *are* moving forward, and I believe there is the potential to make this world a much more equal place – but the onus is on us to make sure that happens.

On Sundays, when we all come together as a family – Andre and I, my parents, my sisters – the house is so full of noise and love. I love that there are so many children now. My sisters both have their kids, and now my babies get to grow up alongside them. It is beautiful to see the children find their own happy places within our home. I have always wanted to create a space that feels like a sanctuary, where these little ones can become the boldest versions of themselves, with all the support in the world. Their presence teaches me so much, too.

I watch my sister Sairah and I love how she is with her eldest boy, my nephew – eleven-year-old Kailum. I study the things she is teaching him, the strength she is instilling in him. I'm taking notes for my own little ones now that I'm a parent, too. One thing my sister drills so hard into Kailum is for him to love his skin, and to love who he is. She tells him he has to *know* he is the best. She boosts him up and pours so much self-belief into him. And you can see the impact it has had. That boy is honestly the most determined, driven, confident character. He plays football and when I watch him flying around that pitch with so much flair and skill, I can just see that inner strength shining out of him. He glows with it. It's because Sairah believes in him so much. She knows the barriers and the walls that are going to try to stop him from getting to where he's supposed to get. As a young Black boy, structural racism is going to make life harder for him. That is the sad reality of the world we live in. But Sairah does everything in her power to push back against this reality, to make sure Kailum is ready to face it. She says to him: 'You're going to know how good you are.' I love that. I'm so inspired by that.

When they're old enough, I'm going to tell my babies they can do whatever they want to do. Literally every day, I'm going to tell them they can be anything they want to be. I want them to know – to really, on a deep level, understand – exactly what they are capable of, that the world is at their feet. It's all waiting for them to grab it, and I can't wait to see what they do with the opportunities they will have. They are my everything. My light, my love, my legacy. My biggest hope is that everything I have learned and everything I am working towards will impact their lives in a positive way. It is all for them, and it always will be.

As well as my love for my babies, I have also grown into loving myself more completely. Over the last few years, I have learned that loving yourself wholeheartedly before you wish to be loved by others, gives you immense power. My journey to becoming the woman I am now has been emotional and painful – unbearable at times – but the one thing I managed to find and hold on to was my power. I am no longer the girl who gets anxious before fan events. I am no longer the girl who constantly questions her position and purpose. I have found my voice and I choose to use it.

# MOTHERHOOD

When I look back at recordings of me performing in the early days of my career, I no longer recognise that person who was so desperate to be appreciated. It is so freeing and empowering to no longer rely on other people's approval. I know now that it's OK to not be everyone's taste, and you need not be everyone's taste either – but you have to make sure that you are your own champion.

Ten years ago, I wish I had had the strength I have now. The strength to recognise what it means to be the Black girl, to embrace it, own it and be an unapologetic representation of my culture. I found my power when I realised it was within me, within my skin and within my soul, the whole time. It just needed to be set free.

# CHAPTER TWENTY-THREE

# Stepping Into My Power

'All that fighting
has made me strong'

'Who are you, Leigh-Anne?' It is a question I have asked myself so many times over the last ten years. And for most of that time, I didn't have an answer for you. I tried to be so many different things, I experimented with so many different versions of myself, and each version was always about how others would perceive me. All those different things I tried – the clothes, the hair, the way that I spoke in interviews – were all attempts to be seen and heard, to please people, to get people to notice me, to appreciate me. No matter what I did, and no matter how hard I tried, it never worked, none of the versions of me were good enough. I was still the one on the outside, looking in. I was still the one pushed to the bottom of the pile, the one people skipped when they were asking for autographs. I was the one they held the camera out to, asking if I could *take* the picture rather than be *in* the picture.

No matter how many versions of me I experimented with, there was always something slightly false about it, a hollowness at the heart of my created identity. That hollowness was caused by hearing the repeated message that I was less worthy, less valuable. I took that message inside myself, and it burrowed deep, creating this void. Underneath all those protective masks and costumes that I used as brightly adorned armour, there were the real versions of me.

She was always in there, somewhere. That nervous little girl hiding behind her dad's legs, mumbling into the microphone. That silly, goofy child making up elaborate games with her best friends and laughing until her face hurt. That love-struck teenager desperate for romantic connection. That determined, hard-working, bright young woman who had everything in front of her, and would stop at nothing to get it. She never went anywhere, but she was pushed down, deeper and deeper inside of myself, until her voice got quieter and quieter, and her presence got smaller and smaller. She shrank herself down to nothing. But now, I'm building her back up. I had to work so hard to find her again, but now that she's back – I'm never letting her go. I will never shrink myself again, not for anyone or anything. I will never again be made to question my worth or my place in the world. The world has changed. I have changed. And there's no way I'm going back.

Recently, I've gone back to therapy again, but it feels different this time. It isn't a reaction to a specific event in my life, or a desperate coping mechanism to help me handle the struggles of being in the band. This time, I want therapy to be a regular part of my routine. Something I do every week to check in with myself, to keep my mind on track, to help me work through and unpick some of the unhealthy habits and patterns of behaviour that I want to improve. It feels like the ultimate form of self-care, and I'm privileged to be in a position to create space for this in my life. It's a space to truly let go of all the tensions, worries and insecurities that creep at the edges of my mind, and I find that engaging with those feelings rather than running from them or pretending they aren't there, really helps. I feel fortunate to be able to have this resource.

Another beneficial thing is having a therapist who looks like me. My new therapist is a Black woman, and I can't tell you how much of a positive difference that has made. As much as I appreciated my previous therapists, in her presence, I feel relaxed. I feel my muscles unclench; my heart feels lighter. I know in a deep way that she is a safe space. I can talk to her about *anything*. I can tell her about an experience that only happened to me because I am a Black woman, and she understands it. I don't have to waste my energy explaining why it was racist, or justifying why I think it was about race, I don't have to worry whether she believes me or if she thinks I am being unreasonable or have a 'chip on my shoulder'. Having that unspoken understanding between us is such a special thing and makes the process of sharing so much easier.

Going back to therapy has been transformational for me. I am loving it and it's exciting to learn more about myself – why I think the way I do, why I behave the way I do. I find it totally fascinating, and it also provides me with the tools to become the best version of me. That always has to start with understanding yourself. We have also done some digging back in time, looking at my childhood, at my family relationships and my upbringing, which has provided some serious revelations too. I believe that you have to know where you have come from to know where you are going, and figuring out my parents is a huge part of that. It has even brought us closer together as a family.

My therapist and I have spoken a lot about how my mum and I are so different. As I've mentioned, Mum can be cold and dishes out tough love. She would be the first person to admit that. Whereas I, on the other hand, am like the opposite of this. I am the most openly loving, emotional, needy person. I need a lot of attention, affection and love, and I give it out too. I have always wondered how I have turned out like this when my mum is not like this at all.

My therapist asked me if I ever felt like my mum wasn't meeting my needs in terms of affection and open displays of love. I thought about it and realised that had been true at points – both during my childhood and as an adult. I thought back to when I was struggling in the band, when I was feeling worthless and unloved. What I needed from my mum in that moment was a hug. I needed an open and fully accepting kind of emotional support and empathy. But my mum's methods of support are tougher. She would say, 'Come on, Leigh, keep your chin up. Be strong. You've got this.' That is still love, it is still support, it's just a different form of it. But my therapist suggested that it was things like this that have made me crave affection. I search for it in every relationship because that was something I didn't feel I had enough of growing up.

We spoke about it on my hen do. My beautiful friends threw me the most breathtaking celebration on Mykonos. I felt surrounded by love and eternally grateful to have such supportive, wonderful people around me. One evening on the beach, Mum and I had a conversation about what I had learned in therapy. She told me she had always been cold, that it wasn't until she had my sisters and me that she learned to open up more, and learned to show more love. But then she told me why she was the way she was, for the first time.

'I hated my dad,' she said to me. 'Like, really, *really* hated him.' Then she started to cry. I pulled her close to me and hugged her tight as all of this emotion flowed out of her. I had known that my grandad didn't behave well towards my grandma, and that was why we were less close to our Bajan side of the family, but Mum had never told me any more details. But now she let me in. He had cheated on her, repeatedly, and he had been violent. My mum witnessed all of this as a child. There was one time when one of the women my grandad was having an affair with had come round to the family home to try to make a scene. My grandad beat her black and blue until there was blood spattered on the floor. My grandma had to scrub the blood from the floor. My mum remembers this. That trauma lives in her body.

Her father was not loving, or kind, or supportive. It was no wonder she ended up struggling to show love if that was what she was shown growing up. It was no wonder she developed a hard outer shell to protect herself. She cried into my shoulder until she had let it all out. Then she told me about her mum, my grandma. She told me about the tiny snatches of joy she used to look for, like this one cappuccino she would always order when they went to this one particular café on bank holidays. She remembers that her mum would say it was the best cappuccino she had ever had. She took so much pleasure in every sip. We spoke about how we wished my grandma was still here, how she deserved so much more joy in her life. It was a beautiful, cathartic conversation, and it taught me so much about my mum.

Therapy isn't only helping me understand myself. It's helping me understand the people around me, the people I love. It is helping me to have more empathy and compassion for other people's behaviour and reminding me that everyone has stuff that they are dealing with, no matter how it might look on the surface. Therapy is helping me navigate life more effectively, and I now feel better equipped to deal with whatever life throws at me. Understanding who I am on a deeper level feels incredibly empowering. I am no longer questioning my purpose, or whether I belong. I no longer have to seek out validation from others in the way I did when I was younger and more insecure. I know myself, and that is a beautiful thing.

Who am I? Well, now I have an answer. I'm a Pinnock. I'm a force to be reckoned with. I'm a performer, a musician, a pop star, but I'm also a campaigner, a force for change and a force for good. I'm a loving daughter, sister and partner. I'm a fierce friend. I'm a mother. I'm a woman. I'm a Black woman. There is so much power in knowing who you are. It allows you to speak up for yourself, and other people like you. Knowing your identity gives you a sense of purpose that's bigger than your own personal wants and dreams. It attaches you to a broader narrative and gives you a sense of belonging within a wider community. Finally having confidence in who I am, and why I am here, gives me a kind of protection. It means that no matter what life throws at me, whether I'm treated differently for the way I look or behave, because of my family, my background or my ethnicity, it matters less than it used to, and it can't hurt me in the same way. I know myself; I know who I am, and nothing can shake that. Not anymore. This is why it is so important to know yourself, to connect with your own sense of identity, and define it clearly for yourself. It isn't something that happens overnight. It took me years to get to this point. So if you're not there yet, don't worry. It will come. Sometimes you have to battle your inner demons first.

I've done my fair share of battling. And I can't see myself stopping anytime soon. All that fighting has made me strong. There is power coursing through my veins, sparking at my fingertips. It has always been there. All I had to do was believe in it. Of course, I haven't got here on my own. It always helps if you surround yourself with people who also believe in your power. My beautiful, inspiring friends who have had my back at every turn, who have listened and learned and been the greatest allies I could have ever needed. My selfless sisters who inspire me to be better, who show me so much about what it means to be strong and remind me every day what I am capable of. My generous, wonderful parents who connect me to my history, my heritage, who have shown me how to create a home that is filled with love and told me again and again to shoot for the stars. Andre, who holds me up and supports my every endeavour, who gives me what I have always craved in a partner – a real, meaningful friendship. My babies – my twin hearts. I look at their faces and I see the future. They keep me going, even when everything feels too hard. Their little smiles are all the encouragement I need to keep going, to keep fighting, to keep doing everything in my power to make this world fairer and safer and kinder for them, and for all the young Black boys and girls who are still at the beginning of everything. They deserve to grow up in a world that sees them, respects them, and allows them to thrive.

Now I know who I am because I know my worth. I know how talented I am. I know how much I have to bring to the table. I also know that I have so much worth beyond my abilities as a performer. I know that my purpose goes beyond simply walking onto a stage and singing. I know what is in my heart, and I know how I am supposed to use that energy to make this world a better place. I have found her – the woman I was always meant to be. The woman who was silenced and tripped up and held back a thousand times. I have finally unlocked her. And I know she is going to be unstoppable.

I'm buzzing about what lies ahead of me, I have so much more to give. I feel like I have an opportunity to release new levels of potential that, until now, have been stifled. I'm itching for it all to begin, and I have thrown myself into this new challenge with the same enthusiasm I had when I was eighteen. That energy is still there, waiting for the opportunity to burst out.

But I have fears about going solo, too. How could I not? Sometimes I wake up in the middle of the night and stare at the ceiling and imagine all the million ways it could go wrong, all the things people won't like about me and my music. My biggest fear is that I won't live up to my potential. I know, in my heart, what I am capable of. I am more confident in my own abilities than I have been for years, maybe ever, but there is still this persistent fear that for some reason I won't be able to show everyone what I can do. But I'm also scared of the things beyond my control. I'm scared that I won't be given a fair shot to succeed. I'm scared that I won't be treated as equal. As we all embark on solo projects, I wonder if I'm going to get the same opportunities as the other girls. Will radio stations play my songs less frequently? Will I have fewer fans, less hype, less media attention? These are the old anxieties left over from my experiences of the music industry so far. I have seen its capacity for cruelty, I've seen how unfair it can be, I've seen how I was treated differently because I'm Black. Will that happen again? I try not to dwell on that thought, but sometimes those fears creep in and I can't ignore them. It's the same old argument, going round and round in my head. I have never desired to be better, brighter, or bigger than anyone else – I simply want the same chance to succeed. I hope that the industry, and society, are finally in a place where I won't be penalised for the colour of my skin. I hope that, this time around, there will be more compassion, kindness and a sense of fairness. I'm stronger now, and better equipped to deal with any hostility this industry might throw at me, but my greatest hope is that I no longer have to be strong.

I'm in my thirties now. I'm experienced and mature. But I am also tired. I have been working hard – ten times harder for less reward – for over a decade. Part of me is scared of going through that again. Will I have to work ten times harder just to put myself on a level playing field? And then there is the pressure. The pressure to not just be good, but to be excellent. Black excellence is something to be proud of, but it becomes a problem when Black people are only recognised if they are excellent, exceptional, stand-out talents, when white people have the privilege of being just good, or even mediocre, and being rewarded for it. I believe that I am excellent, and I push for excellence in all areas of my life. But I am also human. And the pressure of always needing to achieve perfection because I am a Black woman weighs heavily on my mind.

On the other side of fear, there is pure excitement. An adrenaline-fuelled anticipation that sparks in my blood like electricity. I cannot wait for what comes next. The unknown can be a terrifying thing, but it can also be thrilling. I am ready for whatever the universe has in store for me, and I am desperate to throw myself into this new challenge. I want to test my boundaries, push my limits and reach new heights. I have new sounds that I want my fans to hear, a new style that is so entirely me, through and through. I am so excited to stamp my mark on something, to have full creative control, and really see where I can take my music when it's just me at the helm. What an adventure! I can't wait to share this journey with the world.

When those old anxieties start to whisper to me in the dark stillness of the early hours – before the house has woken up and the babies are crying for me and my phone is pinging with a million appointments – in those quiet moments I take deep, steadying breaths and refuse to let the fear take hold. One thing that keeps those whispers at bay is thinking about my fans. They're Little Mix fans, yes, but I'm talking about *my* fans. The beautiful, brilliant little tribe that make up Leigh-Anne's army. I know they will always have my back and they are rooting for me to succeed, because they always have been. I see you, each and every one of you who ever came to a concert and waited for me after the show, the ones who I spot in the crowd, show after show, beaming up at me, screaming support during my solos. You were the ones who kept me going. You reminded me that I was loved when I was at my lowest. You gave me a lifeline and helped me keep hope in my heart, even when everything felt utterly bleak. I will be forever grateful to you, my little rays of sunshine guiding me through the storm. And now I'm on the other side of it, I want to do this for you. I want to succeed for you, for all the people who ever believed in me. I want to prove you right.

This new stage of my career, of my life, is going to be the culmination of everything I have worked for so far. I am still getting my head around how it feels to be entering into this journey on my own. Just me. But so far, I like how it feels. I went to New York for a work trip and from the moment I landed, I could feel it. The magic. I was there visiting Spotify to discuss the new album and new music, and the meeting was being held at one of those dizzying skyscrapers, all glass and shiny metal glinting in sunlight, a vast lobby with marble flooring and tasteful art on the walls. It was all quintessential New York. Ultra-glamorous. I swallowed my nerves and walked in with my head held high. Yes, I belong here. Yes, this is what I am meant to be doing. I repeated the words in my mind until I started to believe them. But I didn't need to be nervous. I saw that the moment I looked up to the far wall of the lobby. On giant screens hanging high above the reception desks and stretching way up towards the lofty ceiling, there I was. My face. And a message that read 'Welcome Leigh-Anne'. I stood in the middle of the space and stared up at the screen, my eyes brimming with sudden hot tears. There I was. They were expecting me. They were waiting for me. It felt like a sign. Well, it was a literal sign, but it felt like a message. Like it was telling me to believe in myself because the industry already believes in me.

# BELIEVE

After so many years feeling forgotten, sidelined, ignored, it was monumental to see myself placed directly in the spotlight like this. My name, and only my name, was there up in lights for everyone to see. I felt a rush of pride and excitement. This was my chance to live life in the way I was always supposed to. This was my chance to show everyone what I have always been capable of.

# Acknowledgements

Writing this book has been a labour of love. I poured my heart and soul into these pages, and I never would have been able to do it if it wasn't for the unwavering support from the people in my life.

Thank you to my mum, Deborah, my dad, John, my sisters Sairah and Sian – I feel eternally lucky to have such an incredible family unit.

Thank you to my wonderful husband Andre for always reminding me that the sky is the limit.

Thank you to my bubbas, for teaching me to be brave and fearless. If I'm ever scared or anxious, all I have to do is think, 'what would the twins do?' Thank you for giving me the most beautiful gift in the entire world – being your mum.

Thank you to my Grandad Steve and Grandma Annette for giving me such a strong sense of identity. With every year I visited Jamaica, my connection to my heritage got stronger and stronger. I have you to thank for that.

I want to thank Natalie Morris for helping me to tell my story so beautifully. I always looked forward to our chats. Thank you for making me feel so comforted and supported. This book is everything that I could have imagined and more. You are a beautiful human and I can safely say I've made a friend for life.

Thank you to TAP Management, to my label Warner Records, to my literary agent Matilda Forbes Watson, and to the incredible creative and glam team who worked on the cover shoot for the book: Oghalé Alex, Jasmine Hamilton, Rudy Betty, Dionne Smith and Joy Adenuga.

Thank you to my editor Yvonne Jacob for believing in my vision for this book and helping to shape it. And thank you to the entire team at Headline who have helped to make this dream a reality – Raiyah Butt, Caroline Young, Tina Paul, Jess Tackie and Louise Swannell.

To all of my beautiful fans and to every reader. Thank you for supporting me, it really does mean the world. It isn't always easy to bare it all and be vulnerable and open. But every time I open up, I feel held and I feel seen. I love you all more than you will ever know. You inspire me every single day. My wish for everyone reading this book is that you never give up on your dreams, erase the doubts, be fearless, and never, ever stop believing.

# Picture Credits

## Plate Section One

1   (all) Courtesy of the author
2   (all) Courtesy of the author
3   (all) Courtesy of the author
4   © Fremantle /Simco Ltd
5   (top left) Shirlaine Forrest/WireImage/Getty Images
    (top right and bottom right) Courtesy of the author
6   (all) Courtesy of the author
7   (all) Courtesy of the author
8   (top left and middle) Chris Jackson/Getty Images
    for Comic Relief
    (bottom left) Courtesy of the author

## Plate Section Two

1   (top left) Richard Ansett, courtesy of Banijay Rights
    (middle) Courtesy of the author
    (bottom left) Anthony Devlin/Getty Images
2   (top left and top right) Courtesy of the author
    (bottom) David M. Benett/Dave Benett/Getty Images
3   (all) Courtesy of the author
4   (top left and bottom right) Courtesy of the author
    (bottom left) Can Nguyen/Shutterstock
5   (all) Courtesy of the author
6   (top) Georgie Gibbon/Shutterstock
    (bottom) Courtesy of the author
7   (all) Courtesy of the author
8   Courtesy of the author